IDENTITY
New Commercial, Cultural and Mobility Architecture

Texts by:
Lars Krückeberg
Wolfram Putz
Thomas Willemeit
Nora Zerelli

Project management GRAFT:
Nora Zerelli, Berlin

Project team GRAFT:
Martin Bernard, Ann-Sophie Heuer, Sarah John, Jan Kadziela,
Théophile de la Presle, Berlin

Illustration editing GRAFT:
Nadine Cordial Settele, Berlin

Editorial supervision and project management Birkhäuser:
Henriette Mueller-Stahl, Berlin

Translation from German into English
(p. 12–19, 40–45, 68–75, 142–185, 268–275, 284–287):
Gareth Davies, Berlin

Copy editing:
Gareth Davies, Berlin
Michael Wachholz, Berlin

Layout, cover design and typesetting:
Proxi.me:
Christian Schärmer, Berlin
Reinhard Steger, Barcelona

Production:
Amelie Solbrig, Berlin

Lithography:
Oriol Rigat, Berlin

Paper:
Magno Volume, 135g/m²

Printing:
optimal media GmbH, Röbel/Müritz

Library of Congress Control Number:
2020937883

Bibliographic information published by the German National Library
The German National Library lists this publication in the Deutsche Nationalbibliografie; detailed bibliographic data are available on the Internet at http://dnb.dnb.de.

ISBN 978-3-0356-1916-4

e-ISBN (PDF) 978-3-0356-1923-2

P.O. Box 44, 4009 Basel, Switzerland
Part of Walter de Gruyter GmbH, Berlin/Boston

9 8 7 6 5 4 3 2 1

www.birkhauser.com

IDENTITY

New Commercial, Cultural and Mobility Architecture

GRAFT

With a foreword by Kjetil Trædal Thorsen
Founding partner, Snøhetta

BIRKHÄUSER
BASEL

TABLE OF CONTENTS

GRAFT founding partners Wolfram Putz (left), Lars Krückeberg and Thomas Willemeit (both right) with Snøhetta founding partner Kjetil Trædal Thorsen and Snøhetta director Jette Cathrin Hopp (center) in Oslo, Norway, in early 2020

FOREWORD

by Kjetil Trædal Thorsen–Founding partner, Snøhetta

For GRAFT to make a book called IDENTITY in 2020 could be misinterpreted as a move back to the roots of local engagement and local solutions. This would not only run contrary to the globalized perspective of architecture and design that has developed in recent decades, but would also be an oversimplification of the message portrayed in this publication. To me, GRAFT's design philosophy is neither local nor global: It is a balancing act.

Their approach to commercial, cultural and mobility architecture represents a truly original position. It counters tendencies that see conservative design methodologies misleadingly postulated as radical. Instead, it reflects on the more innovative aspects of architecture, and so goes to the core of discussions on identity. The locations of GRAFT's first two offices, Los Angeles and Berlin, were no doubt instrumental in this, coloring their political viewpoint, their search for diversity and their belief in the freedom of human creativity.

The meaning of the term "identity" has of course evolved over time, but today I believe that identity is about differentiation. It is the distinguishing character of a person, a place or an object, which in turn leads to individual or collective identification and mutual recognition. The associative aspect of an object or design may therefore be both local and global at the same time.

In other words, identical is the opposite of identity. When something or someone consciously and honestly communicates an identity to the world around them, this object or person becomes readable and thus trustworthy. A unique physical or mental representation can therefore be an identifier of real content that leads to the cultural sensitization of clients, users or the public at large.

For this reason, taking identity lightly can be catastrophic: Architecture is a strong societal tool that influences thinking and experiences in both positive and negative ways.

When GRAFT interposes a project into an urban, cultural, historical or commercial setting, they create new realities. As such, they also define new identities. It is their extensive understanding of how architecture influences and reshapes perception that transforms their projects into cultural events. And while some people might think that this takes us closer to controversial definitions like "brand architecture," the determining factor will always be how well these projects are conceived and realized.

The ethos that characterizes GRAFT within is one of plurality. Like Snøhetta, GRAFT chose a name inspired by its practice, one related to what they do and not merely based on the names of its founders. It is the strategy of a band. It allows for collective approaches, healthy internal discussions and for the diversity that is reflected in the changing conditions of their different projects.

This publication clearly outlines GRAFT's vivid position on the architectural scene. It is an open, honest identifier of them as a practice—and as individuals.

Kjetil Trædal Thorsen
Founding Partner, Architect, MNAL, FAA, AIA, Int. FRIBA, Dr.H.C.

Kjetil Trædal Thorsen was born in Haugesund, Norway, and in 1985 he graduated as Dipl. Ing. Architect from the University of Graz, Austria. The same year he was a co-founder of the first Norwegian gallery for architecture, Gallery ROM.

In 1989 he co-founded the multidisciplinary architectural practice, Snøhetta, which now includes architecture, landscape architecture, interior architecture, product design and graphic design. Since the creation of Snøhetta, Kjetil has been instrumental in the projects developed by the practice, such as the Bibliotheca Alexandrina in Alexandria, Egypt; the New National Opera and Ballet in Oslo, Norway; The SFMOMA in San Francisco; the National September 11 Memorial Pavilion in NY; the Lascaux IV Caves in France; the Busan Opera house in Busan; Under, Europe's first underwater restaurant in Lindesnes, Norway; Shanghai Grand Opera House in Shanghai, China; and the Le Monde Group Headquarters in Paris.

He is a frequent lecturer internationally, and from 2004 to 2008 he was professor of architecture at the Institute of Experimental Architecture at the University of Innsbruck, Austria.

As founding partner, Kjetil has been instrumental in defining and developing Snøhetta's philosophy and architectural ambition. Many of the projects created by Snøhetta have been inspired or led by Kjetil.

Chess boxing is a hybrid that combines the cerebral board game chess and the fighting sport boxing. Blending contrasting skills, competitors fight alternating rounds of chess and boxing. It combines assumed opposites into something ambiguous and new. Chess boxing inventor Iepe B.T. Rubingh was a long-time friend and partner of GRAFT. He sadly passed away on May 6, 2020.

GRAFTING IDENTITIES

Introduction by Lars Krückeberg, Wolfram Putz, Thomas Willemeit–Founding partners, GRAFT

Architecture is a cultural technique. It is never self-contained, nor finite; it is part of a complex cultural cycle in the service of society as a whole. As a result, architecture is always a representation of society rather than an autonomous discipline. The importance of identity within designed space, from individual to community, from city to region, cannot be underestimated. At a time when there is a blurring of boundaries between the real and the virtual, urban and rural, local and global, our built environment plays a fundamental role in defining identity. GRAFT believes in the power of architecture as a tool, best employed not for its own sake, but to represent these ambiguous and diverse identities.

This book features designs for projects in the fields of mobility, digitization, work, branding and urban culture, all of which graft different realities into new, genetic hybrids.

GRAFT is responding to the challenges of the future with an optimistic attitude towards multiple and simultaneous identities, which enables a higher degree of complexity. There is no such thing as one single truth, and we believe that hybridization enhances the qualities of its constituent characteristics. Our design process is evidence-based and human-centered. Our approach stems from scenography and movement rather than tectonics. In this way, we are able to create dynamic, flexible architecture that allows multiple readings.

We have observed a current tendency towards curtailing debate in architectural discourse—leading to a lack of tolerance and a rejection of alternative positions and identities. This polarization robs us of the resilience and joyfulness of hybrid designs that stimulate not only academic exchange but the development of architecture in a pluralist society. A tolerant democracy ought to be reflected in the intellectual debate and our built environment. With this book we are making a case for ambiguity and concurrency, for uniqueness and diversity.

MOBILITY

NEW MOBILITY

A CONVERSATION WITH STEFAN LISKE

A city's development is inextricably linked to mobility—the movement of people and goods. Urban planning in the 20th century was based on the separation of dirty, noisy traffic from the unpolluted, human urban fabric, but global megalopolises today still suffer from the growing implications of traffic. The combination of zero-emission, low-noise mobility with deep digitization and AI will have an enormous impact on the evolution of cities and rural areas, while new mobility concepts are expected to change our understanding of communal spaces and infrastructure.

How can we rethink the mental and physical relationships between the rural and the urban? How will new mobility concepts shape our behavior? How are city planning, architecture and design going to be affected by innovations in mobility? On a societal level, there is much more to these questions, given that physical mobility is connected with social mobility. Movement has always been crucial to GRAFT's spatial configurations and their conception of space, derived from their scenographic understanding of architecture. GRAFT spoke to longtime collaborator Stefan Liske about the implications of progress in mobility and its future milestones.

GRAFT Stefan Liske, our shared history dates back to the time we were setting up our office in Los Angeles. We worked together on the "Moonraker" project for the Volkswagen Group of America, which was about turning societal paradigm shifts and future living scenarios into a tangible spatial experience using built "Life Settings." The fundamental question for these architectural simulations, which were aimed at different user groups, was: How do you recognize the future? This is a question that's increasingly being asked by the research departments of the major global manufacturers regarding the subject of regional and urban mobility—but in much greater depth and with different parameters. Ever since electric motors offered the promise of zero-emission mobility in our urban centers, a rise in intermodality caused focus to be shifted to transfer hubs, and the potential of autonomous driving pointed to a more effective and efficient use of space, the crossover points between real estate and mobility have become much clearer. It's no coincidence that we as an office are now working on more and more projects in the field of mobility, ranging from the branded spaces of traditional automobile companies and service providers to numerous new players in the fields of robo-fleets, drones and maglev systems. In your expert

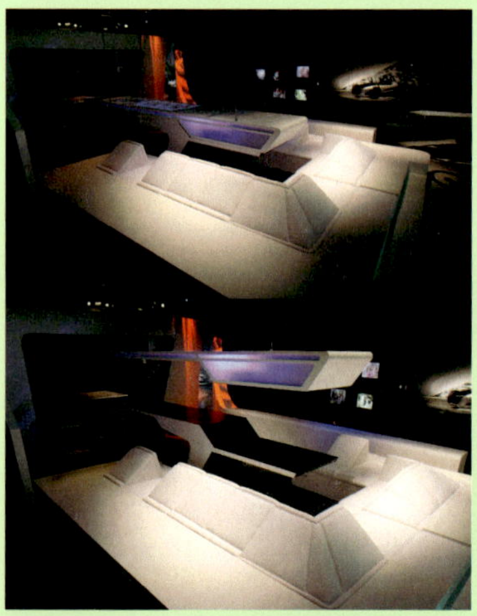

Moonraker, GRAFT (p. 58): Life setting for four avatars to predict the future environment of the target group; a set for movable components of the interior digital interface turns into a kitchen counter and a customized vehicle within a technology driven environment.

The LOCI podcar by BigRep: The fully 3D-printed, autonomous (driving) e-car

GRAFT car with surf equipment at a Californian beach in the late 1990s: Mobility is closely linked to freedom.

opinion, which utopia will establish itself in the field of mobility: Carsharing and intermodality, the maximum expansion of public transport infrastructures or the complete relinquishment of individual control in favor of autonomous vehicles?

STEFAN LISKE I don't think electromobility will be the great savior. This is due in part to the unclear status regarding the recycling of batteries; another reason is that we might be on the brink of a breakthrough in the field of fusion technology, so a step closer to energy abundance. We definitely need to consider entirely new energy scenarios, ones that the major manufacturers are unfortunately reluctant to entertain. Another utopia that probably won't materialize is the idea of a completely autonomous, driverless world before 2030. This is unlikely to happen as mobility still signifies personal freedom to many people. On top of this, there's also the fact that most people want to remain masters of their own routines and continue to define their own rhythms and rituals as much as they can.

GRAFT The concept of freedom in mobility is something that is currently being renegotiated in the political realm. Studying internationally, having the opportunity to travel, founding an office in Los Angeles, Berlin, then Beijing, being exposed to many different cultures and approaches to architecture—all these things have had a formative effect on our thinking and our commitment to diversity, tolerance and heterogeneity, also in terms of form and style. Today, some people want to collectivize mobility and arrange it in large, communal schemes, partly in order to help combat climate change; others, however, say that long-distance individual mobility was only first made possible to the masses with invention of the automobile, and that being able to drive on their own in a self-determined manner is a real achievement of civilization. Anyway, we are fans of all kinds of transport: Collective or individual, surface, air or underground. Do you think that this diversity will decline in the future? A central aspect in the conflict also seems to be the question of how many restrictive rules can survive the democratic process in the long term. Especially when right-wing parliamentary groups such as the Alternative for Germany campaign against such rules.

LISKE I stand on the side of science. And that means that we should be more strictly regulated, more than we can actually imagine—and not only in the field of mobility. Both the EU mobility commission and the Berlin Senate have had initial discussions about introducing quotas for households regarding CO_2, water, waste and consumption. Such quotas wouldn't just affect which medium of transport you use on a daily basis, they would also affect your choice of vacation, the food you eat, how much your order online, etc. Standardized scientific models increasingly show that we'll no longer have a chance if we continue to insist on playing the freedom-of-choice card and allow everyone to do what they want. We might need to consider regulating how much we consume and how much waste we produce, at least to a level that's compatible with democratic values.

Still, we shouldn't undervalue having a range of mobility concepts. There will always be people who want the rugged performance of a gasoline engine, which is why I think that companies like BMW, Porsche, Mercedes, etc., who aren't investing everything in electromobility, will keep doing well. Companies like Toyota will continue to produce fuel cells and other, newer types of engines, even though their profits haven't been that healthy due to the costs of hydrogen production and other technical challenges. In the short term, I think that biofuels such as natural gas are very promising, while fusion technology—which recreates the plasma-based energy production principle found in the sun in small fusion reactors—has the most potential in the long term. These reactors could be produced in a range of different sizes, so even for in-car use, but we're probably talking more like 2050 for that.

GRAFT So, electricity would again be the energy source used in these vehicles?

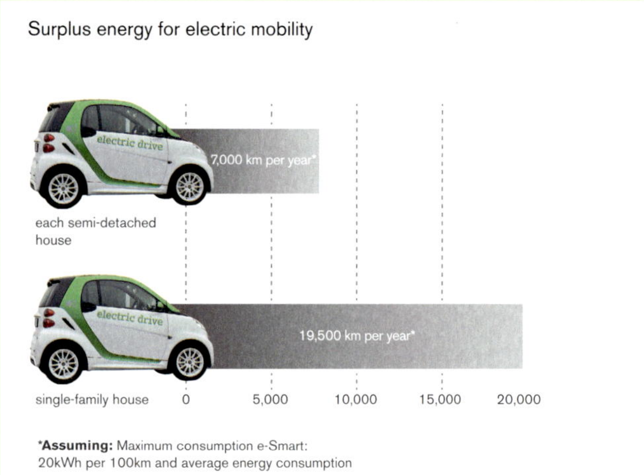

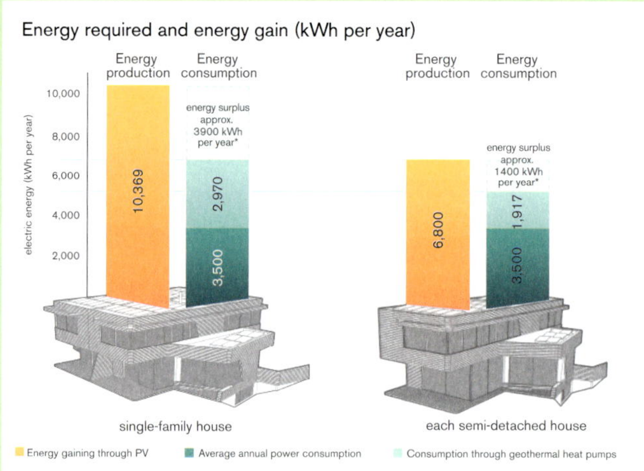

VEHICLES WILL SOON BE ABLE TO ANTICIPATE OUR BEHAVIOR BETTER. JUST LIKE OUR SMARTPHONES, BACKGROUND APPLICATIONS AND AI COMPANIONS WILL REACT TO OUR DEMANDS FASTER, MORE SPECIFICALLY AND MORE INTUITIVELY.

LISKE Yes, exactly. But when it comes to electricity, there is still the problem of storage. Lithium-ion batteries aren't a very sustainable solution. The battery technology roadmaps that the big OEMs[1] currently use as a basis will soon be unviable. But things will look better in the next ten or 15 years if oxygen-based storage becomes possible.

1 OEM: Original equipment manufacturer

GRAFT We are trained engineers, but we're also dreamers. We're interested in using social and technological innovation as a basis for rethinking things, also in terms of urban planning and architecture. You said there would be a number of diverse phenomena and technologies existing at the same time, i.e., different propulsion technologies and multiple modes of mobility: High-speed travel, hyperloop, even new types of air-based transport for goods and people. After a first phase around the turn of the 20th century, when overhead railways and subways enabled intersection-free transport, the use of the third dimension of urban space is becoming a widespread phenomenon again. Elevated maglev railways and drones are now starting to take advantage of vertical space, offering new opportunities for traffic systems in our hopelessly overburdened, ever-expanding metropolises. And when infrastructure doesn't keep pace with urban growth, it results in undesirable developments, such as improvised neighborhoods, slums or unending traffic jams—the opposite of efficient urban density.

Self-driving concepts, in particular, could have a long-lasting effect on our approach to urban planning. Together with intelligent parking systems, autonomous vehicles will be able to free up space that could subsequently be used by the urban community. For some cities, as traffic increases, this will become a question of survival; for others it will be about negotiating what can be done with this overall gain in spatial provision. It's a bit like valet parking, but instead we'll be dropped off at our door, hand over the key to the autonomous vehicle to park itself, which will then pick us up again as needed. This will save on the space required for parking. The more prepared we will be to make our own car available to the community, or to give it over to carsharing schemes, the fewer vehicles there will be in a given urban space. This is one of the most exciting challenges for the future: Achieving a good balance of mobility and high-quality urban spaces.

Holistic living: GRAFT designed three plus-energy houses made of sustainable and healthy materials that are completely reusable and recyclable. The houses generate their own energy and the surplus is used to power an electric vehicle integrated into the technical systems of the house.

At any rate, many of the dogmas established in the 20th century will gradually fall away. If traffic becomes zero-emission in terms of exhaust fumes and noise, and becomes safer due to the application of artificial intelligence, many of the basic conditions of the Athens Charter—which advocated the separation of transportation routes and urban spaces and which formed the basis of urban planning laws across the world—will no longer be applicable. This would mean that many questions would need to be addressed again, right down to the noise reduction standards demanded of building façades. City planning processes could then approach transportation and urban space in a much more integrated fashion.

At the same time, cars have become modern, small-scale manifestations of third places. What about that aspect? What happens in my car when I no longer want or need to drive it myself? This opens up a huge range of new discussions. In 2016, together with other partners, GRAFT and PCH Innovations carried out a feasibility study on the future use of Berlin's Tegel Airport (p.126) and the development of an entire urban quarter. At the time, you predicted that autonomous vehicles would be funded by advertising revenues and in this way be free of charge for the end user. Such a modified mobility model would provide a considerable boost towards the transformation of our urban societies.

LISKE In the field of mobility, vehicles will soon be able to anticipate our behavior better. Just like our smartphones, background applications and AI companions will react to our demands faster, more specifically and more intuitively—this will be particularly noticeable in the areas of in-car work and entertainment. I think the latter will prove to be a better source of revenue than in-vehicle office or retail services. The vehicles of the future will be functional mobile spaces that will accommodate services such as kindergartens, doctors' practices or retail outlets. A concrete example of this: A European automobile company recently sold 200 self-driving "robotaxis" to a Californian coffeehouse chain to be employed as "rolling coffee shops."

I am convinced that the urban environment will profit massively from these developments. We expect to see huge reductions in noise, congestion and the number of accidents on our streets, which will lead to radical improvements in our experience of urban space and thus hopefully in our quality of life. And this is the main reason why autonomous vehicles will be introduced. It is, after all, predominantly about saving lives, not just convenience. On top of this, the cost of transport will go down by around 20 to 30% as drivers' salaries will no longer need to be factored in—which in turn can be repeatedly monetarized using the aforementioned business models. As of January 2020, in China there are 438 mobility startups waiting in the wings. These new players, however, aren't wasting time with service apps, they are primarily developing autonomous mobility concepts.

Predictions regarding app-based mobility services offered by German automobile companies, which they estimated would make up between 15 and 25% of their future revenues around six years ago, have now proved to be somewhat erroneous. In 2020, of the Volkswagen Group's predicted 220 billion dollars revenue, less than a billion will be generated by its mobility services. The turning point that we were all waiting for regarding the monetarization of services never happened. When I look out of my window onto the street today, not much has changed—everything looks pretty much the same as it did 15 years ago. It has sadly become apparent in the last few years that the established names in the automobile industry still aren't really interested in bringing new, exciting forms of mobility and innovative functions onto our streets. Some of the newer players, who are currently trying to shake up the market, are set to score points in these areas.

GRAFT We want to see this new aesthetic on our streets as well as in our homes, and we are constantly on the lookout for new phenotypes—for example those influenced by the need to rethink the future in terms of climate questions—that enable new forms of social behavior on which future mobility concepts can be based.

The Old Mill Hotel, Belgrade (lobby), BRICKS Berlin Schöneberg (entrance): Epigenetic landscapes as representations of people's dynamic rituals in space

Since we first proposed building concepts whose rental price included electric vehicles that could be charged using the positive energy balance of the houses themselves, we have seen that the touchpoints between property and mobility have become more evident and the boundaries of the different areas of planning more flexible. Mobility concepts are now becoming the building blocks for co-working or co-living concepts. We can now imagine having clean, quiet, zero-emission vehicles in the same spaces that we work or sleep in. On top of this, there is also the aesthetic question regarding these vehicles and the space they operate in. Nowadays, a functional space for mobility can also be high-quality environment for personal interaction—there is a more discerning aesthetic expectation relating to these spaces. Our office addresses precisely these topics, and with this book we are trying to ask questions regarding future identities and their aesthetics on a number of different scales—from charging stations and interior branding to houses, blocks and entire cities.

There have always been correlations between the aesthetics of the automobile industry and architectural innovations. For Le Corbusier, the entire formal language of classical modernism was inspired by the automobile and shipbuilding industries. In actual fact, the rounded corners of early modernism were justified by the simple necessity of providing a faster, safer way to take off corners. The opulent car designs present for many years in the United States were a manifestation of the country's faith in its future direction. Besides function, the emphasis was very much on beauty. Individualized mobility and motorized delivery led to the rounded buildings found in the early phase of modernist architecture. Horizontal window bands that suggest horizontal movement, building silhouettes that seem to defy gravity, these things lent architecture an air of dynamism after centuries of tectonic verticality. Sometimes when you encounter modernist architecture, there is a palpable sense of the exhilaration for new technology and mobility and an optimism in creating the structures of the future. Today you can see there is growing demand for architectural quality in the field of mobility.

This is expressed in the architectural projects we have realized for automobile companies like Volkswagen and Mercedes, the e-charging stations we created for E.ON (p. 20), the VoloPort stations (p. 48) we developed for Volocopter air taxis, and the design for Max Bögl's maglev system (p. 40). And that is related to clean energy and a fascination with new forms of mobility. We hope that our commitment to a society in transition, with its new indicators, objectives and associated innovations, will be reflected in the provision of higher-quality architecture and spaces that are more tailored towards the needs of people.

E.ON UF-charging stations (p. 20) and maglev train stations (p. 40): Organic, bionic, dynamic—what will future mobility look like?

A Volocopter air taxi above the skyline of Singapore: Three-dimensional mobility is already here, but how will it change our cities?

LISKE That's my hope, too. But to achieve this, beauty has to become valued as quality once again. Apart from some classic cars and a few sports cars, they aren't many models that can be considered beautiful—in the truest sense of the word—in the automobile industry at the moment. Cars that really elicit a "Wow!" like furniture, watches, art or architecture might. Some of the newer players plan to deliver vehicles in the future that boast completely new material or functional concepts. I predict that Chinese manufacturers in particular will soon overtake European and American companies in the delivery vehicle sector, because production costs alone are 20 to 30% lower. These manufacturers now have all the means necessary to finally express their cultural identity by applying their unique formal language, materials and country-specific functional concepts. The Chinese market is currently in the extremely exciting identity-establishment phase, which will be followed by the identity-expression phase. In Europe, on the other hand, we are in the midst of a huge wave of job losses and are witnessing how the historically nurtured loyalties between automobile companies and consumers are being gradually eroded by environmental scandals, crude lobbying and meaningless lip service.

I could easily imagine that the market shares that European and American companies will lose will shift to Africa. It's currently home to around 800 million people under the age of 30, many of whom want to work and realize their potential and are urgently seeking access to higher living standards, prosperity and free enterprise. Besides energy, water and food, mobility is a fundamental building block for achieving this, but viewed differently from how we know it. And this "thinking differently" is something that the established manufacturers will struggle with once again.

THERE HAVE ALWAYS BEEN CORRELATIONS BETWEEN THE AESTHETICS OF THE AUTOMOBILE INDUSTRY AND ARCHITECTURAL INNOVATIONS.

GRAFT After our experience with the SOLARKIOSK (p. 82), we'd agree with you 100%—everything starts with the provision of energy. The food supply, too, can only be guaranteed if the energy question is resolved. So much food is left to rot in the field because the mobility concepts aren't available to get the food to the places it's needed. The energy supply system in Africa needs to be expanded in a decentralized way: If one were to scale up the SOLARKIOSK system, which currently only produces a small amount of energy using photovoltaics, then things could get really interesting. Regarding mobility, we are really focusing on the issue of last-mile distribution. There's going to be a big breakthrough. As a continent, Africa has already seen large-scale success with its telephone network. Mobile payment is another effective model that grew from the necessity of decentralization. Maybe mobility will be the next great leap forward. It's interesting that we initially developed the SOLARKIOSK because we wanted to provide energy to rural areas, and we're now modifying them to serve as charging stations for drones and e-bikes. These small kiosks have turned into mobility recharging hubs. Such new, decentralized systems create exciting and profitable business cases that could eventually be exported to Europe and the Western world. Over the next few decades, Africa will surely teach us a lot about connected yet decentralized energy supply models based on small, autonomous hubs. And this might be the only way we'll be able to do things in the future.

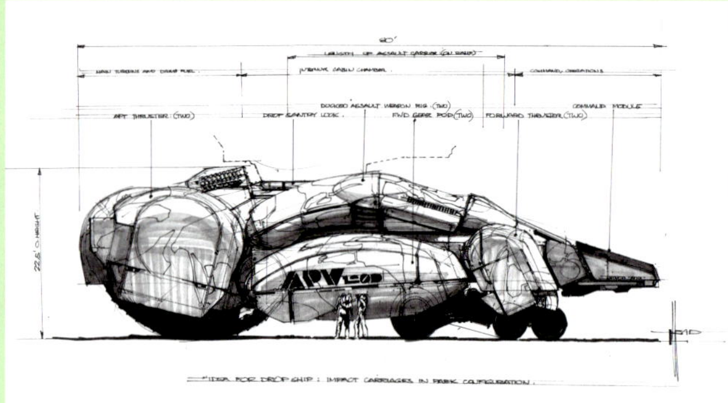

Blade Runner (1982): Three-dimensional mobility as imagined by Syd Mead

LISKE Exactly. What's one of the central economic principles in Africa? Barter and exchange. There are a lot of Western economists today, like Thomas Piketty and Paul Mason, who are developing new, postcapitalist logics. They predict that alongside decentralized, digitized cash flow, bartering and exchange models and other microfinancing systems will become more established in the Western world in the next 15 to 20 years. In the future, the economy will become more community-based, especially in urban centers. To achieve this, though, we will need to establish a new sense of community with new value systems and the corresponding platforms for interaction, exchange, trade, etc.—millennia-old mechanisms and values that have been lost through the process of technological development.

GRAFT Are we talking about ideological tribes here? Does the past still work as a model? Will private transport increase or decrease? This is where artificial intelligence and the autonomy of mobility overlap. In the 1990s, Rem Koolhaas created a European map that depicted the continent in terms of travel time, using distance, speed and accessibility. Today we expect trains to offer an alternative to short-haul flights. Companies like Max Bögl are bringing transport systems onto the market which, based on a similar capacity to a subway, would cost a third of the price and could be built in a third of the time—and, by offering intersection-free urban mobility, would be far superior to any tram. Even the introduction of drone technology as a form of passenger transport is becoming increasingly likely. If we approached it properly, there could be such a high level of competition in urban transport that technology would advance much faster. This is especially relevant when it comes to regional accessibility and intra-city transportation.

To what extent will the relationship between rural and urban areas change in the future? Even in an urban context, people today talk about the reemergence of the rural—the yearning for the village and the neighborhood. At the same time, there's a blurring of the physical and definitional boundaries between the urban and the rural. Connections are becoming more important than boundaries. Cities are changing from destinations into transit areas within a global network of metropolises.

LISKE There will be an increase in individual passenger transport between urban and rural areas. We are already witnessing the first signs of an urban exodus in Germany. Within 15 years it will be possible to carry out a highly paid, highly qualified, demanding job remotely and not have to go to the office at all. I think this will be accompanied by a development in the niche field of mobile living. There is a growing market for caravans, trailers, mobile homes and tiny houses, illustrating an increased desire to lead an off-grid life—with little to no dependence on resources, the state and large corporations. Which means we will see more and more people attempting to live in a self-sufficient manner, providing for their families and communities using independent water and energy supplies, farms and individual-centered sources of income. In the context of climate-change induced floods, droughts, heatwaves, fires and air pollution, and given the development of intelligent, sustainable off-grid solutions in the fields of water, energy, food, health, etc., this phenomenon takes on a whole new significance.

GRAFT Do you not think that this urban exodus might be a transitional trend? New mobility promises us that through the application of artificial intelligence and autonomous vehicles, parking spaces will be turned into green spaces and CO_2 and noise pollution will be reduced to zero. It's ultimately a promise that guarantees a huge improvement in the quality of life in urban areas. In our opinion, these phenomena—the desire for the local, the neighborhood within the city, for belonging, both to tribes and the community—are all clear indications of a yearning for a village character within the urban environment. Maybe if this happens, urban exodus will no longer be an issue, and everyone will be rushing to move back to the city again.

LISKE For many people, these prospective changes to the urban environment have been too long in the making. I also believe that we should really and truly rediscover nature and our rural regions, but without subduing them—it's about protecting, rewilding and restoring.

GRAFT Which would mean an enormous increase in mobility. Let's think about the question of scope and consider distances greater than those between urban and rural areas. At the moment, global travel is a relatively low-threshold activity that is accessible to a large number of people. Not everyone can afford it, but more people than ever before. Now Greta Thunberg is showing us that we should travel to New York by sailboat. From your perspective, are there things in this field that will allow us to maintain this freedom of global movement, perhaps technological advances or innovations that will make flying less harmful for the environment, for example? Or are reducing and doing without really the order of the day, here?

LISKE Behavior relating to global mobility will change massively, especially in the younger generation, as they no longer want to fly because they are aware of the facts and are deeply concerned about the future. They know that they are facing a mammoth task. I can imagine that an interesting, truly innovative set of solutions will be developed, one that could even capitalize on climate change and create new jobs in the process.

GRAFT As for the Moonraker project that we collaborated on, some of the predictions we made in the "Sustainability Earth—Green Topography" scenario really hit the nail on the head. The hypotheses regarding the growing interconnection of IT networks and intelligent building control as well as those on fluid, dynamic interiors were quite accurate. Some of the other assumptions, however, became quickly outdated or didn't prove to be true. If you look at GRAFT's current projects, for example those for urban air taxi service developer Volocopter (p. 48), Max Bögl (p. 40), E.ON (p. 20) or the roof of the Autostadt (p. 32), what identity does our visual language convey today? We believe that our success in these competitions shows that the world of new mobility finds its expression in dynamic architectural forms. It could also be down to the fact that our way of designing is very scenographic, conceiving of spatial experiences as a continuum over time. Of course, even in times of great change, it's also essential to express a certain amount of optimism for the future—albeit with an amount of balance and caution. The starting point for this might sometimes be the future-oriented design language found in the world of sci-fi films; sometimes it might be inspired by organic forms and the language of bionics. We believe that this visual expression will be best suited for creating an awareness that human actions are responsible for changes to the basis of our existence and can no longer be separated from what we have until now understood by the term nature.

LISKE It might sound controversial, but I believe that the biggest and most significant change that will happen in the next one to two generations will be that of humankind.

On the one hand, we live in an age in which we have made inroads into large parts of quantum physics—we can already use quantum computers to efficiently solve complex everyday problems. This might be, for example, traffic flow analyses, AI- and neural-network based analyses that are so complicated that they can only be calculated by a quantum computer.

Looking beyond this, however, the next long-term breakthrough in quantum physics will be in making this phenomenon accessible to everyone. Simply put, quantum logics are logics of energy exchanges between objects and people that have not yet been fully decoded. And I think that as humans, the progressive decryption of these logics will offer us a different relationship to our conceptions of energy and frequency. New, emerging fields of academic research are currently trying to verify and measure forms of energy flow between people. This will lead to a huge increase in the understanding of phenomena that exert control over us as physical beings. The measurability of these phenomena will then be followed by their practical application and the possibility of actually influencing them.

This, as well as all the developments we talked about earlier, won't just massively influence our behavior, it will also shape our entire sense of aesthetics, our sense of language and our sense of a truly functional, objective aesthetics, i.e., an object-bound aesthetics. I think this realm contains a major source of creative riches, and your curiosity and experience make you the ones predestined to unearth it.

Stefan Liske is an innovation designer with 15 years of industrial and entrepreneurial experience and a strong drive to merge the transdisciplinary forces of design, marketing and engineering. He quickly discovered his passion for detecting, and breaking with, rigid and redundant patterns. As a project member, line manager, consultant and innovator, he began questioning inflexible business models, processes and structures, and offering unusual alternatives. He continuously refines his own formula to understand consumers, learn from other industries and analogs, listen to intuition, work counterintuitively and inspire individuals and organizations to realize the highest creative non-standards.

He dedicates a crucial part of his time, passion and hands-on work to social and art-related projects—to tap into new areas and foster ideas that generate sustainable value and joy for people and communities at the "bottom of the pyramid." This teaches him how to be highly innovative in a humble way and create products that meet the very different needs of these markets.

E.ON ULTRA-FAST CHARGING STATIONS

Project: Infrastructure, charging stations, electromobility
Locations: Germany, United Kingdom, Czech Republic, Slovakia, Hungary, Sweden, Denmark, Norway, France and Italy
Client: E.ON
Year: 2018 – ongoing
Status: Design guideline, first implementation

By 2022, an estimated one million customers will be driving electric vehicles in Germany alone. What will happen when electric vehicle technology matures and enters the mainstream? What implications will this have for future patterns of mobility and infrastructure requirements?

Ultra-fast charging station (module system XS)

Option 1
Solar glass roof
Steel lamellae

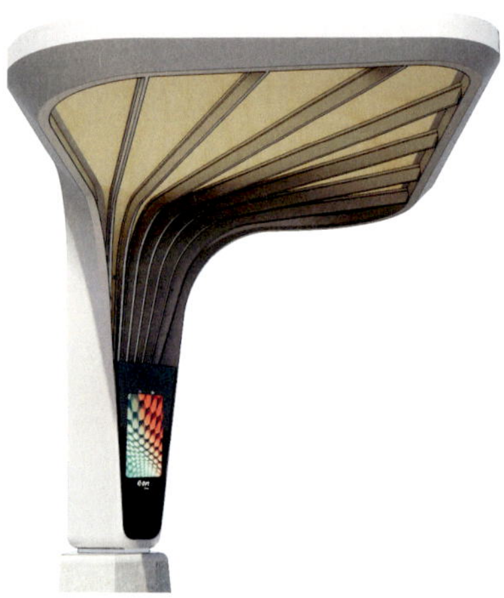

Option 2
Opaque roof
Steel lamellae

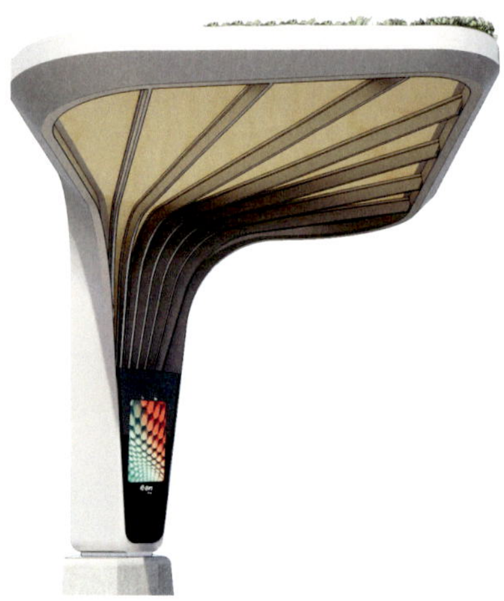

Option 3
Green roof
Steel lamellae

Rendering: Ultra-fast charging station
(module system XS)
Diagrams: Roof types of module system XS/S

As well as developing an intelligent network of fast charging stations, suppliers must also respond to changing customer expectations caused by longer stopover times. The 20 to 30 minutes it takes to charge a car battery changes the sequence of processes within motorway service areas and creates the need for new and alternative facilities. Consequently, there needs to be a fundamental rethink of public charging stations. Together with its partners, E.ON operates one of the largest electric vehicle charging networks in Europe, having installed over 36,000 charging points in customer locations in 25 countries across the world.

For E.ON Drive, GRAFT developed a prototype for an ultra-fast charging station. This was further developed into an innovative, extendable system of modules capable of adapting to future requirements.

The design creates a high-quality stopover environment that provides both customers and suppliers with a range of functions and additional services not commonly associated with filling stations. E.ON Drive and GRAFT's design for ultra-fast charging stations breaks new ground by placing emphasis on user experience, thus contributing to the technology's establishment in society.

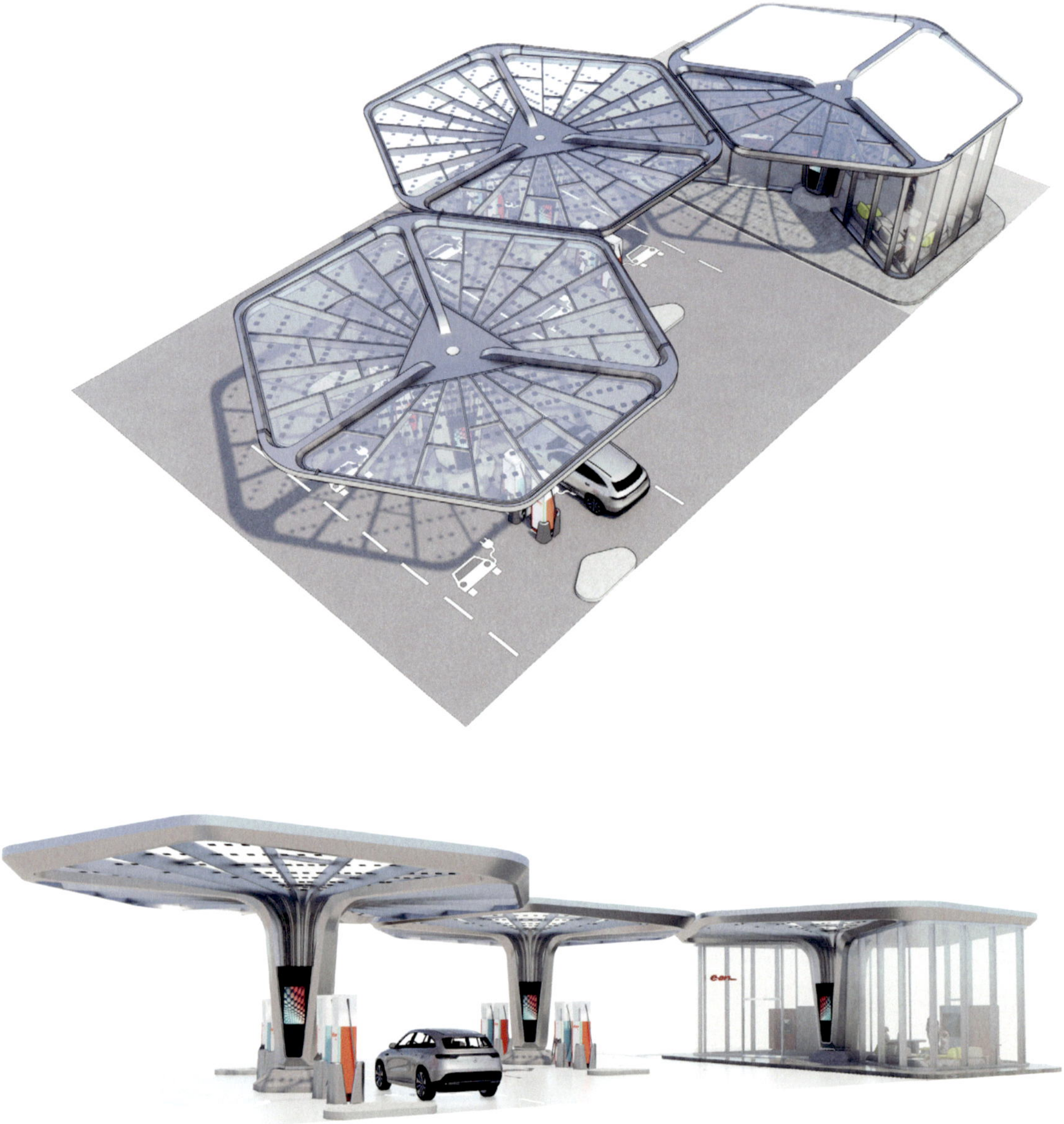

Axonometric and perspective of module system L

With an elegant steel roof construction that extends up and over the user like a bright, airy canopy, the station's design creates a defined space that is protected from the elements, transforming the charging area into a place of rest. Lighting integrated into the frame automatically activates when the charging zone is occupied, creating a clearly specified, safe and comfortable space.

These frames can be configured in different ways: Either featuring an opaque roof with or without greenery; or a glass roof with or without integral photovoltaic panels. When implemented, the photovoltaic system supplies energy for the lounge and the integrated media technology. Slats beneath the roof act as filters, modulating and channeling sunlight into the charging bay area. The precision and dynamism of the construction underlines E.ON's brand identity and consumer experience.

Ultra-fast charging station (module system S)

XS 2B R

XS 2F R

XS 2F L

Ultra-fast charging station (module system XS)

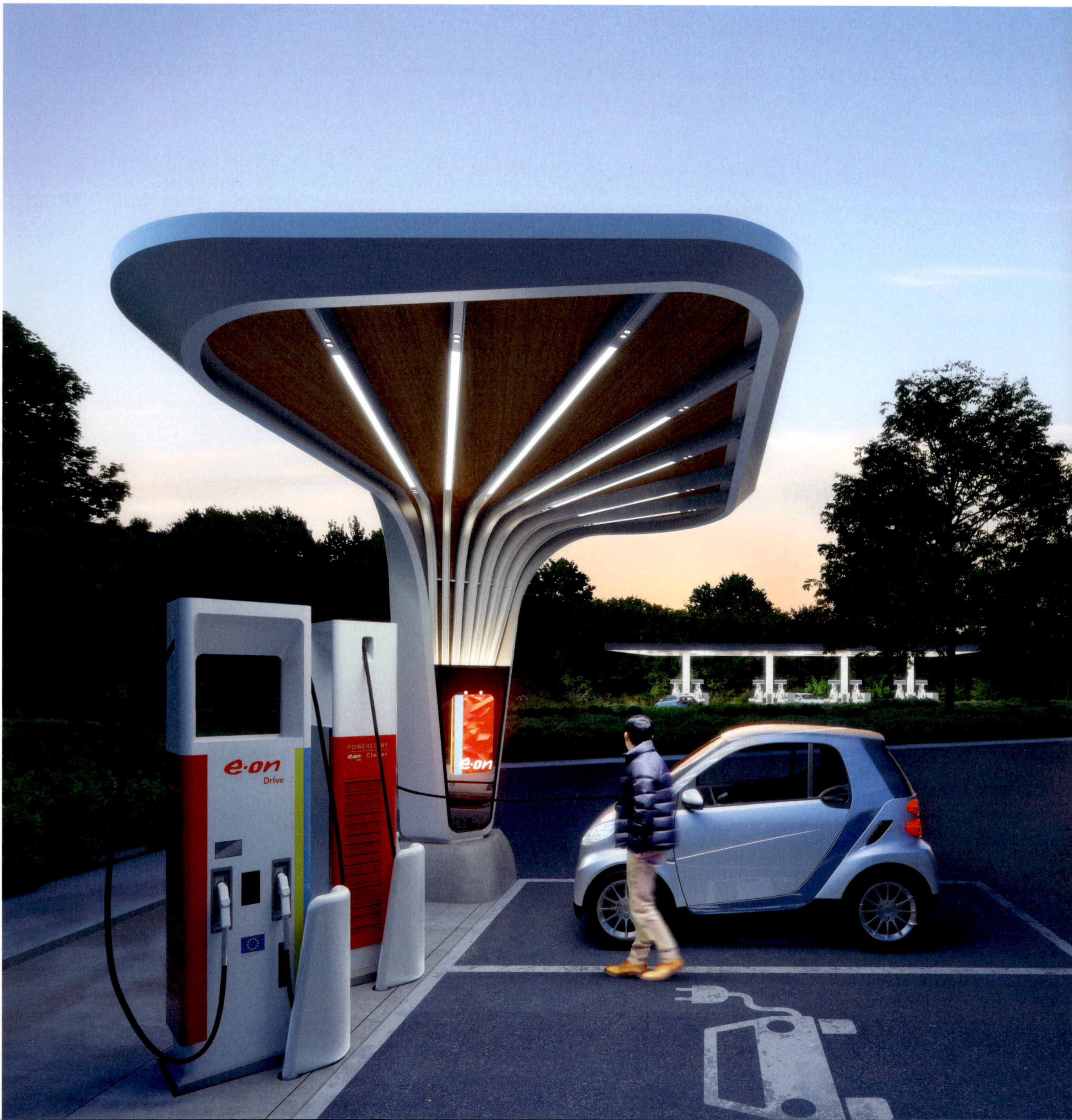

XS 4B X

XS 4F Z

XS 4A Z

XS 4B Z

Matrix of module system XS

Based on two basic modules, the system is able to cater to a wide variety of charging and parking situations.

The smaller of the two modules can be combined to form XS or S stations. With a rectangular footprint of around 3.5 × 5m, it was developed for use in existing car parks and service areas. Its clever geometry makes it possible to provide partially covered parking for one to two spaces in ten different countries. Its self-supporting steel structure allows the modules to be extended linearly to create smaller drive-through options with up to four charging points. Such stations are also suitable for urban contexts, providing covered barrier-free parking in parallel or angled configurations. With a hexagonal footprint, the larger module can be used for M and L stations. The first generation of M stations are designed as drive-through solutions equipped with four to eight charging points, while the L stations, with six to eight charging points, incorporate a customer lounge for use during charging cycles.
In the future, the modular concept can be extended to create XL hubs of varying sizes with additional amenities such as shops, food provision, leisure, spas, fitness and entertainment.
Embodying similar principles in order to ensure a high-quality stopover experience, the station lounges feature fully glazed external walls that create a sheltered space open to the surroundings. Natural materials are used throughout the interior to create a restful, relaxing atmosphere. Media elements are also incorporated into the design, for example touchscreens integrated in the furniture, which enable customers to communicate directly with suppliers.

The recognizable brand architecture of the first generation of E.ON charging stations is scalable, smart and sustainable, and perfectly embodies the company's spirit of innovation at the forefront of technological solutions for society.

A goal of the design is that many of the featured elements, which are primarily aimed at increasing customer experience and user friendliness, will find their way into future government tenders and consequently be made accessible to as many potential users as possible.

Ultra-fast charging station (module system XS)

AUTOSTADT ROOF AND SERVICE PAVILION

Project: Service pavilion, infrastructure
Location: Wolfsburg, Germany
Client: Autostadt Wolfsburg
Year: 2013
Status: Completed
Size: 15,000m^2

The double-contoured roof construction resembles a protective leaf placed over the landscape.

Driver-assistance systems, including automatic parking, traffic-sign recognition and automatic distance control are increasingly common in cars of today. The driving experience at the Autostadt in Wolfsburg offers visitors the opportunity to try out these and other technical assistance systems designed to increase road traffic safety in models manufactured by Volkswagen. The attraction, with an area of around 15,000m^2, was built in only ten months and opened in August 2013.

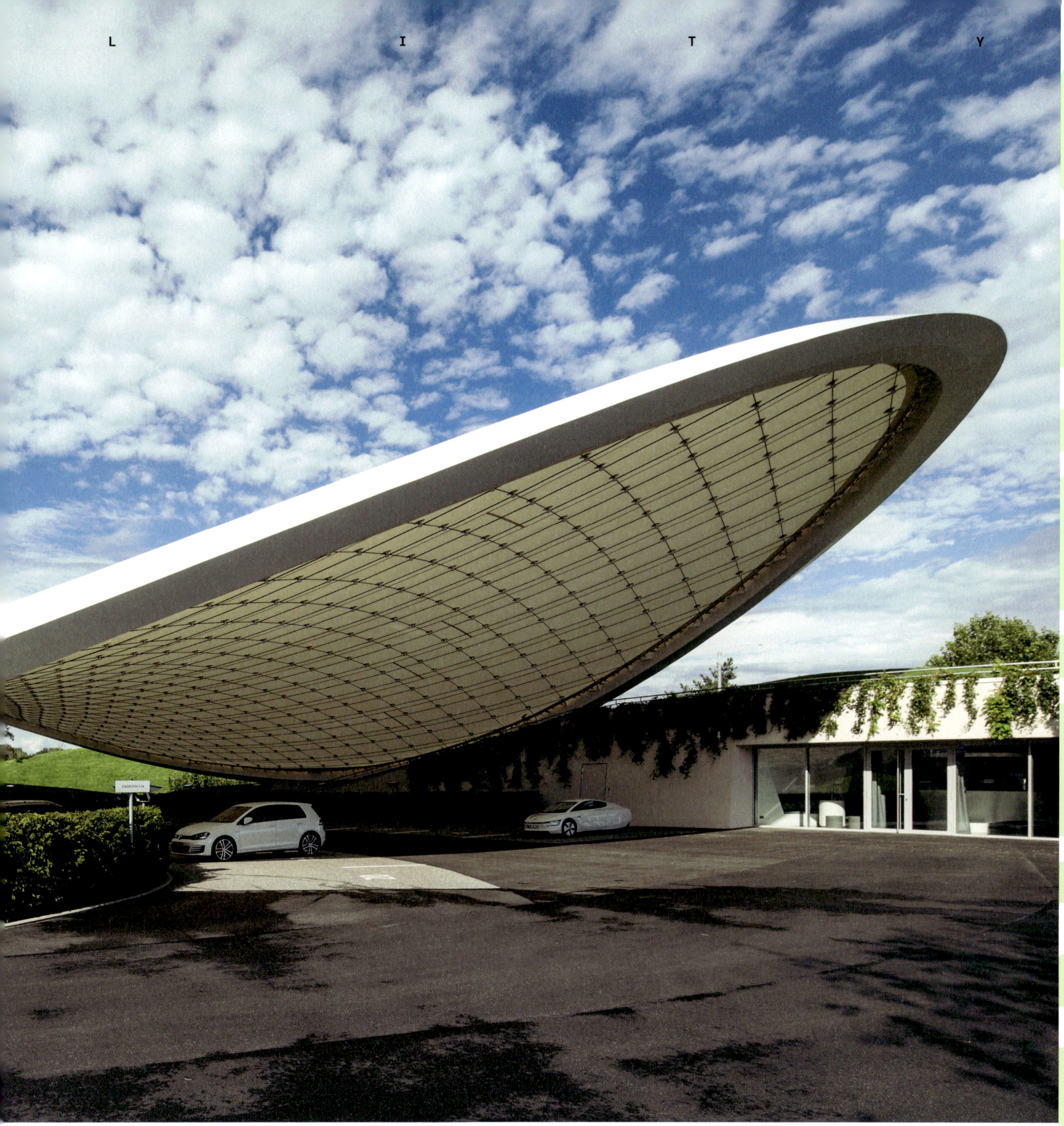

GRAFT was commissioned to create an area where prospective new-car buyers could familiarize themselves with their new functions without the stress of everyday traffic.

The space needed to be sheltered from rain and direct sunlight, but at the same time had to let in enough daylight to prevent the need for expensive and unnecessary artificial lighting.

Nighttime view of the roof construction

The structure accommodates 45 generously sized parking spaces and a pavilion.

GRAFT's concept is based on the idea of a leaf lying on the ground, its organic form sheltering the landscape beneath (designed by WES Landschaftsarchitektur). To adequately capture this idea, the roof construction needed to seem as light as possible. It achieves this by resting on just two points, giving the impression that it is lying on the ground, defining a sheltered space beneath it. The approximately 130-ton steel construction (designed by schlaich bergermann partner) is borne by two concrete foundations anchored 20 meters into the ground.

The arching gesture of the roof and its orientation is welcoming in its nature; the elegant, graceful geometry creates a visual connection between beneath and beyond, between the surroundings and the sky.

All ancillary functions are housed in the adjacent service pavilion: Customers can receive assistance about their new car, purchase accessories or book other attractions and activities in the Autostadt. To avoid detracting from the impression of the roof as a leaf resting on the ground, the pavilion is embedded in the landscape rather than articulated as a separate building. Its interior in turn echoes specific aspects of the roof.

Site plan

Site plan

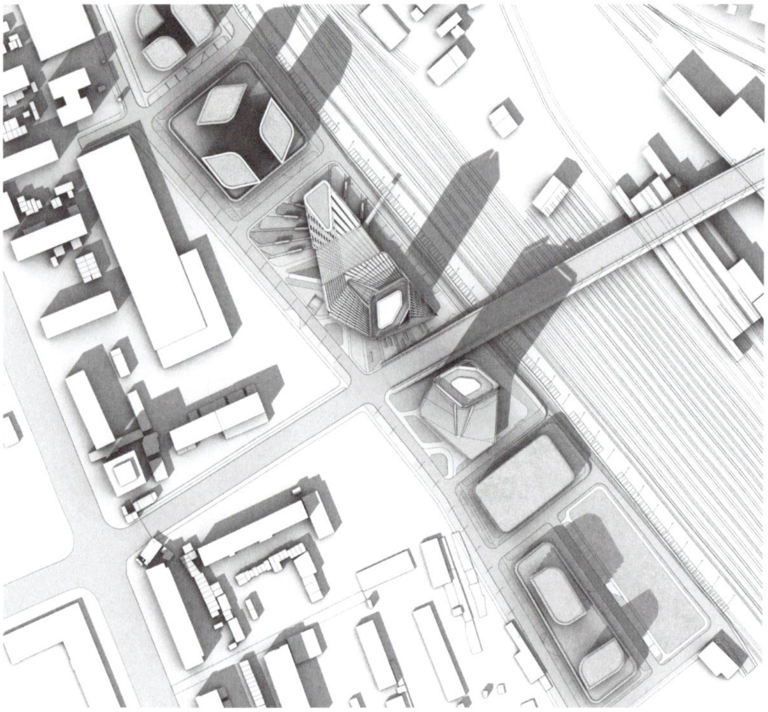

GEORGIAN RAILWAY HEAD OFFICES

Project: Office, high-rise, master plan, urban strategy
Location: Tbilisi, Georgia
Year: 2017
Status: Competition

Densely arranged vertical volumes that culminate in two distinctive towers at the main junction

As part of an innovative business corridor in the northern area of Tbilisi's city center, GRAFT developed a master plan for the Didube Chughureti District that creates a dynamic, scenic landscape and a healthy work environment featuring a wide range of activities for visitors and residents.

The development comprises a series of buildings that vary in scale and composition, reorganizing the site while simultaneously meshing it with the existing urban fabric.

Towers housing the head offices of the Georgian Railway Company

The master plan proposes large public squares that serve as meeting points, business centers and social hubs that, together with the new railway museum and adjoining parks, form a new cultural center.

The architectural gateway defines a new urban landscape.

GRAFT took an integral approach to the design of the site, allowing the landscape to transition into the buildings. The center of this new urban setting is marked by the introduction of more densely arranged vertical volumes, culminating in two innovative towers at the main junction. These two distinctive towers create a new architectural gateway that will serve as the head offices of the Georgian Railway Company and define a new urban landscape.

The façades of the towers branch like a railway junction. In one continuous motion, they move from a horizontal roof covering the railway museum and the adjoining atrium into the vertical sunshades of the towers housing the Georgian Railway Company, fusing the two functions into a single coherent structural element.

The new open-air museum features locomotives from the Georgian Railway Company, and for the first time brings together all exhibits, vehicles and historical artifacts in one place. The atrium combines social areas and cafés as well as a large public staircase that serves as a place for people to rest, meet and discuss—and draw inspiration from the past, present and future of railway transport.

MAGLEV TRAIN STATIONS

Project: Infrastructure, mobility, transport
Location: Worldwide
Client: Max Bögl Stiftung & Co. KG
Year: 2019 – ongoing
Status: In progress
Size: 350m² – 1,000m²

Maglev station at Berlin's main station

With the Transport System Bögl (TSB), the Max Bögl Group has developed a market-ready maglev train that combines innovative technology, everyday usability and intermodality into a new infrastructural instrument.

Through the application of prefabricated features and the integration of track and maglev technology, the company has achieved an extreme reduction in dimensions.

GRAFT was commissioned to propose the implementation of this new technology in an urban or rural context.

This included developing routes and stations for the intelligently controlled, driverless rail system, which seeks to contribute to a low-noise, low-emission future for the city. In addition to designing the routes themselves, the objective was to also ensure their adaptability at intermodal transport intersections.

Taking up the logic of the TSB system, which is produced serially with a high percentage of premanufactured elements, GRAFT's design envisages

Option A

Option B

a modular system that uses prefabricated components that can be applied to meet the different requirements of the various station types. These modular elements can be used to construct stations with one, two or more tracks, center or side platforms or combinations of these.

One modular component is a curved roof section made in two different sizes, which can be used to create smart, functional spaces of varying dimensions. The curved roof becomes a connecting element that recurs in various guises and characterizes the outward appearance of the stations. In their scale and rhythm, these roof sections also establish a formal connection to the city. And while the linear nature of the tracks becomes wider and more sculpted at the stations, in the urban environment it becomes a minimal, static, constructional element. The technical aesthetic of the system stands in contrast to the smooth, dynamic forms of the stations, creating a unique architectural situation at each location.

Maglev station at Berlin's central terminal

The elevated TSB system carries passengers through the city at the top-floor height of its residential buildings. Roof elements define the platforms as autonomous urban zones: For stations featuring a central platform, the curved sections create a central space that is separated from the tracks by a system of automatic doors. Openings in the roof and lateral glazing afford the platforms a sense of spaciousness, providing a clear overview even during periods of maximum use.

For stations with side platforms, the curved roof section forms a space that is separated from the city while still maintaining a visual connection to it.

In certain areas, the façade can also be closed using specially manufactured pieces. To keep the space open and uncomplicated, essential technical features, such as lighting, displays and information systems and seating, are integrated into the roof elements and the sections containing the automatic doors.

Thanks to its self-sufficient technology, the TSB maglev system could be employed globally in numerous locations and across many applications. Besides providing the designs for maglev stations, GRAFT also proposed a fictional but viable maglev route map for Berlin, connecting locations that would unlock huge potential in the development of the city—the main station, the Charité hospital, the Charité Campus Virchow Klinikum and the new TXL Urban Tech Republic. With the stations Charité Mitte and Charité Campus Virchow Klinikum, two central locations could be combined into a joint campus between which patients, staff, researchers and materials could quickly and easily travel.

Side platform

4

Roof elements define autonomous urban zones

Central platform

SUPRAGLIDER

Project: Infrastructure, mobility, transport
Location: Munich, Germany
Client: Deutsches Museum (Nobel prize winners Johannes G. Bednorz and Gerd Binnig)
Year: 2019
Collaborator: Mike Schlaich (schlaich bergermann partner, structural consultant)

Supraglider station seen from the Ludwigsbrücke, Munich

Supraglider station at the entrance to the Deutsches Museum

In a study initiated in 2018 for the Deutsches Museum Munich, Nobel prize winners Georg Bednorz and Gerd Binnig created a protoype "supraglider" shuttle based on superconducting cryostats. Its aim was to showcase the potential of this technology in the field of future mobility. GRAFT was invited to create a design for the shuttle as well as an integrated system of tracks and stations. The proposal envisages passengers boarding via stations at both ends of a 300-meter-long suspended track, that runs parallel to the museum's façade along the banks of the Isar river, while visitors can observe it hovering above against the backdrop of Munich's Museumsinsel.

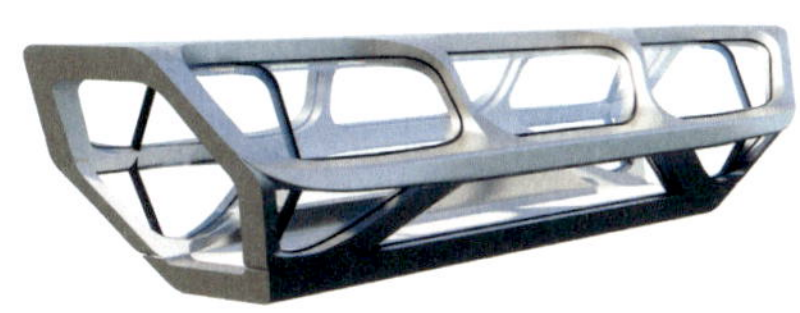

Supraglider shuttle with cryostat wings

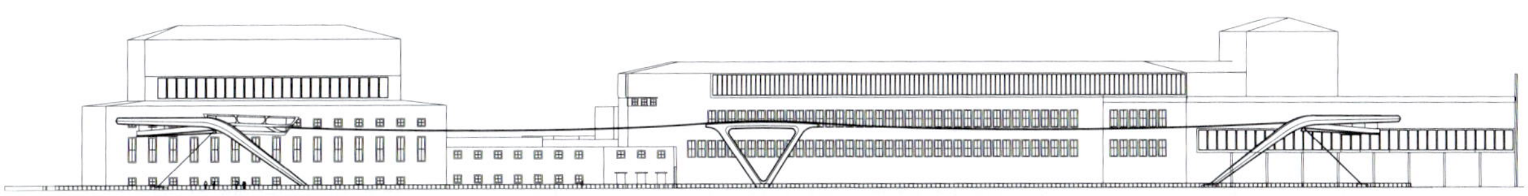

Elevation

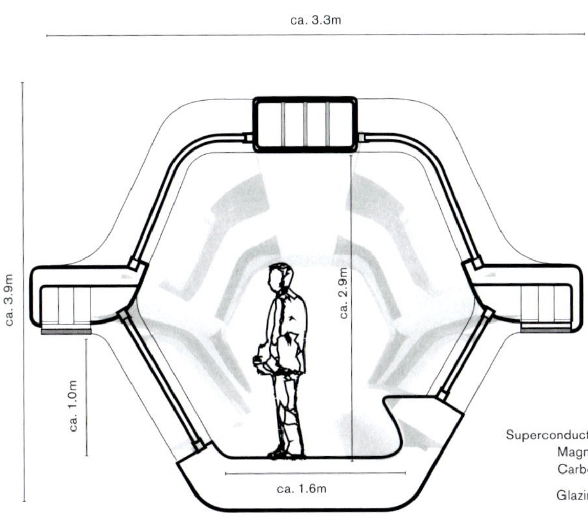

Section

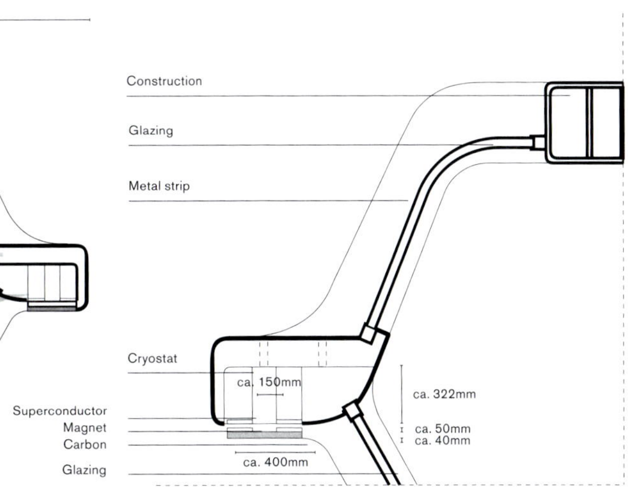

Detail

AIR TAXI VOLOPORT

Project: Vertiports, infrastructure, mobility architecture
Location: Worldwide
Client: Volocopter GmbH
Year: 2018
Status: Competition, 1st prize, together with GRAFT Brandlab and Arup; first implementation

Air taxi VoloPort in Singapore

VOLOPORT

Air taxi VoloPort in Singapore

The German urban air taxi company Volocopter has developed the first fully electronic, autonomous vertical take-off and landing aircraft (eVTOL), an ideal solution for use in urban areas. Together with GRAFT and Arup, the Berlin agency GRAFT Brandlab won the competition to design a modular vertiport concept for Volocopter.

The VoloPort concept combines lounge, security, and departure areas. The result is a flowing space that carefully orchestrates passenger experience and contributes to promoting acceptance of three-dimensional passenger transport. Depending on the specific context, air taxis will depart from the VoloPort's roof or an adjacent landing platform.

Check-in desk at air taxi VoloPort

Volocopter on display in Singapore

Air taxi VoloPort lounge area in Singapore

2X
VOLOCOPTER
VOLOPORT
RESTRICTED AREA

Air taxi VoloPort in Singapore

The modular nature of VoloPort enables a seamless integration of this new form of transport into the existing urban infrastructure. Potential implementation scenarios include railway stations, airports, and unused roof surfaces, as well as floating VoloPorts mounted on pontoons—utilizing space over rivers and other water surfaces.

With their new VoloPort concept, Volocopter is making an important step towards a new airborne form of urban mobility based on electric energy.

M.ICC MOBILITY HUB BERLIN

Project: Mobility, transport, museum, exhibition, infrastructure, e-charging, event space, congress center
Location: Berlin, Germany
Year: 2019 – ongoing

The International Congress Center (ICC) in Berlin-Westend is the largest congress center in Europe and one of the largest in the world. Since April 2014, this acclaimed epicenter of pop architecture has been closed, with potential subsequent uses being discussed in a broad public debate.

To protect the building from demolition, GRAFT initiated a network of advocates and collaborators from Berlin (Trockland, GRAFT Brandlab, Art+Com, Arcadis, Drees & Sommer and many more) to develop a sustainable design concept for securing the building's future as a major mobility hub and innovation accelerator. It proposes transforming the ICC into the M.ICC: the Mobility Innovation Convention Center.

TAXI

The M.ICC will offer pioneering solutions for realizing the complex's untapped potential and approaching contemporary challenges. Overlooking one of Berlin's busiest traffic interchanges—the city's western gateway—as well the former AVUS race track, the ICC is the perfect location for new visions of mobility.

Jointly developed by GRAFT and Trockland, the concept for the vacant colossus at the city's western entry point envisages a museum for motorsport history, a mobility experience center and the realization of Berlin's largest e-charging complex.

Drawing on many years of experience participating in international projects with leading players in the field of mobility, such as Volocopter, E.ON and Mercedes-Benz, GRAFT is aware of the demands and opportunities presented by new mobility concepts.

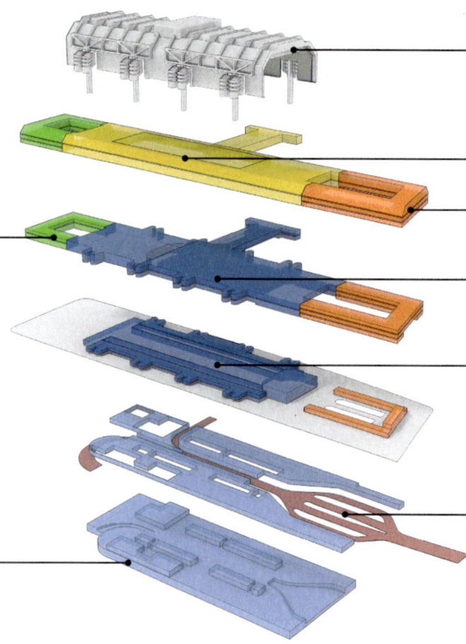

Axonometric drawing

Existing conference hall setup

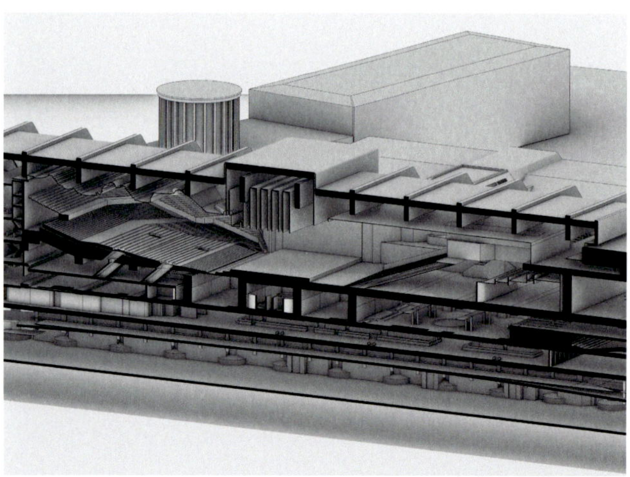

Proposed flexible setup

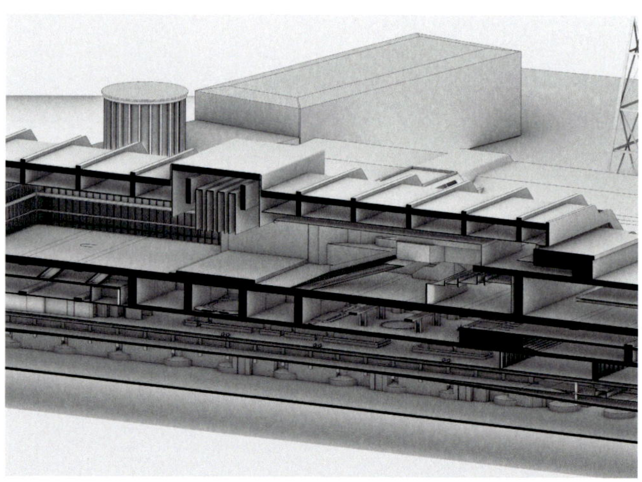

THE ICC HAS ALWAYS BEEN A HUB FOR MOBILITY

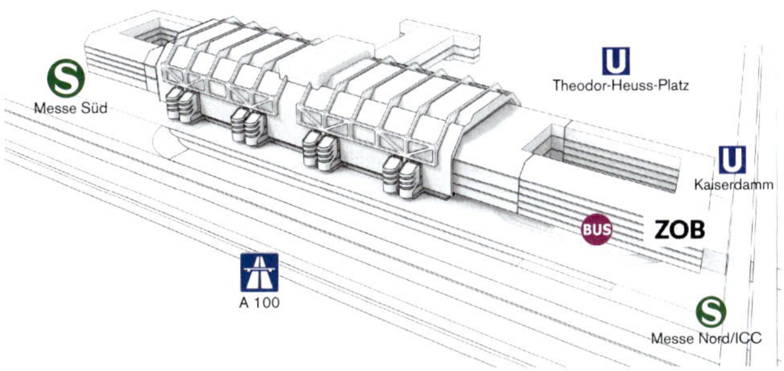

FULLY MODERNIZED CONGRESS FACILITIES

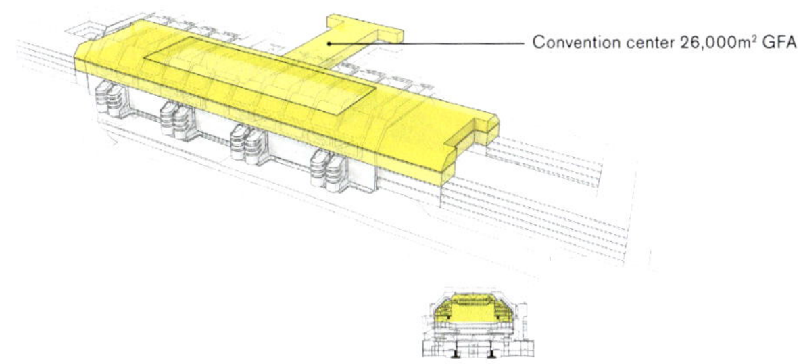

ADDITIONAL HOTEL AND OFFICE SPACE

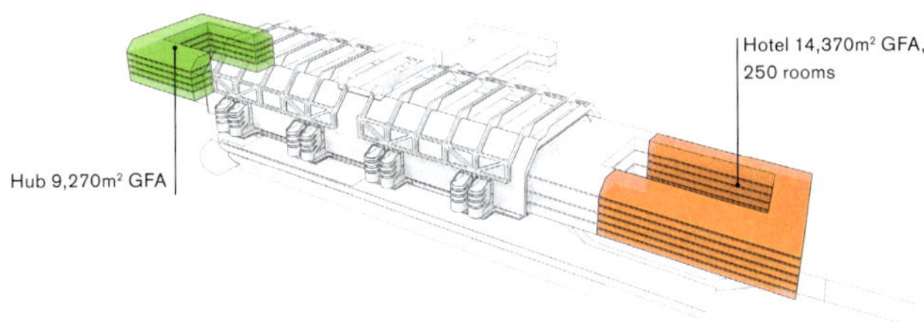

WORLD OF MOBILITY

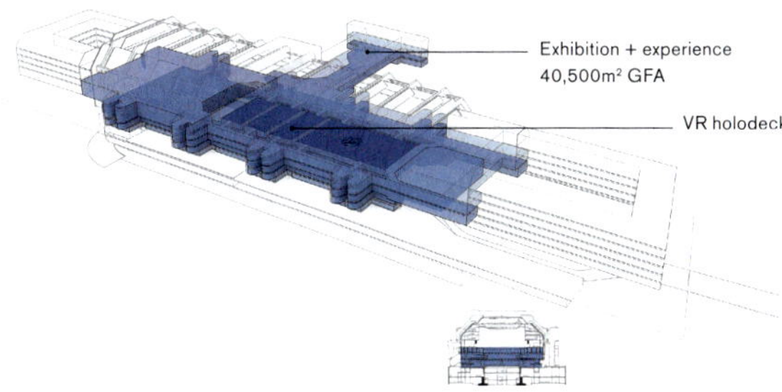

WORLD OF MOBILITY

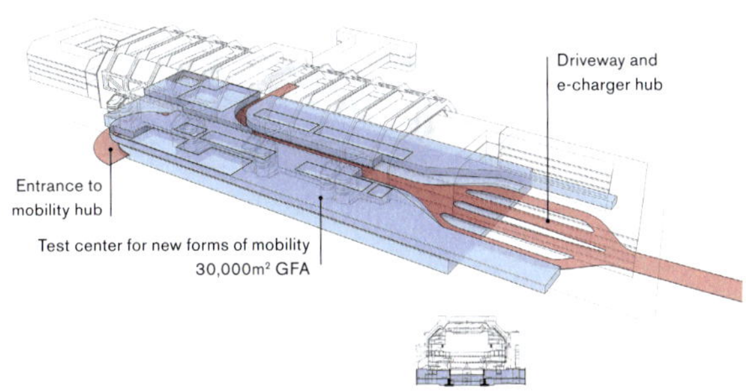

New uses for M.ICC as major mobility hub and innovation accelerator

With a new use and a new lease of life, this architectural icon will not only offer Europe's biggest indoor congress space and a central hub for contemporary mobility solutions, but will also be a place where people, knowledge and innovative technologies will be connected with the world.

Moonraker set 4: Technology driven stage, displaying the occupant's technical prowess, creativity and hands-on capability

Moonraker set 3: Utilitarian workspace and table-centered family gatherings

Moonraker set 4: Design sensibility and customization

MOON-RAKER

Project: Research, experimental interior design installations
Location: Burbank, CA, USA
Client: Volkswagen America/Moonraker Group
Year: 2006
Status: Completed
Size: 1,100m²

Moonraker set 4: System of overlapping horizontal surfaces

What are the future conditions of everyday life?

As the paradigm shift in the relationship between living and working becomes increasingly visible, the idea of the home is changing. People long for a home as a place to be secure, safe and well.

Traditional functions of rooms will merge, known distinctions between space and furniture will blur and identity will be formed differently with the emergence of the modern-day nomad.

Technology will open up new territories of how people interact with space and information. Spaces for mental well-being, meditation and cleansing of the body and the mind will become more and more important. There will be an increased need for rooms for contemplation, peace of mind, recharging and self-affirmation. What will the private spa look like in the future?

GRAFT designed and built future "life settings" as stages of visual communication. Like set designs, these interior worlds are erected within hangar or loft spaces as accessible statements, places of experimentation and inspiration.

As project partners, these concepts will be supplemented with products and consultation by the Moonraker Group.

The future life settings are four built environments representing diverse customer segments that showcase future-appropriate technologies, concepts and products in an engaging way. These four futuristic scenarios illustrate a broad spectrum of user types, interests, competencies and aesthetics. Modifiable in nature, the installation can be adapted to suit a variety of potential scenarios and uses.

SOHO CBD

Project: Master plan, business district
Location: Beijing, China
Client: SOHO China
Year: 2010
Status: Design completed
Size: 300,000m²

GRAFT's proposal for the eastern extension of Beijing's business district envisages connecting all land parcels to follow the flow of pedestrians.

The design features a central park that is partially elevated above ground level, providing space for public, commercial and entertainment facilities beneath. Large openings in the park allow daylight and fresh air to penetrate through to the levels below.

The eastern extension of Beijing's business district

The new railway station connects residential areas to the CBD.

The uppermost indoor level houses a new railway station surrounded by retail areas, while the lower levels contain underground parking. The surrounding towers are articulated by carving plazas out of the podium levels and elevating them above ground. Bridges connect the park level to the adjacent areas, allowing residents to walk to their offices above ground either through the park or indoors through the shopping areas.

By connecting residential areas to the CBD and its retail facilities and green spaces, the railway station reduces dependency on private cars and taxis and contributes to a more vibrant urban environment.

Bird's-eye view

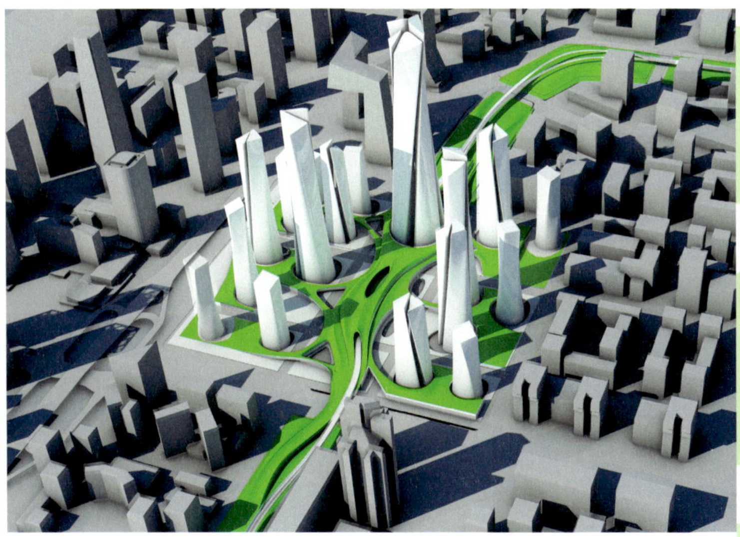

DIGITIZATION

Digitization 4.0

A CONVERSATION WITH GESCHE JOOST

In recent decades, digitization has had a major impact on how architects design, communicate and build. Architecture could become one of the most important interfaces between the analog and the digital—both an embodiment of data and a shelter from it. Either way, designers today are already being faced with questions of ownership and authorship, while architecture is changing rapidly under the increased connectivity of its inhabitants and users. As early adopters in this field, GRAFT has always been eager to foster a progressive environment in which new technologies allow new forms of flexibility and participation. Having realized projects across the globe, GRAFT is aware of what digitization means in different parts of the world. Between the fast-moving Chinese market, a more skeptical Western mindset and underserved communities in developing countries, there are many—maybe even conflicting—lessons to be learned. The rapid adoption of technology, decentralized systems and artificial intelligence will become a significant feature in the future—but in what composition? In conversation with the digitization expert Gesche Joost, GRAFT discusses the varying cultural expectations of technological innovation and its potential for the building industry.

GRAFT Despite having a rich history as a leading technological nation, Germany is very skeptical when it comes to the social implications of technological innovations. There is—and maybe rightly so—a great deal of reluctance regarding the digitization of work environments, as there is an uncertainty surrounding issues such as data protection and social justice. In China, where technological advances are adapted with little regard for their social implications, things are quite different. Do you believe in a designable utopia where digitization is implemented in a good and just way?

GESCHE JOOST Yes, I do believe in such a utopia. But the prevailing skepticism towards digital technologies in Germany has led the country into a dead end. This European perspective, with its developed sense of privacy and humanistic ideals of autonomy and civic participation in decision-making, no longer features in scenarios of the future in China. And that's a bad thing, as I believe in a connected world based on democratic principles—one that can be conceived in positive terms. We should open ourselves up to the discussion of what current technology can achieve and then take this dynamic a step further. It shows that there can be a society in which people have free access to data and in which there is a greater significance placed on the idea of the digital commons as public property. I see a lot of potential in putting forward alternatives that draw from historical cases: How could cooperative models, for example, be used to reimagine digital platforms in a new and fairer way?

GRAFT Aren't these the major gaps in the market that Europe could make use of in the future? How could you generate a wider appreciation of the fact that it's possible to adapt these developments within the framework of a European value system? For the last few years, we've been working on innovations using evidence-based design in healthcare architecture, which is why we're interested in the example of digital health: Using anonymous medical data, it's possible to compare many different clinical pictures and thus achieve valuable insights. But even here you have to accept that there are certain risks regarding data protection. And in view of Germany's history, which saw the existence of two illegitimate and unjust state systems in the 20th century, it's a very sensitive topic. What would be a good starting point for

Access to large data sets will become one of the fundamental prerequisites if we are to make a difference in the fields of digital health and artificial intelligence in the next few years.

society to understand that server structures with incremental security systems actually represent a new field of commercial potential? And how could sufficient checks and balances be built in to guarantee basic democratic rights?

JOOST To consider such concepts from a purely German perspective would be too limited; in the digital world we need to think on a European scale, which is already determined by the continent's internal digital market. I would like to see a European platform that is politically regulated, guarantees secure access to data on mobility and health, for example, and is also designed with AI applications in mind. Access to large data sets will become one of the fundamental prerequisites if we are to make a difference in the fields of digital health and artificial intelligence in the next few years. Without data we'll be left behind in an international context. There's currently a lot of impetus from the scientific world to build on some very good German AI research and rethink public-private partnerships. Under these adapted conditions, we could shape the future in the fields of healthcare, city planning and mobility.

GRAFT In this sense, cities were already cultural models over a thousand years ago, where, in contrast to rural areas, anonymity and the idea of freedom were achievable and readily sought. There's a famous saying in German, "City air sets you free." [1] Cities offered the opportunity for people to free themselves from the social control present in smaller societal entities.

This raises the question of how we should categorize social accounting in China and other regions more inclined to innovation. Modern technology enables us to establish individual control independent of urban spatial structures and the anonymity they offer. To what extent can this be undermined, either now or in the future? Is digitization something that has to be kept in check using data protection; wouldn't it also be possible to control it technologically within the boundaries of certain communities? From the point of view of an architect, there are two observable phenomena: On the one hand, there is a group of technologically versed people, perhaps with an actively defined purpose, who are convinced that the smart city is the future. And this conviction is relatively clear and understandable in the fields of mobility, heating and energy. On the other hand, there are those scared about the hackability of their private spheres, who want to ensure that their property is self-contained. The building might have to be provided with some energy, but the basic principle is, "My home is my castle." This means that, as needed, it can be disconnected from the grid and become totally self-contained. We encounter these two extremes in our everyday work, and it highlights the large degree of uncertainty in this field.

Can forests and cities own themselves?

Terra0 started as an art project initiated by design students from Berlin University of the Arts and is now run by developers and researchers from the FZI (Research Center for Information Technology). "The idea is to use blockchain technology combined with machine-learning, remote sensing and smart contracts to give a forest the ability to own itself." To make it into the first self-owned, augmented biological unit, the team bought the land and sold it to the forest. It is now a non-human legal entity that can act as an economic unit.

"With the help of drones and satellites, the forest evaluates its growth and economic value, giving it the capacity to interact with humans as peers." The team researches questions including: What kind of economic activities does such an entity choose to take on? What is its perspective on human interactions? What will happen when it is capable of self-replicating?

The concept behind Terra0 could be transferred to many kinds of autonomous agents, potentially leading to self-organized infrastructure instruments.

1 The saying "City air sets you free (after a year and a day)" describes a legal principle from medieval Germany: From the 11th century onwards, freed serfs and other members of the third estate began establishing settlements around castles and monasteries. Often situated next to old Roman or Germanic developments, these settlements began developing into new cities. More and more serfs started settling in these cities, where it was difficult for their landlord to find them. As such, it became a legal custom that an unfree person who had lived in a city for a year and a day could no longer be recalled by his master and thus became an inhabitant of the city. But if the master, along with seven witnesses, could prove that the serf was his property, then they would have to return and serve the master again. This rule was abandoned by the *statutum in favorem principum of 1231/32.*

JOOST We examined two models in this context. Borrowing from Benjamin Bratton, I'll call the first "The Stack": A vision of a completely interconnected infrastructure in which physical and national boundaries are no longer relevant. The model uses blockchain[2] technologies to create a DAO, a decentralized autonomous organization, as a new form of organization based purely on code. People no longer play a role in this model; they are merely part of a network. Buildings, infrastructural instruments and mobility concepts govern themselves autonomously by using blockchain calculations to achieve the optimal balance between economy and ecology. Terra0 has used the "stack model" to create a forest management system. In this autonomous, self-governing forest, it is no longer the ranger who decides how many trees will be cut down: The forest as a system monitors the global price of timber, the level of bark beetle infestation and the weather forecast and then decides whether or not to cut down trees. Humans are no longer involved in the decision-making process—it's a fascinating concept!

The second model is a networked system. I saw an extremely interesting example of this in Togo in West Africa: The WoeLab. The idea envisages a network of small labs set up ten kilometers apart. Each lab provides local neighborhoods with access to communal gardens, solar energy, a 3D printer and an even more decentralized network, offering digital technology to a small community. These systems are potentially hackable, but that's not really relevant as they only have a local range and form a larger network in this way—peer-to-peer.

GRAFT But this begs the question as to whether a forest in itself automatically offers a good framework for representing ecological equilibrium. What principles are guiding the ecology of this forest, which "laws of nature" apply? According to this, blockchain is a system solution for the self-determined, a kind of digital self-defense.

JOOST This autonomous self-management is founded on sustainability—in the ecological, economic and social

3D printers made in Africa: WoeLab in Togo is turning e-waste into 3D printers and robots.

2 A blockchain enables the sending of modification-proof information using a widely shared, decentralized database, thus eliminating the possibility of copies.

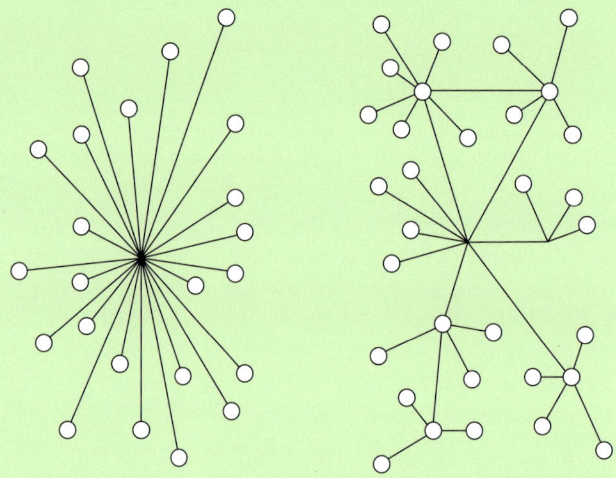

senses. Blockchain is simply the technology that lends itself to the realization of the system, and it has many advantages—including its decentralized nature and its security. But what we really need for the development of such future-oriented concepts is education. For the next phase of digitization, it will be of utmost importance for people to develop an increased data competence and learn how they can protect themselves, as well as being aware of who has access to their data and who they want to grant access to. There's a huge lack of these competences at the moment, which is another reason why we are falling behind with developments in this field.

GRAFT Do you also see a desire for anonymity in the international academic debate on digitization? Is anonymity equivalent to freedom, or is that a typical European phenomenon? As architects, we see the opposite in Asian countries, where everything happens so quickly, but where there are also no participatory models or democratic consultation processes. Urban planning there is authoritarian and centrally controlled, but despite the negative social effects, in some ways it can be seen to facilitate pioneering architectural work. Due to its top-down planning principles, innovative concepts can often be implemented much more quickly and more directly. In view of the increasing challenges we are facing, such as climate change or the corona pandemic, we're not sure if these social-dynamic models predominant in Europe will be able to remain competitive given the current pace of developments.

JOOST The desire for privacy is definitely a European phenomenon—this became clear to me after spending time in Shanghai, where the idea of a system of social credits is gaining ground. In China, the question of privacy versus security is viewed in a completely different way. Humanism and the values of the Enlightenment had less of a formative influence on Chinese society, which can be attributed to historical factors. By employing video surveillance in public spaces, Shanghai has become one of the safest cities in the world. But the people there are well aware that they value security and stability more than we value privacy and freedom.

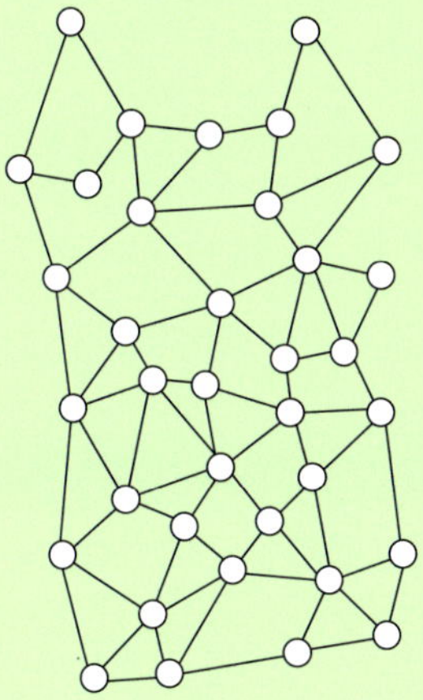

Centralized, decentralized and distributed networks

GRAFT In order to try and preserve this humanist idea, you could channel these democratic parameters into technology. We wonder whether there's too much doubt and dogma in Europe to find new ways of implementing technology, ones that will allow experimentation without ignoring questions of security. We hope that our work manages to constructively break down the alleged contradiction between an enthusiasm for technological advancement and the retention of social freedoms. Either way, preemptive misgivings and dismissing ideas are certainly not a catalyst for innovation. While we certainly soaked up some optimism for progress during our founding years in Los Angeles, our values are firmly rooted in European humanism. We were recently part of a delegation to New York with Ramona Pop, Berlin's Senator for Economics, Energy and Public Enterprises, and saw how few barriers exist when it comes to collaborations between academia, public funding and the private sector in the USA. The Massachusetts Institute of Technology (MIT), for example, effortlessly combines commercial and academic research relying on public funding. What do we have to do here to see the emergence of influential startup incubators that are funded by both public and private money?

JOOST I think that politics has less of a tendency for creative thinking than a lot of companies. At MIT there is a prevailing awareness that they are addressing major societal challenges, and everything is done to ensure that any new developments move forward quickly. Here in Germany, collaborations between industry and universities always seem to be a bit stuffy. But we are currently facing such huge questions in the field of digitization that we need to develop answers through cooperations between industry, politics and civil society and not only through purely academic research.

But we shouldn't underestimate the part small initiatives can play. A very vivid example of this can be found in Agbogbloshie, the biggest electronic waste disposal site in the world, located in Accra, the capital of Ghana. It's an awful place, a city made up of electronic waste from affluent European societies. Around 40,000 people live there, trying to salvage reusable elements from the discarded material, like copper from the cables. Two architects set up a local maker space there, featuring 3D printers, tools, an internet connection, etc., enabling the residents to take their upcycling to a new level. They wanted to provide access to technology and knowledge and highlight ways in which people could earn a living. Even though it's small and completely underfunded, it's a future-oriented initiative that provides a glimmer of hope.

GRAFT As architects, besides being interested in virtual and mental space, we are primarily concerned with the space in which we physically interact with one another other. When it concerns digitization, we look carefully at how navigation is altered within a space. We used to use maps to gradually familiarize ourselves with the physical reality in places we didn't know very well. Today we experience a very different mode of "seamlessness," as we are often aware of the physical information in advance. We are provided with detailed information from a wide range of interfaces, search machines give us recommendations for shops, restaurants or whatever it is we might be looking for—we perceive the physical environment increasingly through its continued presence in the virtual realm. On the other hand, screens are becoming increasingly larger, and multimedia walls have become a

Connected solar schools: SES and SOLARKIOSK bring power and the Internet to education centers run by UNICEF in the Al Zaatari refugee camp in Jordan. The camp currently hosts more than 80,000 refugees, including around 25,000 children of school age.

The connected solar schools utilize solar energy provided by SOLARKIOSK's E-HUBB technology to deliver broadband connectivity enabled by SES's Astra Connect broadband platform, which in turn enables teachers to use quality e-learning materials sponsored by UNICEF. Teachers and pupils can also charge solar lamps, laptops, printers, mobile phones and tablets. SOLARKIOSK was initiated by GRAFT's founding partners and Andreas Spiess.

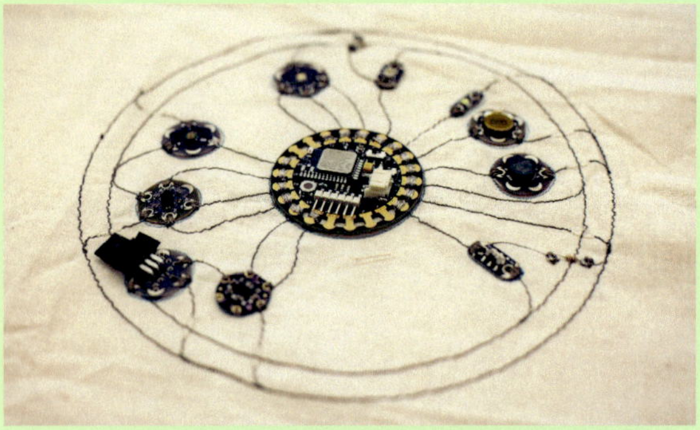

Gesche Joost conducts the interactive textiles research department at the DFKI (German Research Center for Artificial Intelligence), which develops research projects on the future of human–machine relationships from a user-oriented perspective.

Her department focuses on interactive textiles and smart materials that enable new combinations of textiles and electronics. Interweaving traditional methods of textile production and microelectronics, the researchers design smart materials that function as sensors and actuators. These are then employed in wearables, finding their application in the fields of health, sports, future work and connected environments.

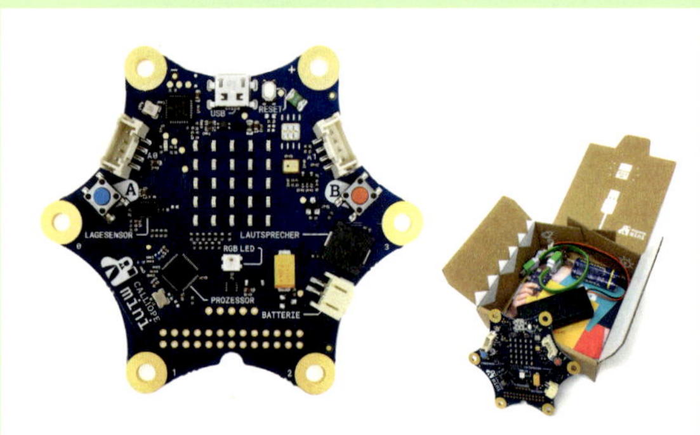

The Calliope mini is a single-board computer aiming to show children the joy of programming and helping them to start coding in a playful way.

permanent part of daily life in many contexts—in airports, for example—with the consequence that real shapes are fading into the background. Media interfaces take up an extremely large amount of space, meaning that all of a sudden, the question of designing surfaces has been completely redefined. If you think about this phenomenon in terms of urban space, you quickly encounter the question of individual customization. Will there soon be a time when everyone will be presented with their own individually customized media environment? How do you view this new, marked overlap of the physical and the virtual world? Do you think the boundaries of the two will continue to converge and perhaps blur even more?

JOOST In the field of research, the city has been viewed as an interface for a long time. And in the last few years it has increasingly become a reality—in the form of ubiquitous computing, the omnipresent potential of interaction. Virtual reality has also been hyped a great deal in recent years, but I am yet to be convinced by the applications I've seen. This so-called customization you mentioned is based on a far too limited perception of human beings. If I look for a printer online today, I will be shown adverts for printers for weeks afterwards, even if I've already bought one. We are reduced to specific, mostly simple—or not sufficiently complex—needs, and this is problematic because it frequently just defines us in an economic dimension. We are simply impelled to buy more. I don't really see much potential in this shopping bubble that we've become accustomed to. For me, it will only become interesting when it's combined with social elements, games, creative experiments and the element of surprise.

GRAFT It's probable that the whole spectrum will be on offer. An augmented reality program can either be a creative approximation of my environment or an interface with a purely commercial use. Maybe that will be a source of social conflict in the future: Only those with the financial means will have access to realities free from commercialization.

JOOST You're describing a dystopia that already applies in many areas. We already know that algorithms are extremely biased and perpetuate inequalities like racist and sexist discrimination. To name just a couple of recent examples, there was a soap dispenser that only recognized the palms of white people but not those of black people, and a piece of image software that identified the eyes of Asian people as closed although they were open. We have to decisively counter this perpetuation of stereotypes, as well as the risk of a total reduction of our needs. We have to ensure that it remains possible to break out of the system and wander round.

GRAFT The other fear is the fear of being rendered obsolete by technology. The chess computer demonstrated this, and even pilots rely on computer-assisted systems. At the same time, as human entities, our worldview is based on the idea that, as masters of our own reality, certain things can't be taken from our control. Are there hurdles that an AI application can't surmount? Or is it a lost cause if we don't restrict and regulate these things in their potential usage scenarios at some point in the future?

JOOST There's no real consensus on this. I'm the head of the interactive textiles research unit at the German Research Center for Artificial Intelligence. Rather than talking of artificial intelligence, we play it down a little and refer to it as machine learning, because it's not about intelligence, it's about learning systems.

This already works extremely well with very narrowly defined tasks that consist of a fixed set of rules—like chess, for example. In such a situation, a human doesn't stand a chance against a well-trained AI system. And it's the same with the processing of large data sets, for example comparing images of tumor tissue. Algorithms are simply better at these things.

At the same time, you have to be more nuanced when it comes to other applications. When you see how long an AI system needs to learn how to tell the difference between a cat and a dog using a neural network and how high the initial error ratio is, then you look at everything in a more relaxed way. Intelligent systems are light years away from mastering complex tasks like social interaction and creativity. Or playing football.

GRAFT Creativity in the digital field is something that has accompanied us from the very beginning. While training at the TU Braunschweig, people's final designs clearly showed which medium they used in their sketches—pencil, ink or watercolor. And from their architecture you could tell who thought in black and white and who in color. The instrument is built into the feedback loop of our thought process and helps to define it. At the end of the 1990s, after we'd finished our German degrees, we headed to the USA to continue our studies, filled with curiosity and a longing to learn new tools. We encountered the exponential possibilities of digitization first-hand while studying at the SCI-Arc in Los Angeles and began to employ them immediately after founding our office in LA in 1998. When we opened our second office in Berlin in 2001, we maybe had a slight advantage over other offices in Germany at the time, but we learned very quickly that the code of the person who had actually programmed the 3D architectural tool had more influence over what could be created. The first digital revolution in architecture saw a lot of people who just "played with the buttons," but this nevertheless gave rise to some interesting blobs.

It was a euphoric phase; with a few clicks you could achieve results that would have taken weeks to produce by hand in analog form. The debate was quickly reduced to purely formal considerations and only addressed the social and societal factors presented by digitization around ten years later. There was an early resistance to this technology because it was difficult to apply the criteria of beauty—the programmers were clearly no aesthetes. And then more doubt crept in, above all regarding the frequently random aesthetics: How were we deciding which computer-generated designs possessed actual architectural qualities? What functions was this new architecture fulfilling?

With Calliope, you have founded a non-profit organization that has the aim of teaching children how to program. Do you think the next generation will program their own design tools?

JOOST I think whoever writes the codes holds the reins. In other words, virtual freedom is entirely dictated by its framing. That's why I believe that the Calliope mini should be introduced as early as the third grade, so that children can learn that they can create things themselves—and know that rather than just consuming YouTube or setting up a channel, they can hack it and program creatively. My argument is that architects and designers should also learn how to program—so they too can achieve a greater degree of self-determination.

GRAFT Another feature unique to architecture is that, unlike other areas in which digital processes can be employed, the final product is not a digital one. We have seen designs with extremely complex, dynamic forms that then have to be painstakingly formed using timber board and almost medieval techniques to ensure that they can be cast at all. A certain degree of standardization is beneficial when considering the debate on sustainability, as lavish, unconventional production methods produce enormous amounts of waste. There are now several branches of research that focus exclusively on how houses can be made using 3D printers. Even here, contrary to all expectations, you mainly find ordinary, repetitive forms.

JOOST I agree. The huge promises of the virtual design process didn't fully materialize. But have there been gains or improvements in the areas of sustainability or energy efficiency?

GRAFT Yes, it resulted in major improvements regarding safety and precision as well as the speed of the planning process. These new means have also given rise to a completely different culture of photorealistic simulation, one that eats into an area of potential savings. Now, even in the very early stages of a project, you are expected to produce a large number of 3D renderings providing detailed information right down to the design of the door handles. We don't just see this as a technological revolution, but as a communication revolution, as clients can now be integrated more closely. We also witnessed this in the corona crisis—with a few hardware and software updates, the whole office was able to work from home. Despite the many stresses and strains that our employees surely experienced during this time, we were able to carry on our project work to a large extent. To do this, we took advantage of all the technological options we had at our disposal. The technology, however, wasn't new. What was new were the communication tools that made it possible for 150 people to work together efficiently despite being separated by large distances.

JOOST This crisis has changed my perception of things in many areas—for instance, the importance of public space, interactions with friends, family and colleagues, and having a place for collective exchange. I was very taken aback by the rapid adoption of digital platforms to enable dialog. In no time at all, we were all communicating by Zoom, Skype, Hangouts, Teams and Slack, and had even introduced joint online yoga sessions—in addition to the countless virtual meetings. Design in times of crisis has become a central theme for me, as it helps me to understand the power of design and what really matters. I was also deeply impressed by the political capacity to act and the level of solidarity in society.

GRAFT In the field of digital environments, there is currently a great deal of potential in the development and application of virtual reality. Beyond the creation of realistic materials and a physical tangibility, we might also see the emergence of an experiential dimension created especially for VR.

As users of VR technology, we are aware of the fact that our data might be used or even sold on. That also affects our clients, i.e., the users of a wide range of buildings. This brings to mind the former Apple engineers who developed

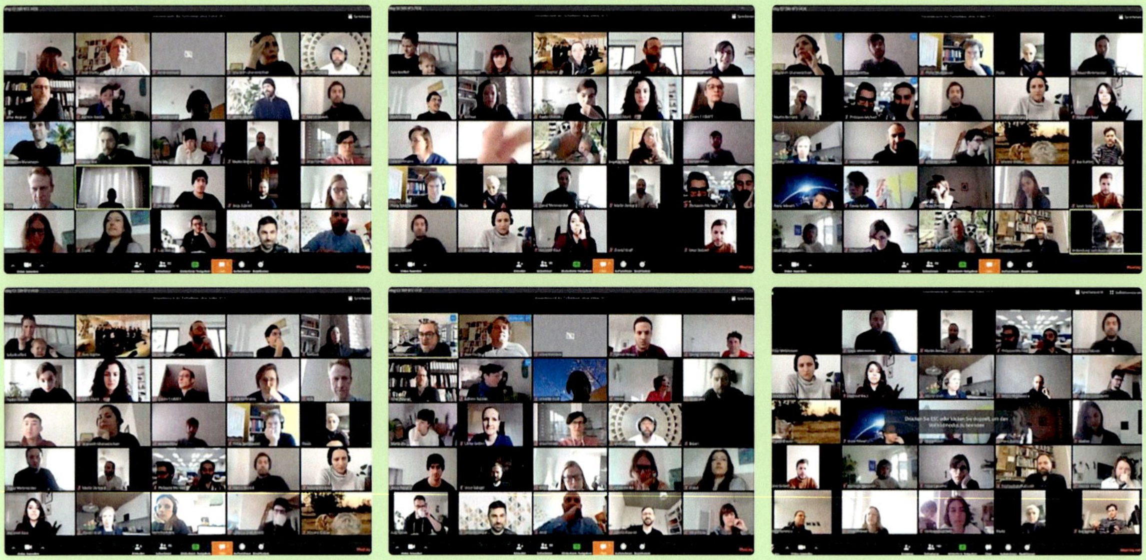

Technology and communication tools made it possible for the whole GRAFT office to work efficiently from home during the crisis surrounding the Covid-19 pandemic.

the Nest Thermostat, whose functions far exceed those of a normal thermostat. The sensor isn't only capable of measuring how warm a room is, it can also read many behaviors of the occupants and relay this information back to the developers. Such instruments are often fronts for very lucrative business cases—what is the extent of awareness for the phenomena that hide behind these digital interfaces?

JOOST Indeed, there is an emergence of new business models based on big data analysis. In Germany, though, we are still a bit cautious when it comes to developing such services. In the field of the smart home, for example, you can employ data analysis to increase potential savings in electricity and water use, or you can implement smart grids that can optimize supply and offset fluctuations. In recent years, more and more smart products have found their way into our homes, from the networked lamp to the router in the cloud. This has become a relatively normal thing, and our strict privacy laws help protect us against misuse. At the same time, there is an increasing demand for security—who wants their smart home to be hacked? Here we need security-by-design solutions that are easy to operate.

These interconnected networks generate huge amounts of data, which in most cases companies haven't utilized until now. Due to the high level of uncertainty caused by the EU General Data Protection Regulation, the market here has been slow to develop. The opposite case is true in China, where—especially during the current corona crisis—the system of social credits is demonstrating the potential of the complete analysis of networked data. For example, at the start of the outbreak, a patient from Wuhan was tracked and his path traced so that everyone who had been in contact with him was placed in quarantine—at least that was the version in the official media. In South Korea, too, healthcare and motion data are being used for the purposes of prevention during the crisis. In Germany, the debate has just begun as to the extent to which this would interfere with our basic right to informational self-determination. Finding a suitable approach to European data policy is of utmost urgency—for one thing, to allow access to the market; and for another to safeguard our high standards of data protection and the right to privacy.

GRAFT Many people give in to the temptation to hand over their personal data to multinational corporations, even though they have no idea of what these companies are doing with it. We also see this in architecture. In the city, due to digitization, the mechanism that distinguishes between the private and the public has been transformed a great deal. The fact that the boundaries between the private sphere and the public realm are no longer easily drawn can be illustrated using two simple examples that have probably proved to be true for most people during the corona crisis. The first is a person sitting in bed making a video call: Doing so they might be having the most open, social moments of their day in their most private environment. The second is someone passing through public space wearing noise control headphones—though public in the physical sense, they are existing in the most autonomous of acoustic private spheres. We think that the more easily, accessibly and interactively we can control whether we feel private or public, the more tempting, successful and acceptable it becomes.

JOOST But isn't that an exciting new field of activity for you, being involved in the design of data environments? You are quite farsighted if you already view this as a future field and are able to formulate a vision of how data environments can function in conjunction with the built environment. Is that a layer you consider?

GRAFT Certainly. Only yesterday one of our employees showed us a new product: A plaster–graphite render that stops any kind of telecommunication signals from passing through, thus creating a data shelter—a kind of digital panic room. We don't know whether these kinds of ideas will prove successful, or if the designer will ultimately be able to maintain control of the data in the building. In the end, it's maybe the smart washing machine whose intelligent software creates a user profile based on your personal data that poses a bigger problem. The corona crisis has really forced us to address the challenges of these transformations between private and public, working and living.

JOOST I'm extremely interested in wearable computing. Maybe you're familiar with this: There's no wireless signal in the kitchen because it's too far from the router. As a result, a lot of people have those ugly repeaters that you plug into the wall. As an alternative solution, we created a rug that makes the wireless signal travel further. You could also integrate

In the city, due to digitization, the mechanism that distinguishes between the private and the public has been transformed a great deal.

something like this into wallpaper or even a guest towel. In the future, we will no longer differentiate between what is technology and what isn't, we will simply integrate new smart materials into our everyday lives.

GRAFT We will probably also have to learn new decision mechanisms relating to property. We are particularly interested in the regulation of increasingly diffused authorship. After all—and we spoke of this earlier—in the planning process, different planners and architects all work in one and the same file, which in turn is based on logarithms whose copyrights are somewhere else completely. We know that every radical shift in society is accompanied by a change in the concept of ownership. Our approach to property will undergo a lasting change in the approaching age of full-scale digitization.

JOOST Roland Barthes was already celebrating the death of the author back in the 1960s. Authorship is something that we like to construct retroactively in order to create the image of an artist. In my opinion, this fabrication of creative authorship, with all of its associated attributes, is no longer up to date. I see a great beauty in collaborative processes, in sequential reworkings, interventions and reinterpretations. And I would also consider a change in the concept of ownership to be a positive thing. In terms of bringing about a fairer access to resources, the sharing economy proved to be totally overestimated. The ideas that are now popping up during its second wave, however, are much more interesting, borrowing from cooperative models and the concept of the commons. In Sweden, for example, every apartment block built since the 1970s has featured a communal laundry area. Now there are collaborative online platforms like Fairmondo and Enspiral. Such concepts of sharing will certainly be reevaluated in the context of the debate on sustainability.

GRAFT But where will responsibility lie if the concept of ownership is broadened? The architect currently has the role of controlling, monitoring and ultimately being responsible for the many processes relating to a highly diversified authorship. This kind of communalization is nothing new in the field of planning—if anything it's how it operates. What we build represents a balance of interests between the client, the planner, the legislature, the local authorities and the public interest.

JOOST That brings us back to the concept of identity. We construct communal identities and collectives. This also leads to a collaborative accountability that we refer to as shared responsibility and shared ownership. If we begin to understand spatial concepts and cities as collective networks, then such categories are necessary. The DECODE project in Barcelona impressively demonstrates how the smart city and smart data can be consolidated in order to rethink the city as a network. For me, it's a perfect example of a European approach to creating a digital society.

Gesche Joost, professor of design research at Berlin University of the Arts, is a researcher, founder, political advisor and tech consultant. Her work focuses on digital transformation and its implications for our society, both in her research practice and on a policy level. She runs a research lab at the German Research Center for Artificial Intelligence that specializes in human–computer interaction and wearable computing devices. From 2014 to 2018, she served as the German government's federal internet ambassador to the European Commission. Since 2015, she has been a member of the supervisory boards of SAP, ING and Ottobock. In 2016, she founded Calliope gGmbH, a non-profit organization offering digital learning to children.

Traffic Alert
Congestion detected
Traffic optimized routes

Virtual city model and gaming tool

HERE

Project: Dynamic parking systems, traffic scenarios and real-time navigation, gaming, augmented reality, virtual reality
Location: Worldwide
Client: HERE
Year: 2014 – 2018
Status: Completed

HERE is the market leader for navigation software and location intelligence. Using cloud technology and highly accurate 3D maps of our cities, they enable qualitative positioning in real time across connected devices.

To illustrate their services in a simple and comprehensive way, GRAFT Brandlab developed a range of exhibits for HERE to use at worldwide events and trade fairs or as mailings and gifts. Users can, for example, experience how the company employs cloud technology as part of a virtual city model or interact with traffic scenarios using a gaming tool, thereby witnessing the complexity and competence of HERE's products first-hand.

HERE MODEL

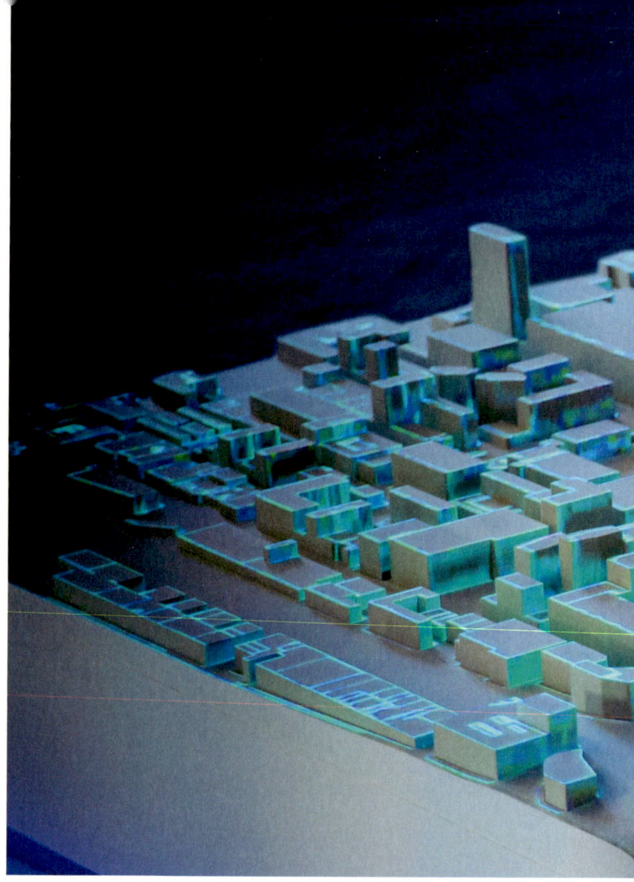

Responding to HERE's brief for an entertaining and flexible exhibit that outlined the company's services and mission statement, GRAFT Brandlab developed a minimalist city model that serves as the canvas for a projected mapping animation enhanced with sound.

The projection model has been in use since 2014 and is regularly updated with new stories. It is presented at trade shows around the world and is on display at the company headquarters for demonstration purposes.

The city model allows HERE to demonstrate how they employ cloud technology.

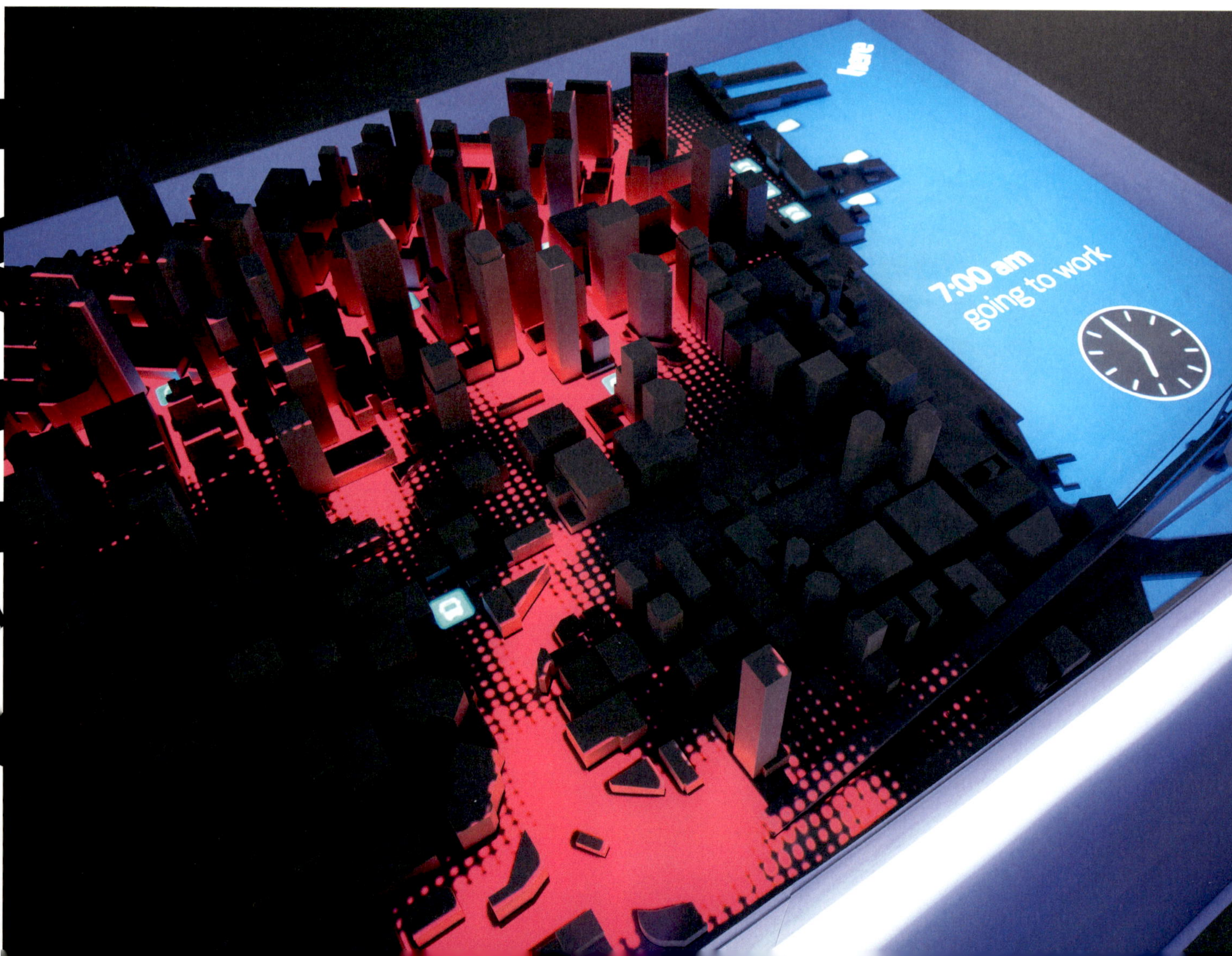

Projection model for trade shows and demonstration purposes

A projected mapping animation ...

... uses the city model as a canvas.

AR app developed for CES 2018

HERE APP

For HERE's presence at the 2018 Consumer Eletronics Show (CES), GRAFT Brandlab used augmented reality to craft an immersive experience that showcases the power and potential of HERE's entire automotive portfolio. Visitors received a beautifully printed map of San Francisco that provided the canvas for an entertaining augmented experience. The AR app was developed to be used by HERE's sales staff worldwide.

The result was a fascinating 3D experience that conveys HERE's automotive portfolio in a playful and compelling way.

HERE CUBE

Also for CES 2018, HERE asked GRAFT Brandlab to create their booth's centerpiece, where visitors could experience their core offering: The open location platform. "The Cube" presented a gamified demo of the platform, in which two players trigger changing scenarios by placing RFID-connected tokens onto a table.

What happens when a drone encounters rain? How do autonomous cars find parking spots? The Cube is essentially a catalyst for new partnerships and business models. Industry professionals can make simulations of future services and collaborations in the Cube and see how HERE can serve as their backbone.

HERE cube for CES 2018

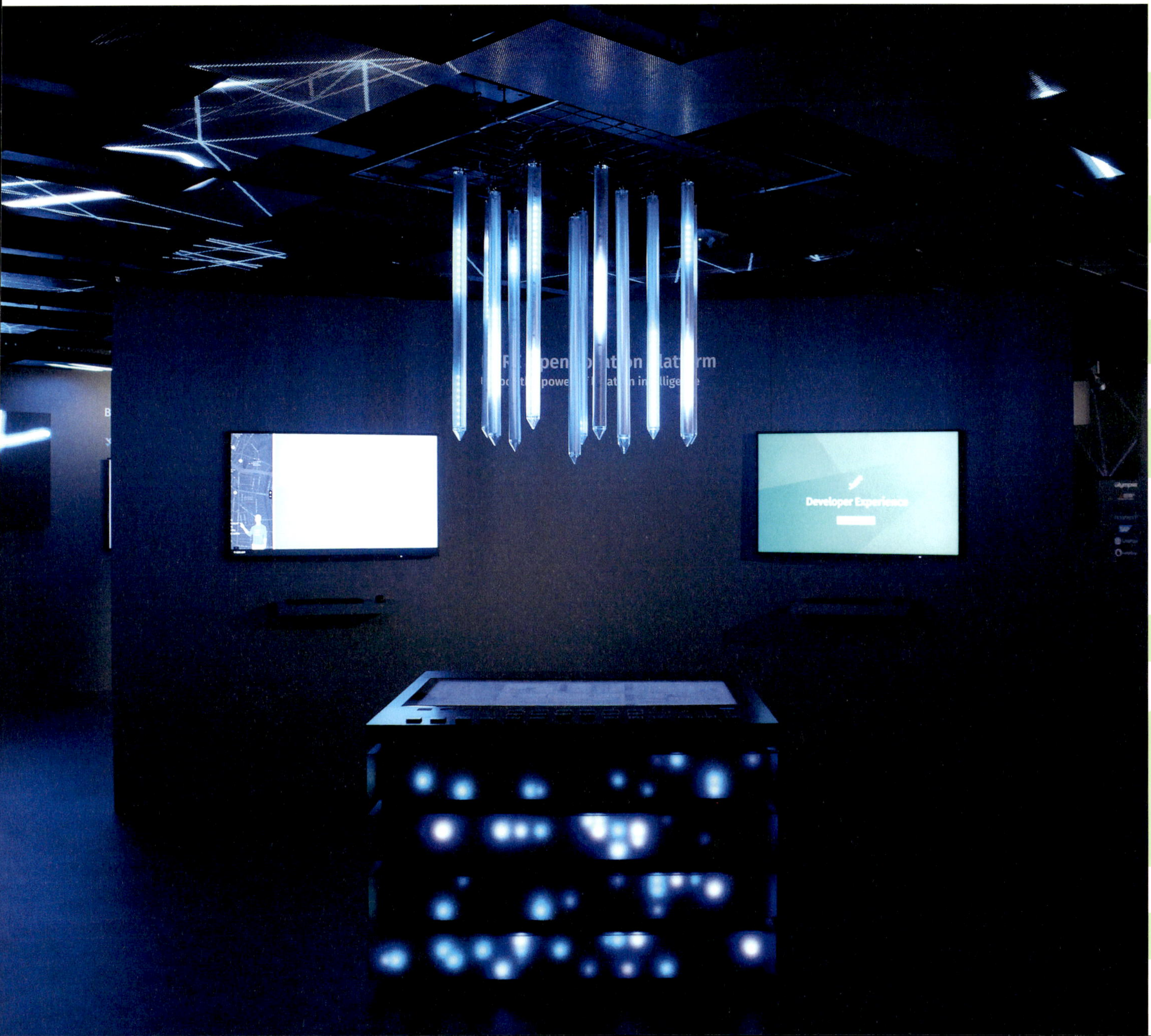

GRAFT ENERGY CONNECTIVTY HUBS

Project: Off-grid and clean energy provision, drone technology, solar power, sustainable business, rural communities, architecture activism
Year: 2009 – ongoing

GRAFT Energy Connectivity Hubs offer autonomous energy solutions and space for drone providers.

For approximately 16% of the world's population, most social and economic activity effectively ceases with nightfall. Worldwide, around 1.5 billion people live without electricity—600 million in Africa alone.

Ironically, these "off-grid households" spend an average of 40% of their income on alternative, non-sustainable sources of power, such as kerosene, diesel generators, charcoal and dry-cell batteries—a significant hazard for health and environment.

To have any chance of being part of future global developments, remote communities in Africa need affordable and clean sources of energy and reliable infrastructure systems.

With SOLARKIOSK, GRAFT and Andreas Spiess have developed an infrastructure instrument that creates an ecological and economic impact from the bottom up. The kiosks give local people the opportunity to acquire new skills and gain economic stability, safeguard their health and the environment and gain access to modern technology and communication. While the electrical components are procured and preassembled centrally to ensure quality and durability, all other materials can be manufactured and assembled locally. SOLARKIOSK has established local manufacturing sites in Ethiopia, Kenya and Ghana, covering both East and West Africa.

On-site construction of a SOLARKIOSK

SOLARKIOSK is an infrastructure instrument that creates impact from the bottom up, cooperating directly with local people and developing their community.

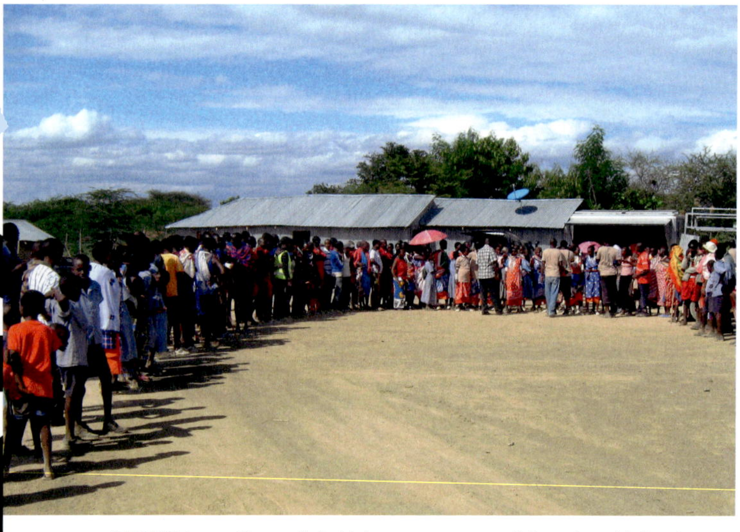

GRAFT Energy Connectivity Hubs encourage creativity and enable low-income communities to create their own value chains. An operator in Kenya uses the clean energy supplied by the hub and extended her business to power an adjacent restaurant, a butcher's shop and a movie theater.

Operating SOLARKIOSKS in a vast number of countries and designing the required technological solutions as an inclusive business model that provides energy, connectivity and communication even in remote regions, GRAFT gained in-depth insights into what is needed to increase access to essential services and promote development in isolated locations.

GRAFT is currently rethinking the business model, providing autonomous energy solutions and space to clients such as drone providers, refugee camps, health stations, schools and other services.

At the African Drone Forum in Rwanda in early 2020, GRAFT and DroneMasters presented a new concept that would enable the fast and easy implementation of a decentralized drone, energy and education network.

1.5 billion people (16% of the world's population) still lack access to electricity.

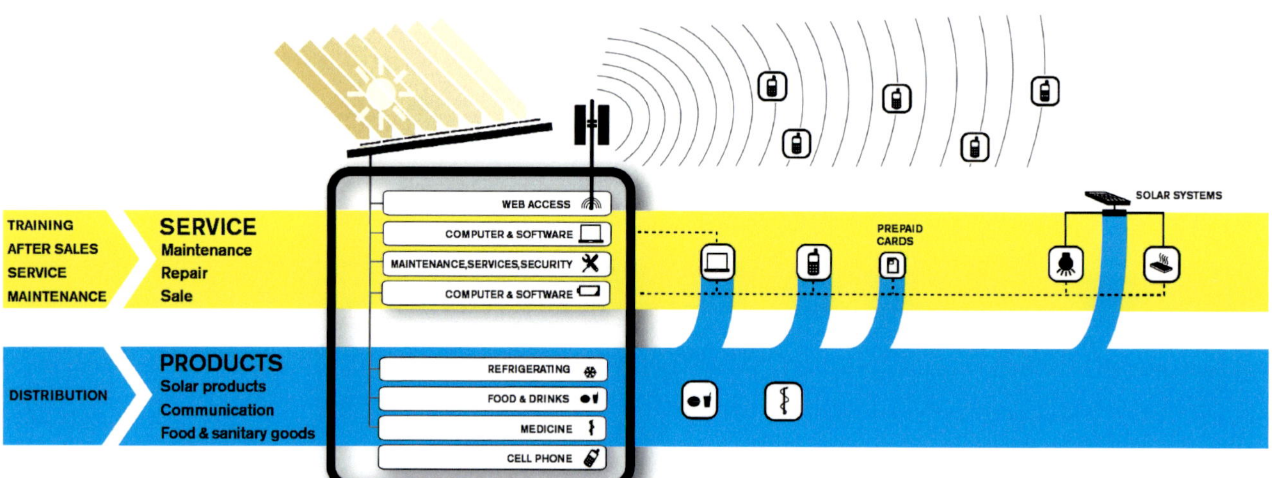

SOLARKIOSK business concept

SOLARKIOSK provides a clean energy supply, connectivity and communication, even in remote regions.

GRAFT Energy Connectivity Hubs offer autonomous energy solutions and space for refugee camps, health stations or schools.

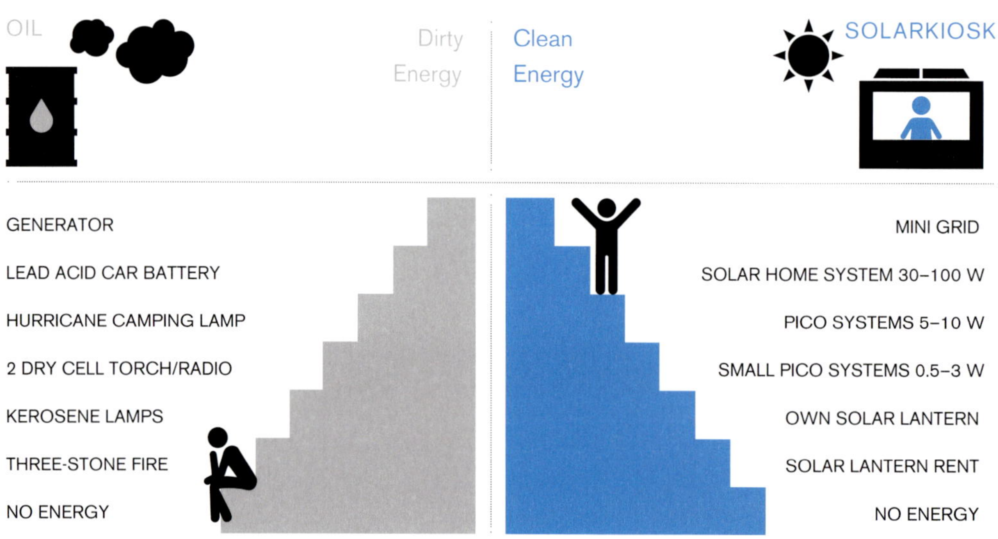

Energy ladder

SOLARKIOSK within a busy market in Ethiopia

The idea is to link the existing functions of the SOLARKIOSK with drone infrastructure to increase rural connectivity in Africa.

The GRAFT Energy Connectivity Hubs network is geared towards direct cooperation with local people.

Besides providing clean solar energy, the hubs serve as charging, take-off and landing platforms for delivery drones, creating a resilient, decentralized network with an enormous range that even encompasses far-off and underdeveloped regions, thus tackling the problem of last-mile distribution. Connected off-grid communities form larger networks with extended educational and medical functions.

SOLARKIOSK at night, Ethiopia

SOLAR
KIOSK

With the energy and the technology already on-site, the GRAFT Energy Connectivity Hubs unleash the potential for exploring and researching what prospective infrastructural systems based on drone technology might look like.

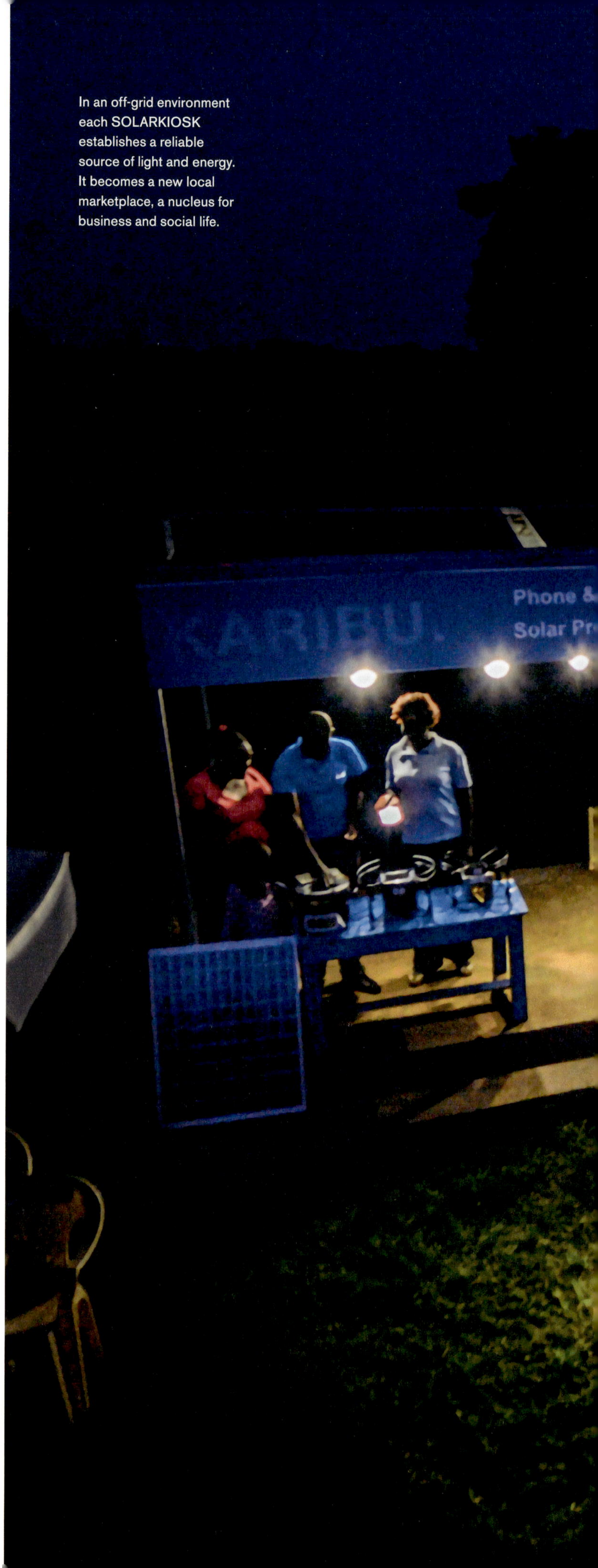

In an off-grid environment each SOLARKIOSK establishes a reliable source of light and energy. It becomes a new local marketplace, a nucleus for business and social life.

SOLAR
KIOSK
ENABLE. EMPOWER.
SOLAR
KIOSK

ICU ROOMS, CHARITÉ

Project: Healing architecture, evidence-based design, intensive care units, hospital, healthcare architecture, scientific research project
Location: Berlin, Germany
Client: Charité Facility Management (CFM)
Year: 2013
Status: Construction completed; research ongoing
Collaborators: Charité (Prof. Claudia Spies, Alawi Lütz), Charité Facility Management (CFM), Art+COM
Consultants and partners: LichtKunstLicht, Fresenius, Philips, Modultechnik, von Bergh, Guldmann, Barrisol
Funding: This project was funded by AiF research and development funding (Federal Ministry of Economics and Technology)

Paradigm shift from abstract, technical considerations towards the design of healthy human environments based on empirical data

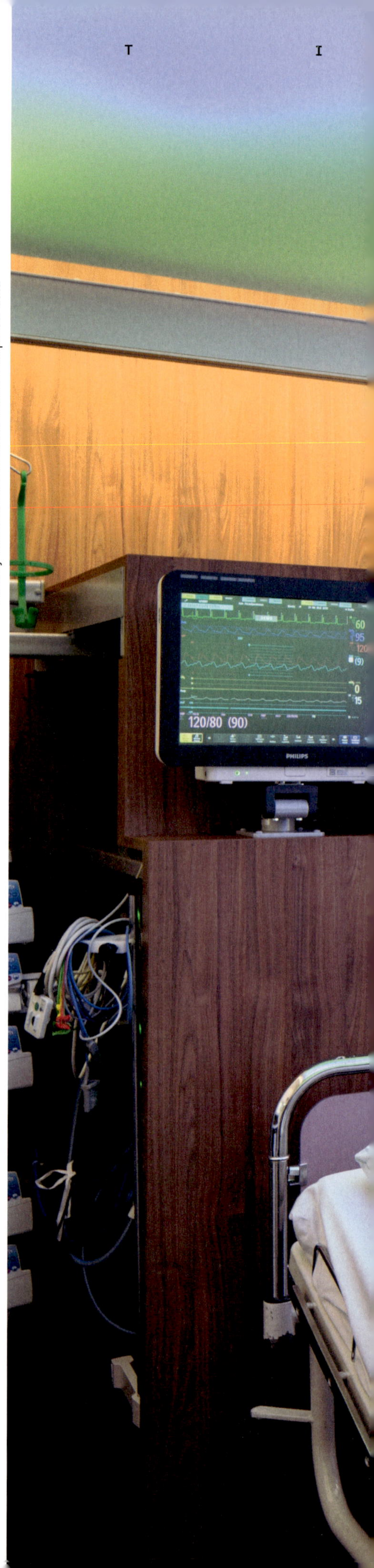

Circadian rhythm, sleep and cognition

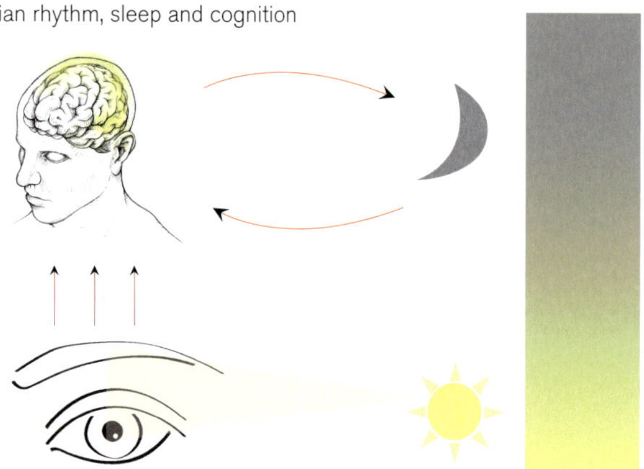

Geis S et al., Nat Neurosci. 2000,3(9):1335–39
Figueroa-Ramos MI et al., Intensive Care Med. 2009,35:781–95.

Medical environments are still considered self-contained, predominantly functional and technical spaces, far removed from everyday life and its routines. The extreme conditions and sense of physical vulnerability felt in ICU rooms are experiences that have largely been neglected in the design discourse.

In their five-year "Parametric Dream Room" research program, GRAFT has revealed the huge potential for collaboration between doctors, designers and the healthcare industry in the design of beneficial medical environments.

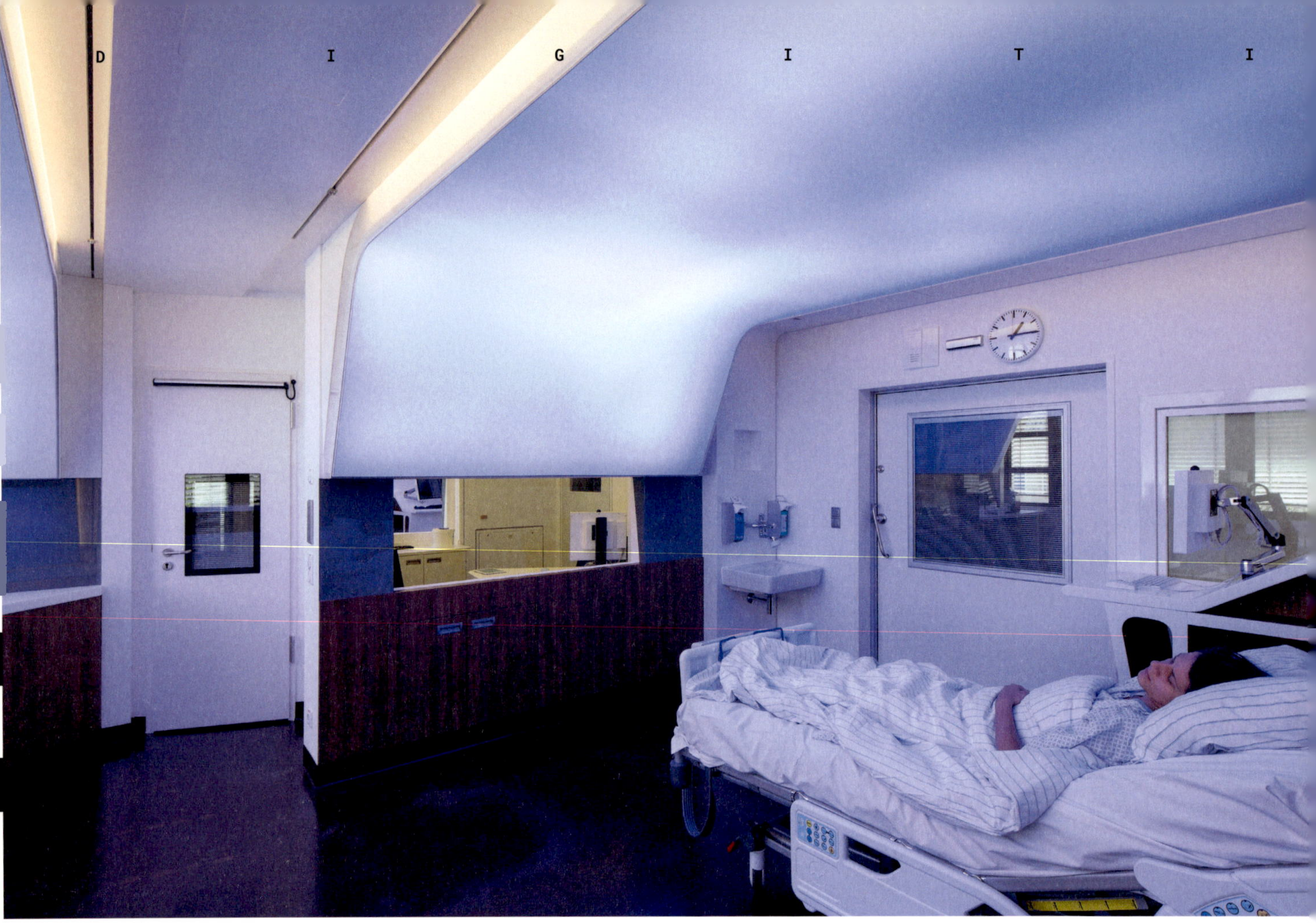

The two ICU rooms focus on lighting conditions,
noise control and new approaches to healthcare.

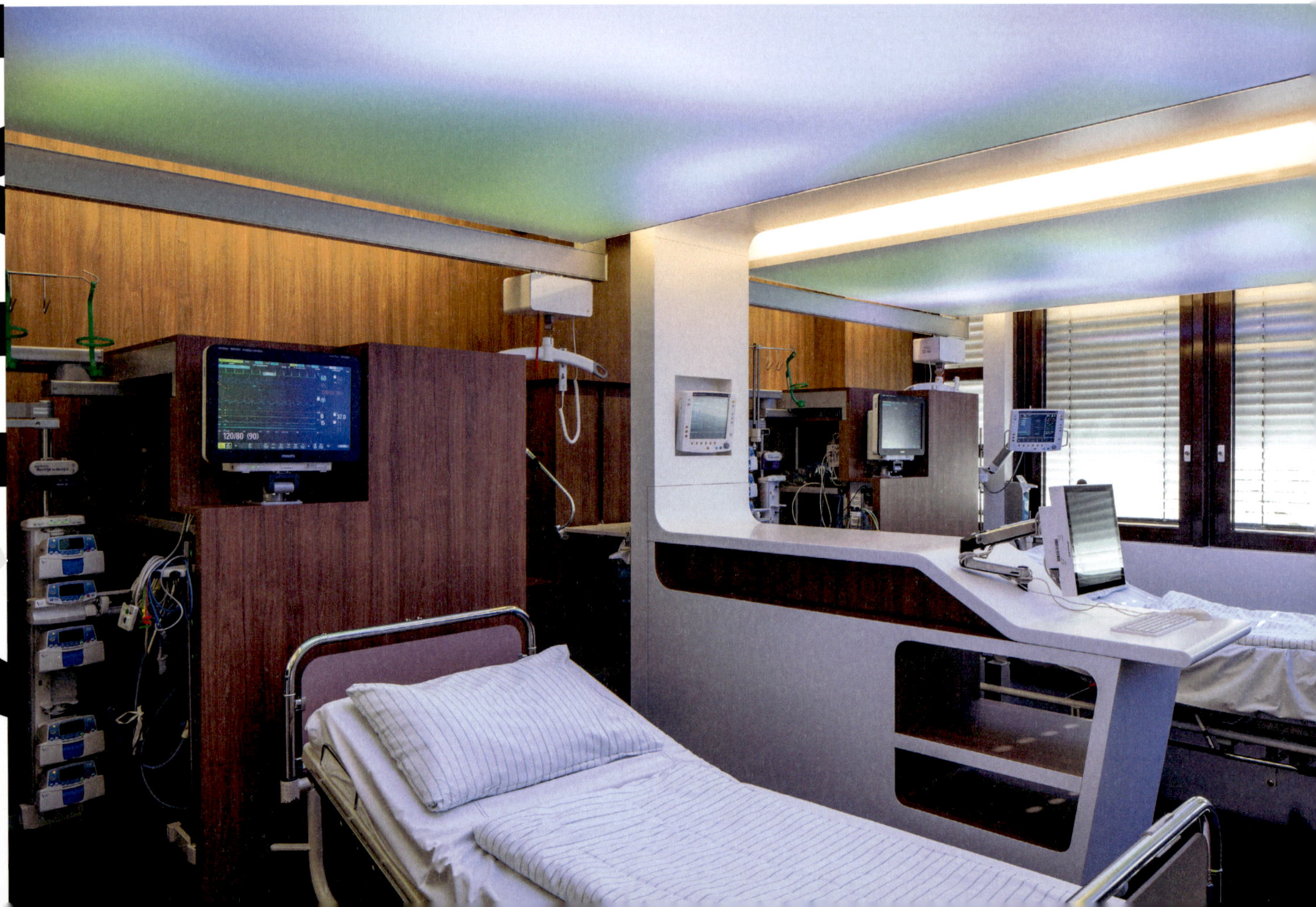

Noise level in an intensive care unit

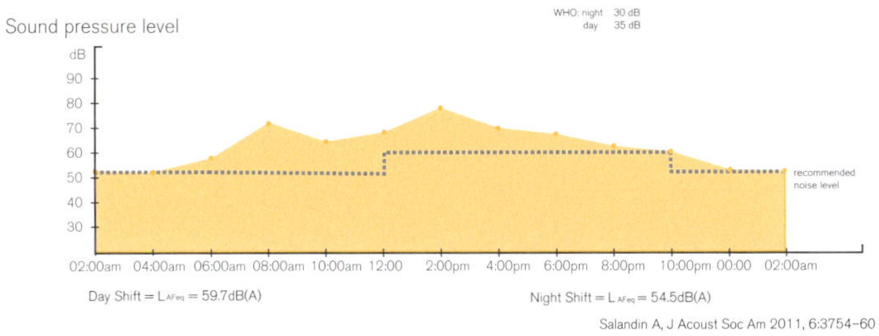

Disturbed melatonin secretion of ICU patients

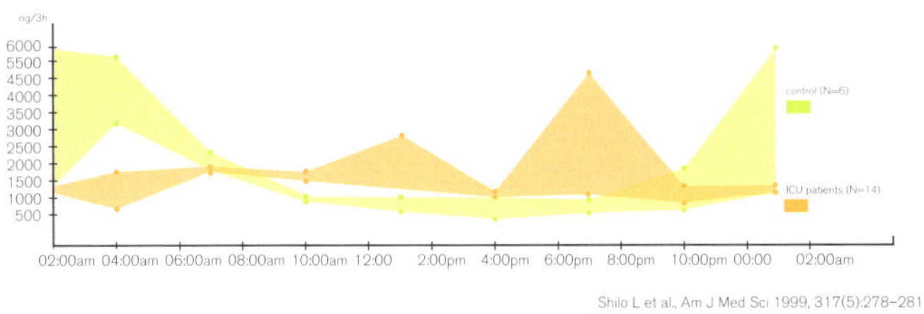

Physiological sleep profile of ICU patients

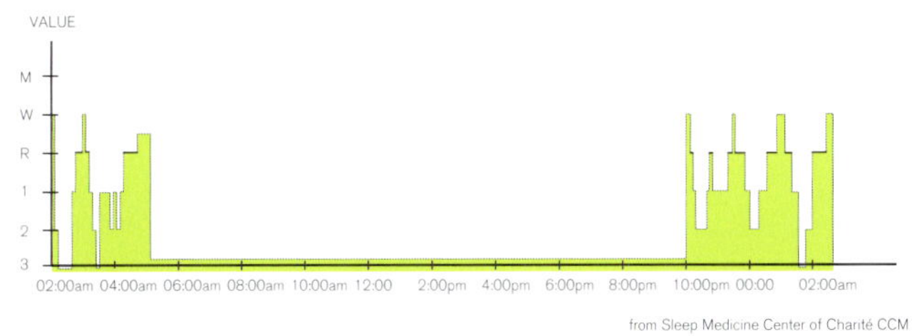

Lighting calculation

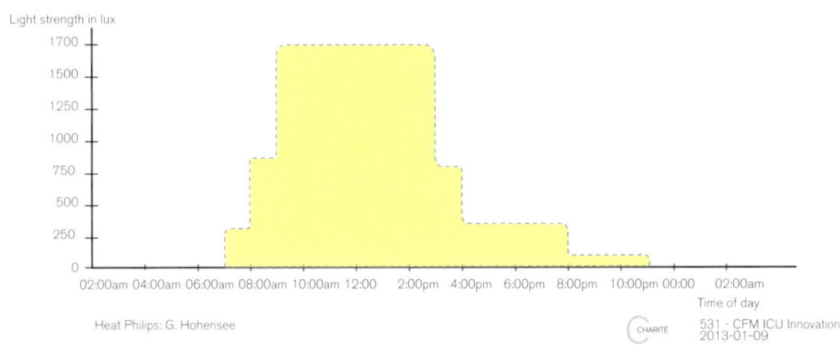

The two new ICU rooms focus on noise control, lighting conditions and new approaches to healthcare, and represent a paradigm shift from abstract, technical considerations towards the design of positive human environments based on empirical data.

The core component of the concept is a purpose-built interface that can be controlled by doctors and healthcare professionals as well as the patient, who can also personalize its content. This interface adjusts automatically in response to ambient environmental parameters and the patient's vital signs. The ICU design arranges medical equipment and related apparatus within a modular wall system located behind and above the patient while ensuring that measured data can still be read and the equipment is immediately accessible. A reduction of audible signals and warnings also contributes to reducing stress, as does an improved air climate in the room.

The research project started in 2012 and two ICU rooms were completed in 2013 in collaboration with the Charité hospital in Berlin, the Charité's facility management department and Art+Com.

Observation room

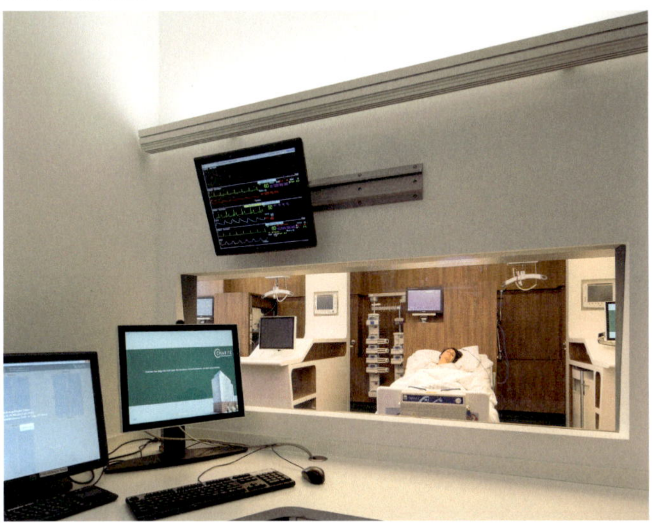

A scientific study confirmed the positive effects of the patented ICU room architecture on the healing process: The delirium rate of patients treated in the ICU rooms designed and planned by GRAFT was significantly lower (46%) when compared to patients treated in the standard rooms (76%).

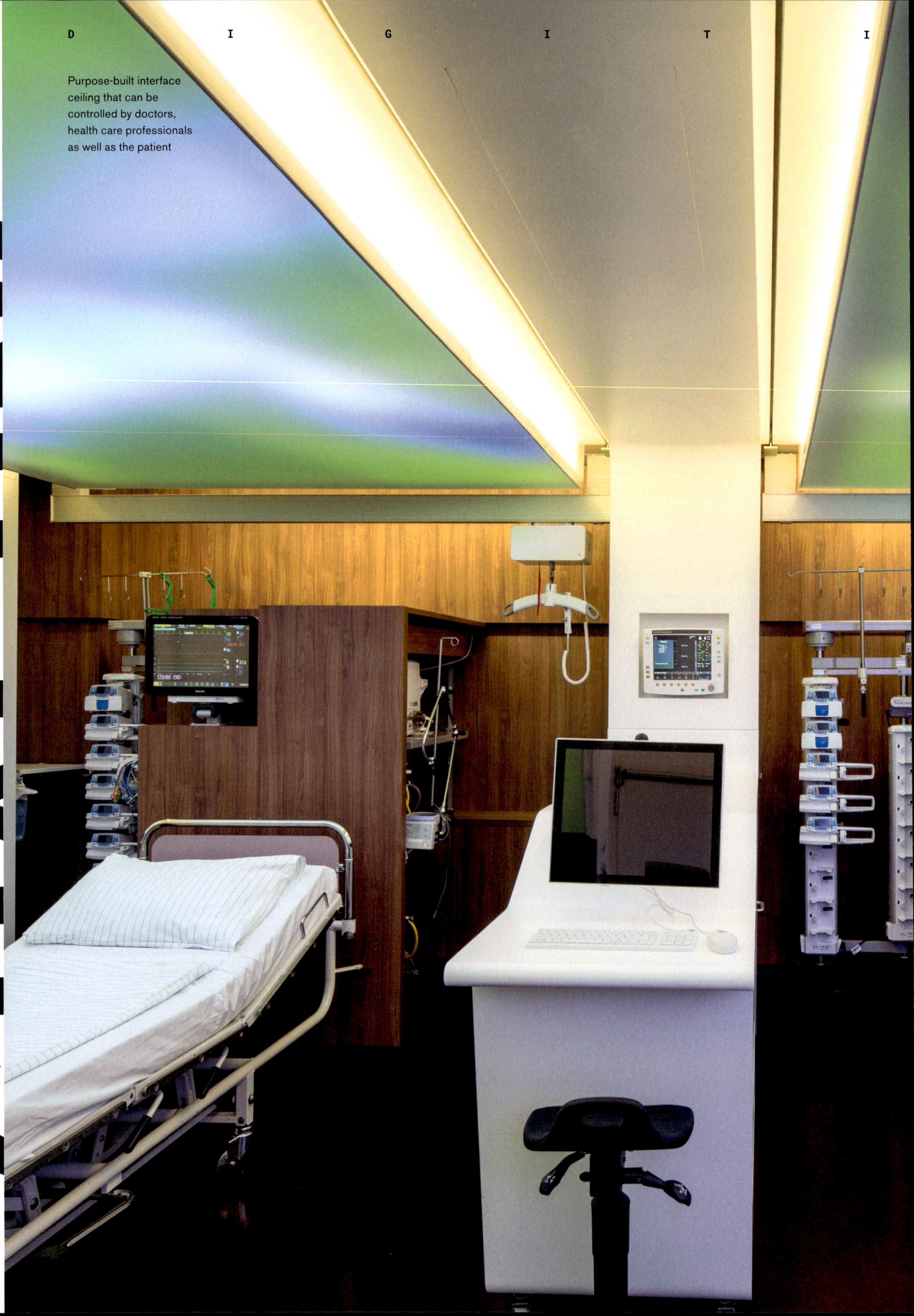

Purpose-built interface ceiling that can be controlled by doctors, health care professionals as well as the patient

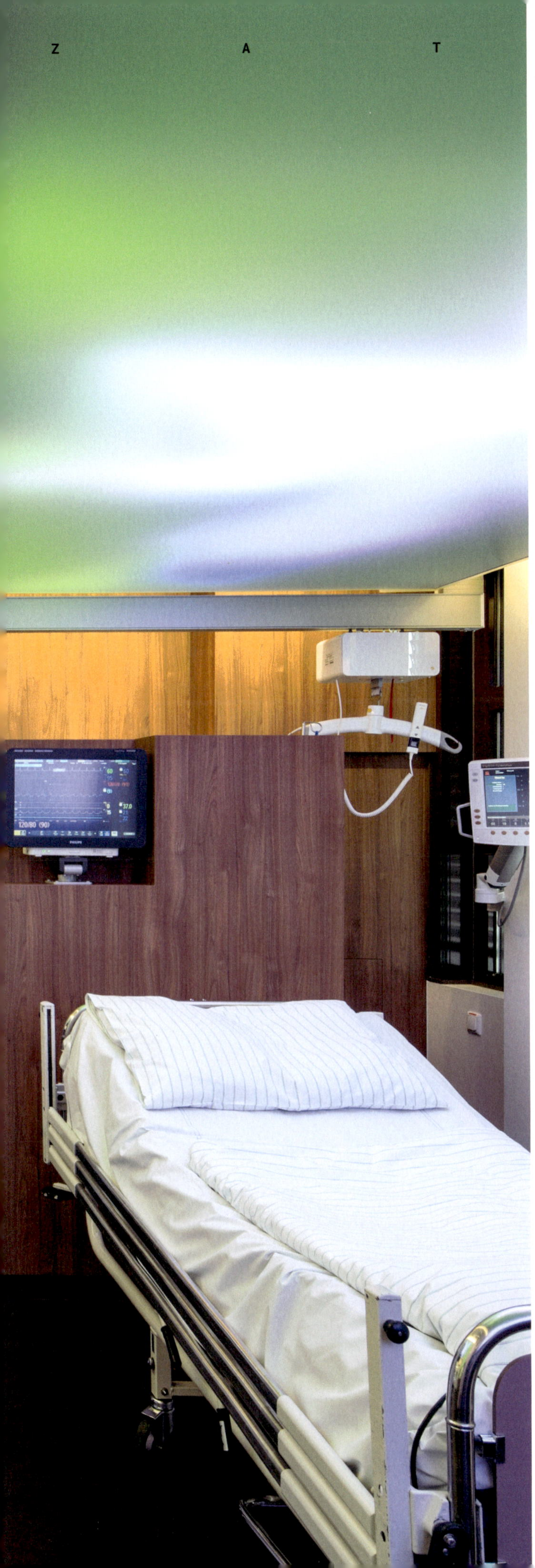

This project reveals the huge potential for collaborations between designers and the health industry and the need for a shift in paradigms: From the abstract terminology of sustainability towards an intelligent design of healthy human environments based on empirical data.

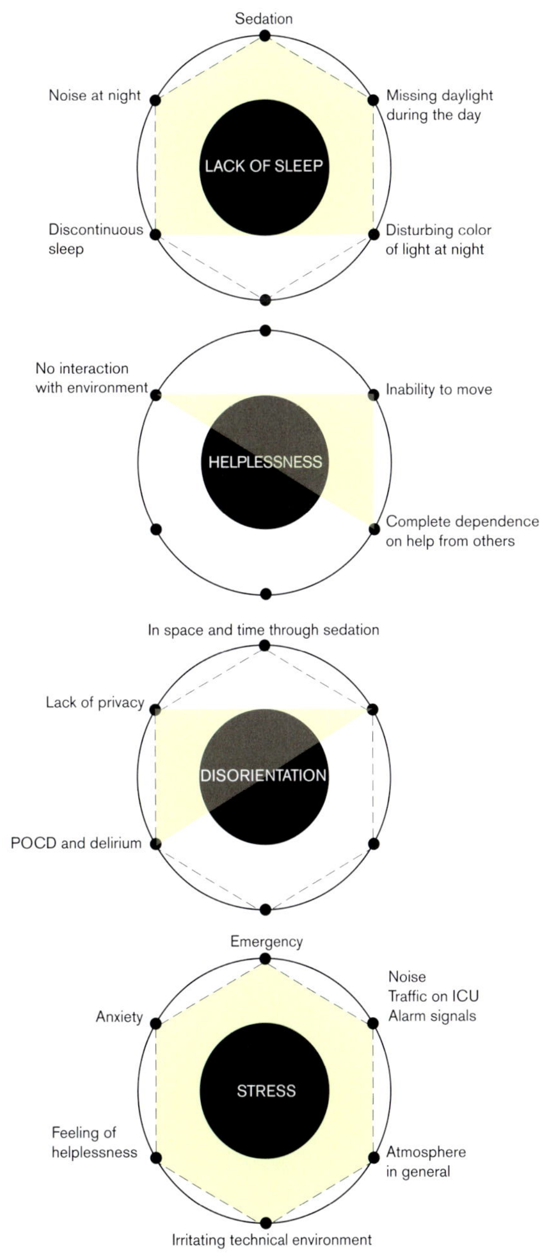

Patients in intensive care suffer from abnormal secretion of melatonin, resulting in lack of sleep, anxiety and even temporary psychoses.

WORK

REINVENTING WORKSPACES

A CONVERSATION WITH MIGUEL MCKELVEY

Common areas at WeWork blend work and leisure zones to provide diverse workspaces.

Tiny booths for calls are one of eight use cases at WeWork and are popular among WeWorkers.

This publication was produced under the conditions surrounding the global Covid-19 pandemic—a time in which many of us were subjected to unprecedented spatial experiences in the public and the private sphere. Our working environments, in particular, underwent drastic changes as a consequence of remote working and a subsequent shift to digital tools.

GRAFT has always been a close observer of transformations in the work sector, whether they originate in the processes of digitization or are rooted in the radical mindsets of new generations renegotiating their priorities between living and working. With many aspects of work becoming increasingly diversified, GRAFT's office designs experiment with flexible and adaptive spatial models for an evolving range of requirements while respecting the need for resilient solutions. How will these major changes manifest themselves in architecture and interior design? In this dialog with WeWork founder Miguel McKelvey, GRAFT sought to uncover new approaches to work environments and to work itself.

GRAFT When we visited WeWork in New York, we went to see your WeLive space right next to the East River on Wall Street. The project, a refurbishment of a classic 1960s mid-rise, functions like a city, it's a really interesting concept of sectioned neighborhoods. Your architecture team explained that the names given to the different areas are terms borrowed from city planning: Your users navigate through neighborhoods and communal areas, with staircases becoming connectors and meeting points.

MIGUEL MCKELVEY We were indeed trying to implement a neighborhood that resembled the feeling of our hometowns. As a kid, you knew if your neighbors were home because the doors were open, and you felt—and were—overseen by the community, of which everyone was a part. We thought about putting in screen doors on the apartment floor and seeing how many people would leave their doors open. Unfortunately, this idea didn't comply with the New York City fire code and we weren't able to implement it. With WeLive, we experimented with things we'd learned from the work environment. How do these findings translate to a residential setting? How can we actually encourage new behaviors in people? How can we add notions of surprise?

Trilux Light Campus (2020): The grand staircase in the foyer is an adaptive space that is also used as an auditorium and a place for informal meetups.

GRAFT Learning from the reorganization of work through ideas of community and applying it to a completely different typology, for example living, is also of great interest for us. Since it was founded in 1998, GRAFT has planned and realized a large range of hospitality projects. We learned to experiment with ideas from such commissions and apply them to other typologies because, after all, hospitality also concerns living environments—even if they are temporary. As a designer, you can test out a lot of residential scenarios in a hotel. Things that work well in this field, for example how hotel guests organize themselves within a space—both functionally and regarding communal aspects—are usually introduced in the residential domain a couple of years later.

We are currently working on a highly flexible startup cluster. The underlying idea is to avoid defining where users should live or work, because these lines are becoming increasingly blurred anyway. The design is heavily based around the idea of community. People live and work in five wooden towers that are situated on a plinth where all the communal amenities are located: Cooking, cleaning and eating are done collectively in these communal areas, positioned around a large, covered marketplace. The cost efficiency gained in concentrating kitchens and washing machines in communal areas is quite interesting. The real efficiency, though, is a social one, as people are smarter, healthier and happier in a dynamic community. We also ran into problems with zoning because German law demands that an area be designated as a place for either living or working. For us, the beauty lies in the hybridization of functions.

MCKELVEY I'm always so perplexed and frustrated as to why zoning regulations aren't more adaptable. I'm sure current technology would allow us to compensate for everything.

GRAFT It seems that it's not necessarily the regulations per se, but the way they are interpreted and translated. In a bolder, more innovative environment, you can actually experiment a lot within the regulations and really push the envelope. The sad thing is that official authorities usually have working environments that are opposite to this—hence fostering a mindset of always covering your back and creating a silo mentality. If we could change their working cultures regarding the idea of exchange and communal encouragement of innovative thought, our cities might then reflect that. It would be a very interesting task to rethink the workflow and collaboration through space in a city planning department.

But suggestive spatial layouts are just one part of how innovation will challenge our working environments. Technological and demographic changes will cause major shifts in the labor market, with new emerging careers and modes of work. With machines doing more and more predictable and routine tasks for us, the future of work seems to be rooted much more in the notion of "purpose." How will work be perceived, as digitization moves along and we are replaced by robots or algorithms?

MCKELVEY I haven't really ever gotten to a place where I feel super comfortable proposing or suggesting any conclusions, primarily because it feels so imbalanced what those proposals would mean for different people. When you look at it from a typical perspective, you think about the elimination of jobs that are labor, which aren't necessarily occupied by knowledge workers. In this case you're actually talking about a class issue and fair access to our economic system. This issue will not be solved by architecture or design. It's different when I think about it for the people who might benefit from less work, like myself: What would I do if I only needed to work four hours a day to maintain my lifestyle? It's a fantasy at this point, but I could follow all these other intellectual pursuits or a healthier lifestyle. For that you could design great spaces to support new purposes, interacting in different constructs of physical and intellectual discourse. Still, there will always be this affordability line that excludes people. So, what do we do about that? You would have to go deeper into racial or class discrimination and other societal aspects, which are also part of the whole story.

GRAFT We agree. It's definitely going to raise major questions of social justice. But what if you had to look at it from an idealistic viewpoint? Let's say that all these inevitable developments would open up multitudes of resources and more people would be able to nurture the uniquely human trait of being creative. If work itself were to become more purpose-driven, in contrast to money-driven, how would that change the working environment? If people specifically went to work to be creative and solve problems, it would allow the emergence of a new aesthetics of physical workspaces that promote the uniquely human skill set of creating meaning through social and emotional intelligence, collaboration and creativity.

WORKING COMMUNITIES AND INDIVIDUALS HAVE NOT YET UNLOCKED THEIR FULL POTENTIAL WITHIN CREATIVE STRUCTURES AND SETUPS.

Neue Sentimental Film (2001), p. 120: An early GRAFT office design in Los Angeles integrates leisure and communal activities into the workspaces.

MCKELVEY In our construct of WeWork, we have seven or eight different workspace case typologies. For example, we have very small phone booths, which are one of our most popular use cases. I wouldn't use them personally, except to make a quick call, but some people will go in there for the entire day. They get in early in order to claim it, and they are happy to be in this little box for eight or ten hours straight. You have to acknowledge that there's a huge diversity in the way people show up in space and what they feel comfortable with.

I think people have a passive relationship with themselves, meaning they don't actually choose the spaces that are most conducive to their planned activity. We have all these amenities that aren't used in the "right way." How do we get people to use this array of amenities that we offer?
In this context we are actively tackling thresholds. It's similar to the online marketing rule: The more clicks, the less sales. We want to remove the number of steps towards a decision. How do you remove those thresholds and those numbers of clicks in real life to actually get to that activity? That's a big premise of why we started. We are trying to make our spaces really multifunctional. So, when you walk in one morning, there might be a bootcamp exercise at 8am in the common area. The next day you can just wear your shorts in the morning and join in. Or rather than putting a speaker with an audience in an auditorium, we put a keynote presentation in the foyer, so you have to walk by and can't avoid it. Maybe you pause, spend an hour and a half there and then there's a happy hour afterwards, where you meet someone really interesting to discuss the subject with. That's the ideal case for us. It's part of the challenge to find out over time what the perfect configuration is, the one that will result in fulfillment. It's hard for people to break out of old habits.

GRAFT As architects who derive inspiration from user-centered design thinking, we want to know what the people who inhabit or use our spaces really need and want.
But it seems that working communities and individuals have not yet unlocked their full potential within creative structures and setups.

If we look at the architectural history of workspaces, we notice a reinvention or a trend hypothesis appearing approximately every ten years. Since the turn of the century, for the first time, there seems to have been no homogeneous idea about how the next generation of work will evolve. You are suggesting that working itself, as well as working environments, will become more eclectic and open. The seven use cases you mentioned could probably be broken down into even more variations.

Why are we increasingly becoming migrants between different identities and communities that seek to hop around, even commuting within a workspace? Is the grand experiment that scouts different forms of life and work the new reality or just another trend?

MCKELVEY The first dot-com boom, which was around '98 or '99, switched the mindset for a lot of people. It became clear that you didn't need to follow a certain, well-known path in order to become successful. During that explosion, there was a detachment among young people, who discovered that they didn't have to wait 20 years to move up the ladder if they just started their own company. At the same time, the companies that became more corporate were responding to that vibe. All these people who were unleashed from the cubicle then needed a lot of new spatial programs and entertainment to engage them.

GRAFT We were very lucky to be in California at that time. The guys you just mentioned were our first clients when we started GRAFT in 1998. They were younger than us, and we were only 30 ourselves. We designed those dot-com offices. The design brief was often like: "Our employees work nonstop. They basically live here. How do I keep them? How does boy meet girl and vice versa?" Knowing that most employees spent almost all their time at the office, we basically tried to create an environment that embraced work, leisure and life. That was new. At the same time, the workforce was still expecting cubicles. When we were done, the companies were either so big that they had to move into a bigger building and we had to start all over again, or they had collapsed. When we came to Germany a few years later, nobody had even heard about these developments. No one understood our designs either.

MCKELVEY I think first and foremost people want to do something that they feel is purposeful, and they want to be directly connected to that purpose. Secondly, they actually want to have fun, especially young people, pre-family. Their social network is often where they work. If they move to New York City without knowing anybody, as early employees at the company they're working for they'll form friendship groups that they'll probably have for life. I don't know how many generations back, but probably before the dot-com boom, their expectation wasn't to have fun.

GRAFT We agree. We think they expected that their life would start at the end of the working day. They didn't envisage that it might be otherwise. The permanent shift of this understanding makes sense, even more for employers. Efficiency and efficacy are not based on squeezing everybody to the core. Fun and health equals productivity—with that formula in mind, everything changes for the better.
In Germany, it is regulated by federal law that certain workspaces have to be equipped with natural light and ventilation. These regulations are based on the simple scientific fact that biological entities require natural light and air. As architects, we always think about how buildings can be made more efficient. What does this mean besides placing zones that don't require daylight in the center of a building? It's not something that should only take money into account; it should also consider people's health and well-being. If you understand that better buildings bring better results, everybody wins because productivity increases.

Urban theater: Children's Games by Flemish Renaissance artist Pieter Bruegel the Elder (1560); urban public life as a beguiling spectacle

ONE OF THE MOST IMPORTANT CHALLENGES IS DIVERSITY— ALSO IN THE DESIGN OF OUR WORKSPACES. THERE'S SO MUCH COMPLEXITY FROM A MORE HUMAN SOCIETAL PERSPECTIVE. AT THE MOMENT, WE ARE CLOSELY EXAMINING OUR STRATEGY WITH REGARD TO DIVERSITY. STUDIES SHOW THAT DIVERSE TEAMS ARE STRONGER.

MCKELVEY As architects, you are in control of your environment. To very few people, very few leaders, does the physical space ever occur to be pivotal. They would easily walk into a horrible conference room that feels super claustrophobic and has ugly furniture and accept it as it is. They don't question whether this is actually the best place for great energy to come from in a meeting. How do you break free from your mental construct and continue to grow and change and evolve? You probably need some input that will inspire you to do so. And where do you spend all your time? In the workplace…

GRAFT When we look around your WeWork office here in Berlin, we wonder if you were inspired by the *Urban Theater.* It's like what you might imagine Florence to look like in the 15th century, when everybody was out on the street.

MCKELVEY I think authenticity really matters, and it flows through when the people who started the business continue to be there and lead it. I was and still am super-interested in this challenge of getting people to be more open to each other. You can look at it from an event perspective and create peak experiences that bind people together. The combination of the physical space and the social programming needs to be really good. Our starting point wasn't a business model; we came up with an experience and a connection to an energy that we wanted to spread.

GRAFT A synonym for authenticity might be identity. Talking about identity besides your own, who do you work for? You are providing a home for their career paths. That's a big responsibility. And given that you host people from many cultural backgrounds across the world, what's around the corner? What's next? For us, repetition is the most boring ingredient. We try to design different typologies for different communities on different continents. That's difficult, but we're happy when there are challenges and problems we haven't solved yet. What do you think is the next big challenge in the new workspace?

MCKELVEY One of the most important challenges is diversity—also in the design of our workspaces. There's so much complexity from a more human societal perspective. At the moment, we are closely examining our strategy with regard to diversity. Studies show that diverse teams are stronger. I certainly designed the first WeWork in my own image, meaning my own personal style was the inspiration for it and I made the choices I made within the context that I existed in. Still, I don't want our spaces to be made by white people for white people. We are actively examining and making steps as to how we can make our spaces more inclusive.

We were also looking into large supermarkets in rural areas of the USA. They are often situated within complex socioeconomic divisions and their employees are facing job losses through automatization. We are asking: What could we do to strengthen these large retail centers as places of learning, of growth, of the future? The aim would be to expose employees and customers alike to their diverse potential. What if you developed these places as reskilling centers that aren't just about learning low-level technology but about connecting to a much broader set of things?

GRAFT The rise and fall of the mall was already a big topic when we studied at SCI-Arc in the late '90s. Such spaces are highly interesting because they are the modernist, somehow aseptic translation of medieval marketplaces. The reappropriation of real estate and its original spatial program into other hybrids in the transition phase is even more interesting today.

Eventually, due to automatization processes, we won't need as much office space as we did before—how are we going to transform these spaces then? Is it actually high-quality inner city or not? There is a similar discussion about the former industrial sites that exist all across Europe, a relic of industrialization over a hundred years ago. Among them are many beautiful "cathedrals of labor," monuments of industrial architecture. Many of these amazing spaces are now being reused. They're wonderfully built and are thus of great architectural value. I believe that malls could be of great value too, as they have a different connection to younger people.

Kraftwerk Berlin: Industrial cathedrals of the 19th century hold enormous potential for new work environments.

MCKELVEY I wonder what would happen if you unleashed young kids and artists on one of these empty malls. What would they do? How would they occupy it? This has actually happened in neighborhoods in New York City, whether it was SoHo or Dumbo or even Red Hook. You had these places that were made for manufacturing and then the artists came in, took them over and started producing work there.

GRAFT There's a reason why the street-art scene is still so big in Berlin: They had the Wall, the biggest canvas in the world. Sometimes it is exactly these obstacles in a community that foster innovative and disruptive thinking as a rebel response. The Wall was given a completely unforeseen new urban use, it became a place of free communication. When the Wall was finally overcome, the experience not only established a strong part of a global art scene but the true identity of the city of Berlin, the city of freedom. We envisage the emergence of new urban identities once we are liberated from the modern dogma of separating living, working and manufacturing in our urban centers. Before modernism, urban areas worked exactly like this. Imagine the reduction in mobility and energy needed if these functions were to be hybridized again, clustered around temporary communities and neighborhoods that can easily change and regroup. We believe that we are in an extremely interesting moment in time when it comes to reclaiming our cities.

While working on this publication, however, the world has been going through the crisis surrounding the spread of Covid-19. Experts from different fields predict that it will have a profound and lasting effect on the entire world—the workplace included. Deborah Tannen, professor of linguistics at Georgetown University, predicts that the idea of "the personal" will permanently be associated with danger. She says, "Instead of asking, 'Is there a reason to do this online?' we'll be asking, 'Is there any good reason to do this in person?'"[1] Our digital work routines, which used to be an unwelcome alternative to physical encounters, may become the norm. And companies will be better prepared for remote work. This development could potentially lead to a bigger emphasis on tech, such as telecommunication and artificial intelligence vs. travel. The relevance of New Work services lies in the many ways of creating New Work communities and unleashing their social power. This is challenged in times of social distancing. But another important aspect of New Work environments is the facilitation of these working communities via telecommunication, meaning connecting many people smoothly through new augmented and virtual realities, lowering thresholds of digital co-working. Do you see a paradigm shift in the future of New Work environments, as Tannen does? Will the meeting table be more virtual in the future?

MCKELVEY While the world is going through a paradigm shift, I think the effect will be a more purposeful use of space and time. As we all emerge and begin to create the new normal, we will evaluate the cost of our commutes and the associated risks of being surrounded by people. In doing so, we will value our time spent with people even more. We will see our time at the office with co-workers as something no longer to be taken for granted, but rather something to be cherished. We will have more appreciation for the spaces designed for work, because our homes are certainly not conducive to the wide range of use cases we've identified. As nice as it is to be home, many of us would admit that the static environment can be stifling.

For me, I desperately miss the buzz of people moving around space, as well as the random, casual conversations. On top of that, seeing less overall, absorbing less, will reduce openness and empathy, which is certainly essential for our path forward. Those who live in bubbles or closed communities are known to be less open-minded and less interested in diverse thinking. We will need to encourage people to engage again in open, diverse forums and to take risks—with their ideas and their actions.

[1] https://www.politico.com/news/magazine/2020/03/19/coronavirus-effect-economy-life-society-analysis-covid-135579

Miguel McKelvey is the co-founder and chief culture officer of WeWork, a platform for creators that helps people make a life, not just a living. Miguel oversees diverse initiatives across the company, ensuring that WeWork's founding values are infused into all aspects of the company's culture, design, products and operations.

Miguel and co-founder Adam Neumann started WeWork in 2010 in New York City. Before WeWork, Miguel and Adam started Green Desk, a turnkey eco-friendly workspace based in Brooklyn. Previously, Miguel worked on the international rollout of American Apparel's retail stores.

Miguel began his entrepreneurial career by co-founding the company English, baby!, an English language learning platform and social network that is still thriving today.

Originally from Oregon, Miguel studied architecture at the University of Oregon, where he also played basketball.

New Work design, GRAFT and GRAFT Brandlab (2019): By employing communal spaces and different work scenarios, New Work environments create communities using the potential of public interface and interaction.

TRILUX LIGHT CAMPUS

Project: Office building, new construction
Location: Cologne, Germany
Client: Trilux GmbH & Co KG
Year: 2019
Status: Completed
Size: 2,794m² (GFA)
Collaborators: Lobby light sculpture and Parelia LED lighting system in collaboration with Felix Monza

Lobby with sculptural light surface

TRILUX
SIMPLIFY YOUR LIGHT.

Continuous, staggered glass façade

Taking inspiration from the client's creations, GRAFT's design for the new location of German lighting company TRILUX in Cologne incorporated light, reflection and refraction.

Southeast elevation

Northwest elevation

The continuous, staggered glass façade reflects—in the truest sense of the word—the precision of lamp manufacture. The rectangular building presents a changing pattern of reflections from different viewpoints and is inspired by the aesthetics of spotlight reflectors, which optimize the optical distribution of the light source. To achieve this, each façade module is rotated at the same angle about its central axis, which creates an overall impression of a monolithic building that produces different light and depth effects depending on the perspective from which it is viewed.

Foyer of Trilux Light Campus

The main entrance to the TRILUX Light Campus makes an inviting gesture, its glazing going from one to two floors to wrap around the corner of the building. The new building frames the site on its western edge, defining a space for interaction between the new and existing buildings. With their landscape design, Lill + Sparla have created an outdoor plaza that is green all year round, using delicate grasses that contrast with the building's uniform overall impression.

The theme of the plaza is continued into the building's interior.

Open staircase
in the foyer

The spacious, two-story foyer and reception area extend the public areas into the building and, together with the gallery on the first floor, provide generous space for exhibitions and communal activities.

Similarly, the open staircase in the foyer also serves as a further meeting place. The ceiling features a sculptural light surface especially designed by GRAFT and Trilux, at once an architectural detail and a lighting element. As a sculptural luminaire it unfolds from the ceiling, cascading gently in the space above the auditorium.

Sculptural luminaire above the auditorium

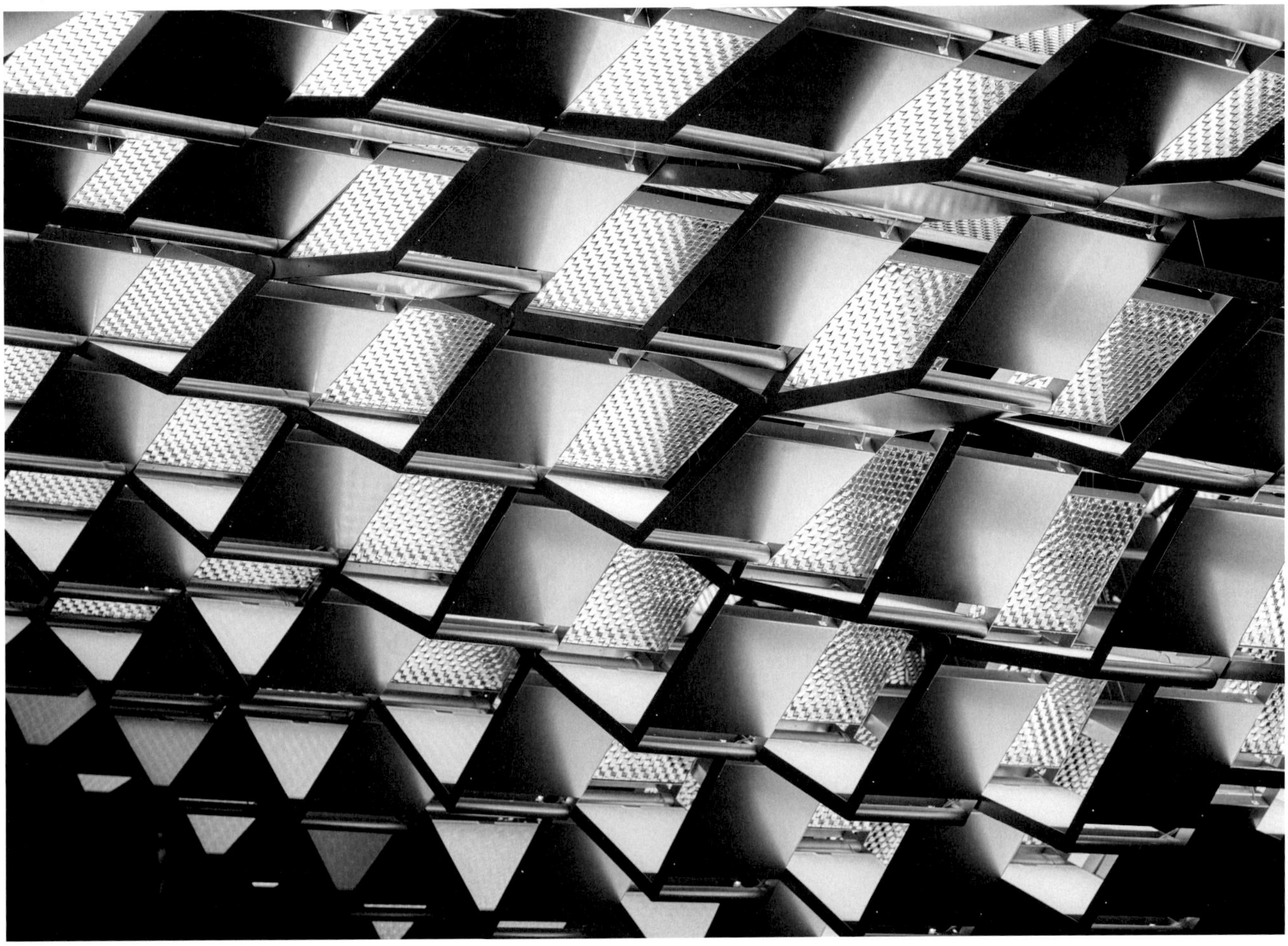

1 1

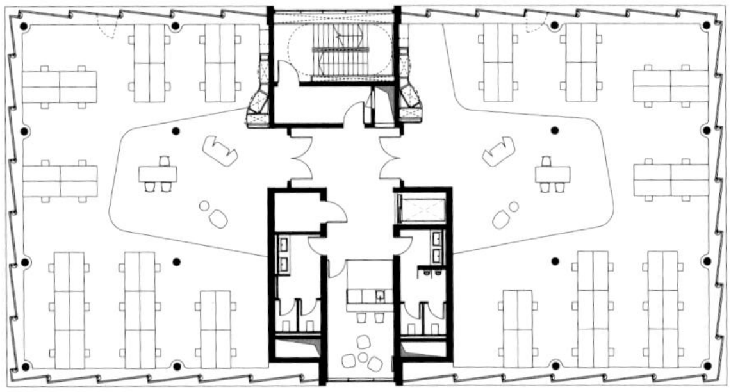

Second floor plan

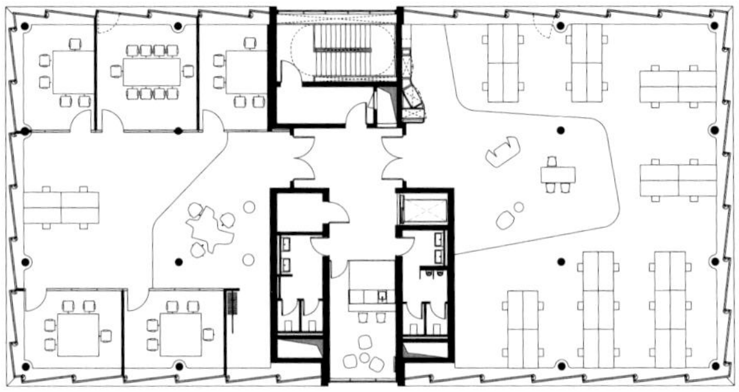

Third floor plan

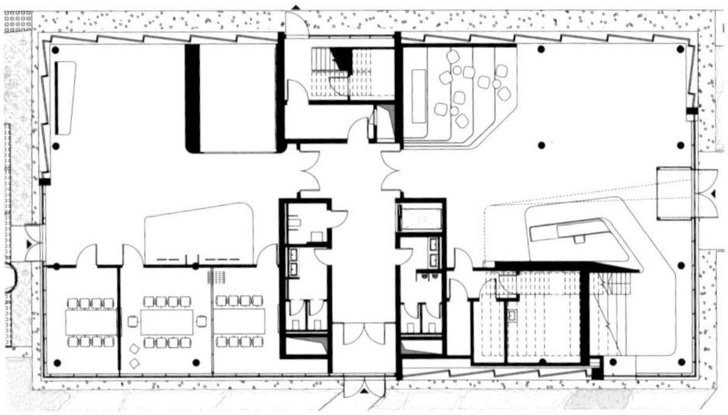

Ground floor plan

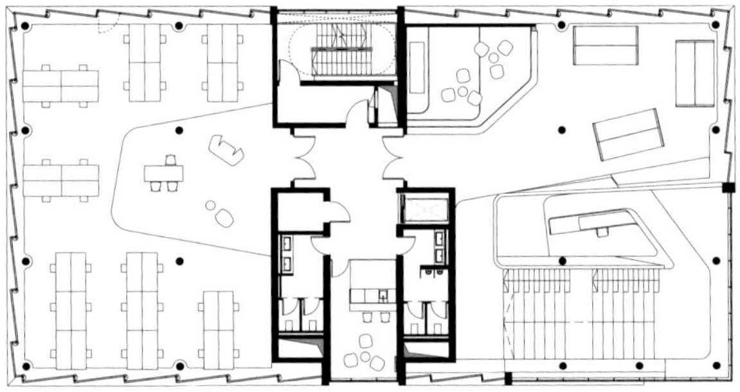

First floor plan

Section

Free-flowing floor plan for enclosed work and open communication zones

The building's upper floors house the company's office space and product exhibition areas, thus forming an essential part of the company's competence center, which already partially existed on the site.

The free-flowing floor plan continues in the upper three office floors and extends the entire depth of the building, interrupted only by three service and washroom cores. These so-called smart working spaces comprise both open communication zones and enclosed work zones equipped with hybrid furniture elements that can be combined in a modular fashion.

NEUE SENTIMENTAL FILM

Project: Office
Location: Los Angeles, CA, USA
Client: Neue Sentimental Film
Year: 2001
Status: Completed
Size: 1,200m² (GFA)

The West Coast headquarters of the Neue Sentimental Film company

Boat suppliers, dot-com companies, storage warehouses and numerous branches of the film and advertising industries define the surroundings of the new West Coast headquarters of the Neue Sentimental Film company in Los Angeles. Operating globally with many subsidiaries, the company requires the space and infrastructure for office-sharing with both permanent and temporary affiliates.

The challenge of the project was to provide the client with facilities for the entire spectrum of commercial film production—from concept to postproduction—all in one place, as well as being able to accommodate independent working groups of two to eight people at short notice.

To meet the challenges of such a fluctuating demand for space, GRAFT devised a concept that offered each unit an independent "office tower" alongside shared conference rooms, a reception area, a cafeteria, a library and a lounge. These five freestanding office towers were located in a 1,200m² warehouse site at Marina Del Rey. The first tower serves as the company's headquarters while two are permanently rented out to subsidiary companies; the remaining two are available for temporary teams.

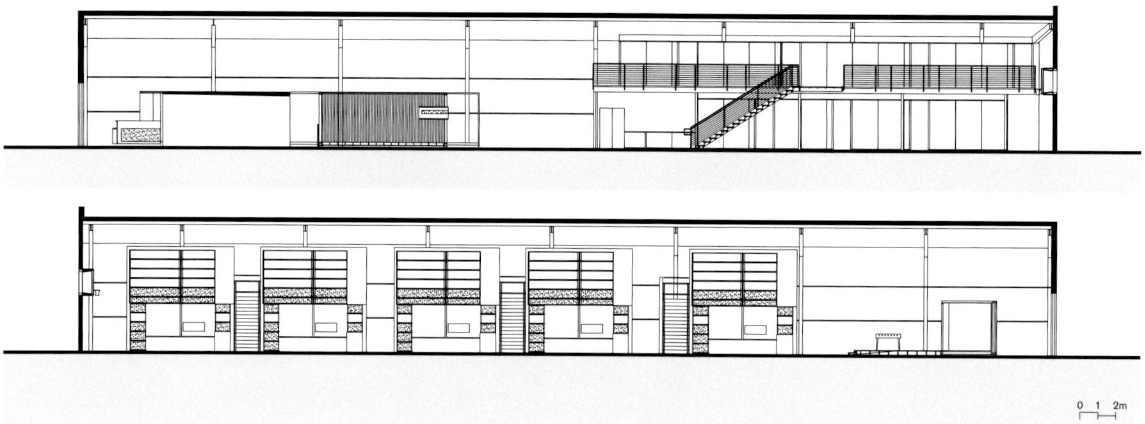

Sections

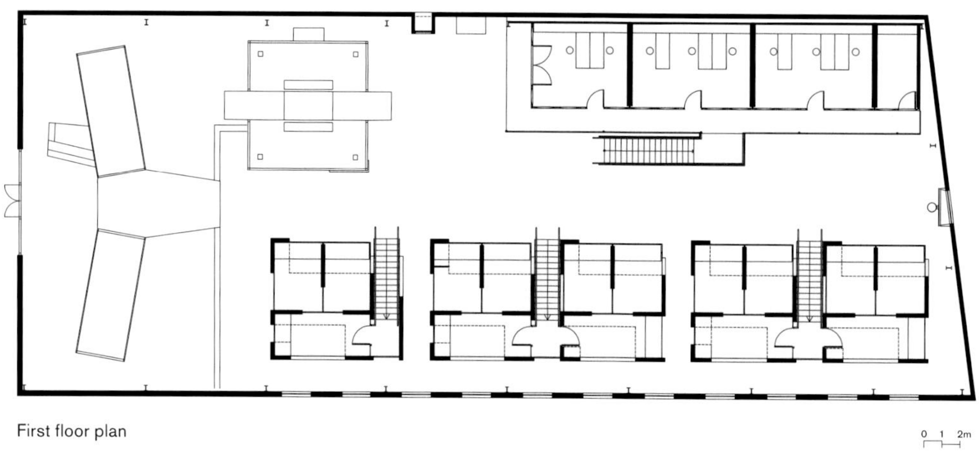

First floor plan

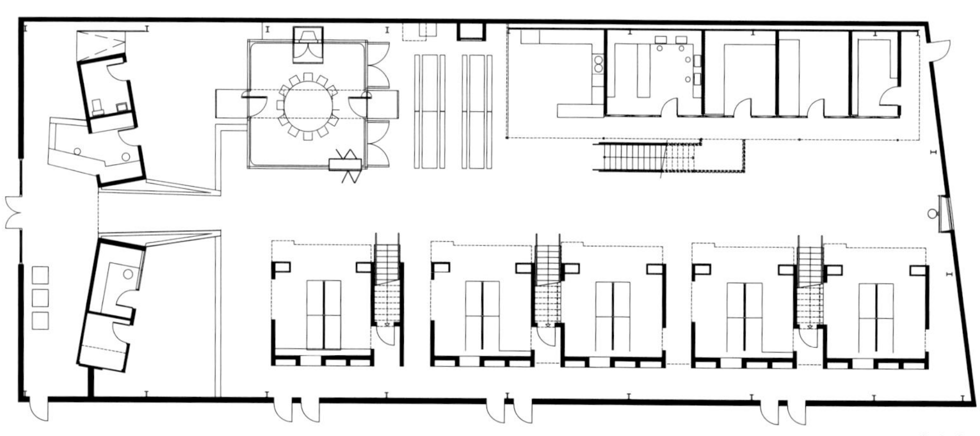

Ground floor plan

R K

Communal area

Conference room

1 2 3

A social hub, consisting of the communal kitchen and dining area, forms the "marketplace" of the establishment. Two shipping containers house conference rooms and create an entrance portal to the dining area. They embrace the concept of temporary occupation and toy with the idea of worldwide trade and wanderlust.

From a practical standpoint, they allowed construction to begin before a planning permit was received, as it was possible to pre-fit them before they were installed in the space.

The passage over the threshold into the sheltered area beyond the entrance is emphasized by a change of floor surface, as polished concrete gives way to a realm of recycled rubber granulate.

Flexible work environments accommodate independent groups of two to eight people.

Independent office areas for fluctuating spatial demand

Reception area

TXCHANGE

Project: Feasibility study, mobility, Internet of Things (IoT), building technology, sustainability
Location: Berlin Tegel Airport, Germany
Client: Tegel Projekt GmbH
Year: 2017
Status: Completed

Extract of feasibility study

TXchange poster

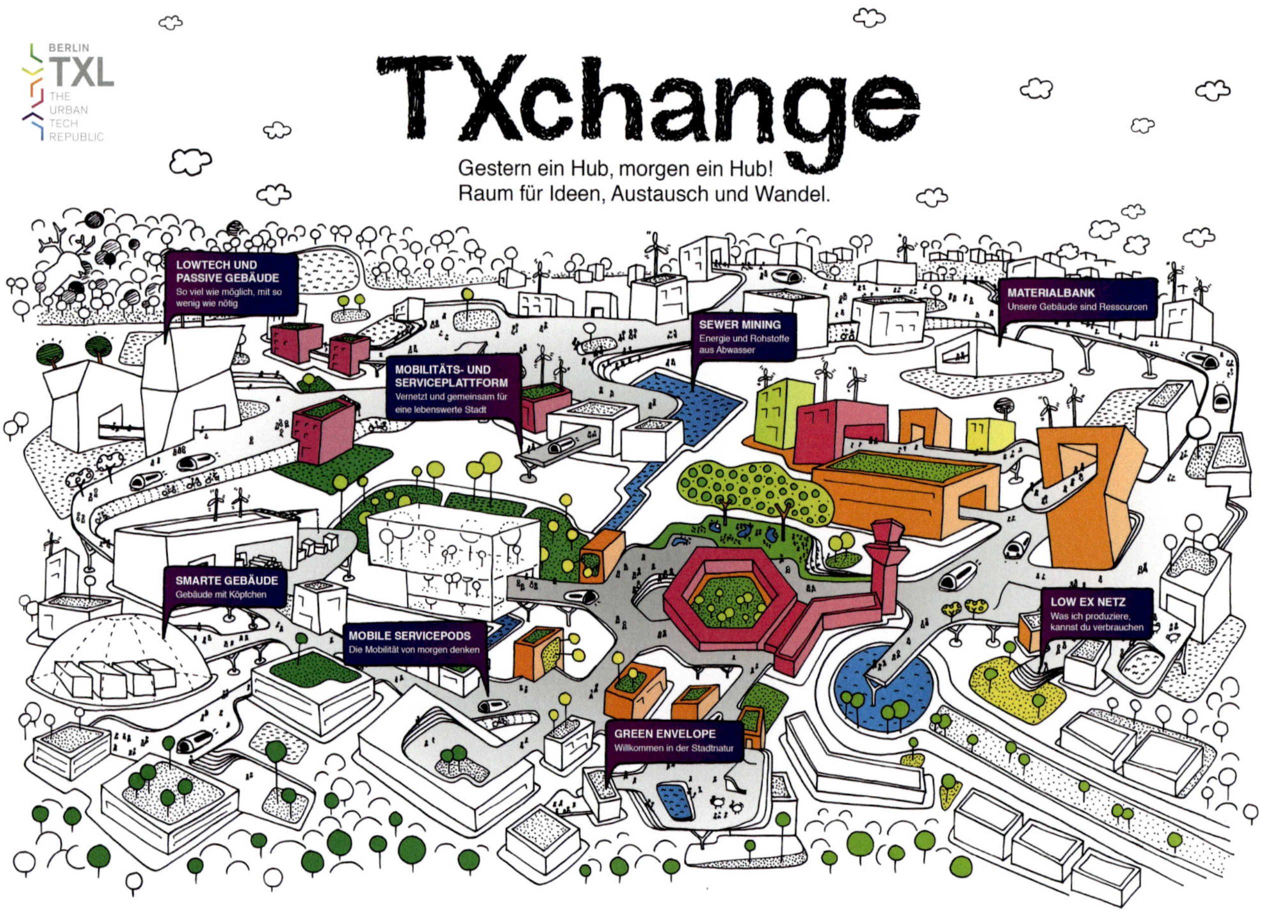

R K

TXchange booklets

Extract of feasibility study

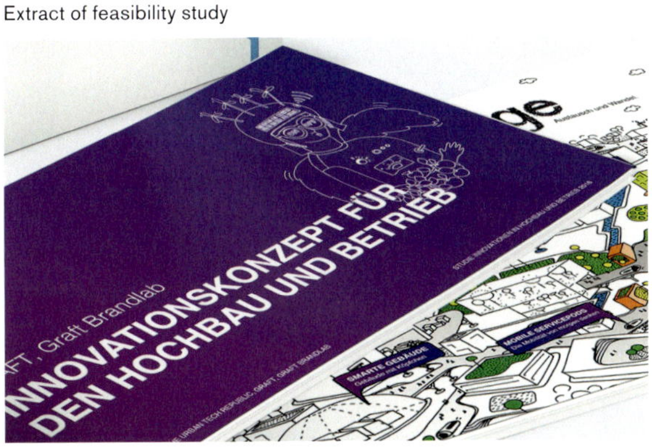

Tegel Airport is scheduled to close, and a research and industrial park is set to appear in its place. Berlin TXL will offer a space for entrepreneurs, students, investors, producers and scientists to develop urban technologies for the cities of tomorrow.

1 2 7

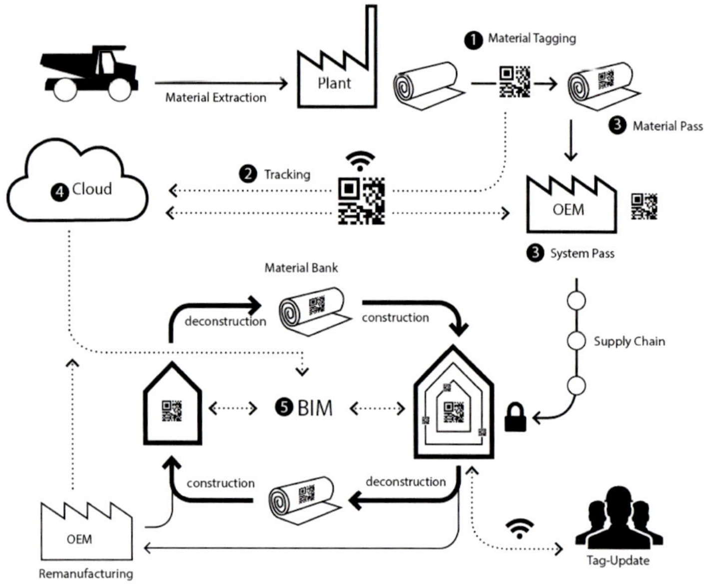

The material bank system

1 TAGGING
Materials and semi-finished products are tagged at the beginning of their life cycles, enabling information about them to be stored.

2 TRACKING
This tagged material is then trackable from a centralized location. Tag and cloud are in continuous communication.

3 MATERIAL PASSPORT
A material or system passport documents all relevant data according to standardized criteria.

4 DATABASE
All material and system information is stored in the cloud. These data are constantly updated and accessible at any time.

5 BIM
With the help of BIM, systems (e.g., buildings) can be planned in a way that allows all individual components to be mapped within the entire system. Among other things, this makes their replacement easier.

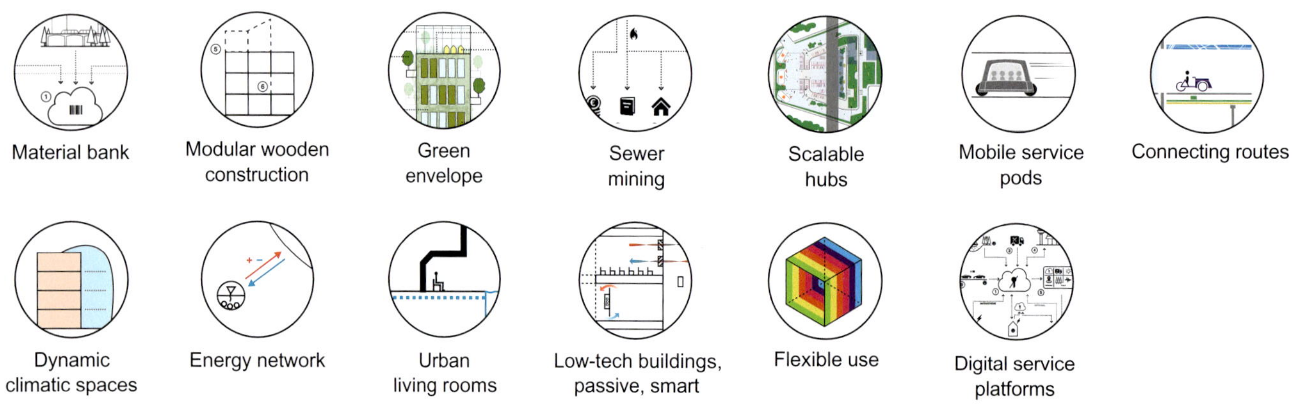

Potential fields of action
Our analysis identified a range of potential fields of action that were prioritized and examined further during the course of the study.

PROJECT PARTNERS:

Led by GRAFT and GRAFT Brandlab, the project saw a unique collaboration between engineers, architects, scientists, UX designers and mobility experts. Arup, EPEA, GRAFT, GRAFT Brandlab, PCH Innovations and Transsolar joined forces to generate original approaches for the site, resulting in a study that presents an overarching concept for future developments, a planning manifesto and a catalog featuring innovative solutions for smart, sustainable cities.

URBAN TECH REPUBLIC

Project: Feasibility study
Location: Berlin Tegel Airport, Germany
Client: Tegel Projekt GmbH
Year: 2013
Status: Design and study completed

Conversion of Terminal D at Berlin Tegel Airport

GREEN
ROBOT
DESIGN

W

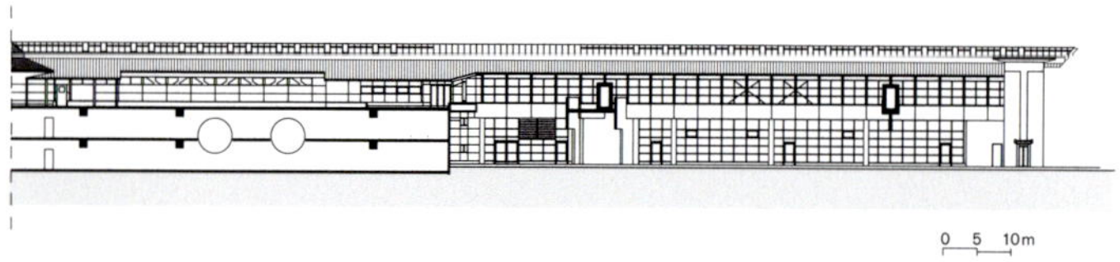

Section

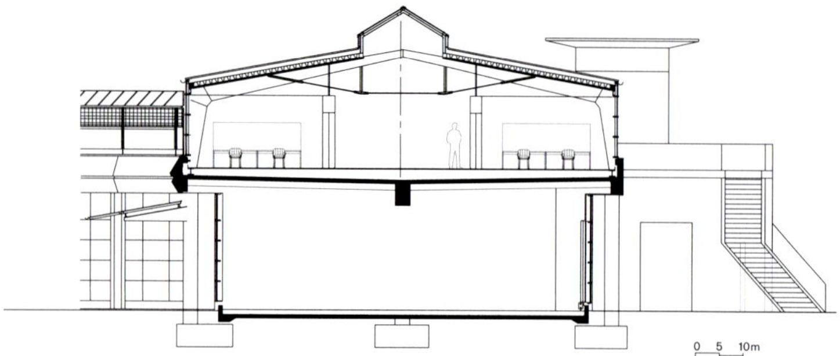

Section

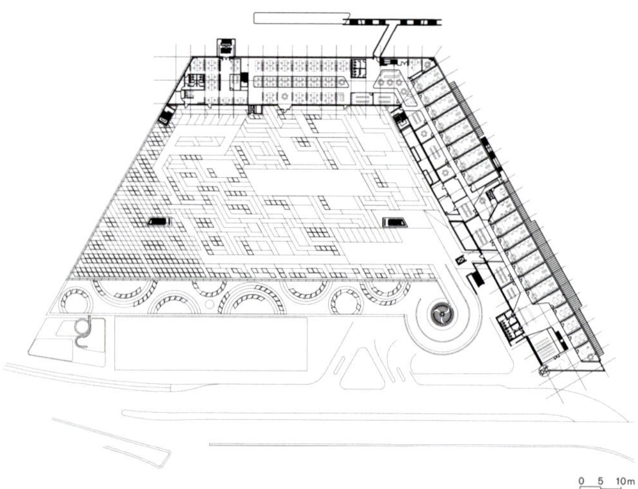

First floor plan

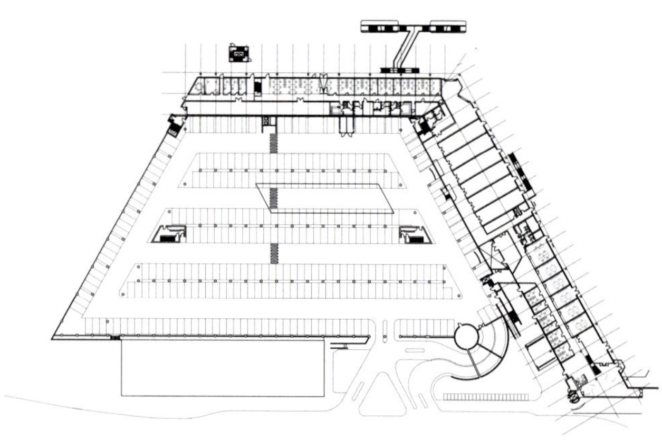

Ground floor plan

O

1

3

2

Flexible co-working areas for start-ups and tech companies

GRAFT won a competition for a feasibility study to develop a concept for converting the existing Terminal D at Berlin Tegel Airport into a startup hub for tech companies.

Together with the planned university in Terminal A, the building's intended function is to serve as a nucleus for the development of the entire Urban Tech Republic site. The high standard of design in the initial phase at Terminal D is intended to act as both a focal point and a stimulus for future phases of the Urban Tech Republic project.

New outdoor area

Tegel Airport's Terminal D affords ideal conditions for its conversion into a startup incubator: Its historical importance, its excellent transport connections, its established status as an industrial center and its existing infrastructure all combine to make it an unparalleled location.

Modular conference and presentation areas

Flexible set-up for presentation area

W

Flexible set-up for conference area

GRAFT's design features flexible co-working areas, group work and conference rooms, communication zones, office spaces and a nursery for up to 50 children. The multistory car park will be transformed into another kind of nursery, in which trees and bushes will grow into a young forest and later populate the new TXchange urban development.

1

Abflug / Departure
BERLIN
TXL
THE
URBAN
TECH
REPUBLIC

The terraced landscape creates a multilevel marketplace.

ECKWERK

Project: Office, new work, residential, high-rise, new construction
Location: Berlin, Germany
Client: Eckwerk, GuK cooperative (Genossenschaft für urbane Kreativität)
Year: 2014 – ongoing
Size: 34,000m²

In collaboration with Kleihues + Kleihues architecture office and the Genossenschaft für urbane Kreativität (Cooperative for Urban Creativity), GRAFT developed the exemplary Eckwerk project, which sought to find solutions to current social, economic and ecological questions.

The central idea of the Eckwerk was to create a vibrant, inspiring place that sets new benchmarks for the relationships between work and living and public and private life.

The site, located in the northern section of the Holzmarkt area on the River Spree, was home to the legendary Berlin nightclub Bar 25 until 2011.

Drawing on the characteristic qualities of the location, the Eckwerk takes up features from the surrounding area, making particular reference to the railway viaduct as a defining feature of the site. A central element of its design is a two-story plinth that follows the course of the street on one side and the railway viaduct on the other. The space between the viaduct and the plinth becomes a passage, a place of interaction where public functions and the building's main entrances are located. The plinth elevates the main level of the complex to the height of the viaduct, and acts as an urban terrace with a view out over the water. On top of the plinth are five independently accessible towers, each providing highly flexible spaces for working or living.

The terraced landscape of the interior space is designed as a publicly accessible, multilevel marketplace and serves as a hybrid indoor–outdoor area, mainly for co-working spaces.

Covered by a delicate steel and glass construction, it lets in natural light and can be used all year round.

Breaking up the built volumes into separate towers was implemented not only to fulfil the requirements of Berlin's zoning laws, but also to create a sense of openness by revealing a variety of views and vistas, dissolving the boundary between the house and the city (the private and the public). With their staggered arrangement, decreasing in scale towards the river, even the towers to the rear are afforded direct views of the Spree.

The five towers are linked by a publicly accessible walkway, the so-called "mountain path," which connects the ensemble's component parts and opens into semi-public spaces of interaction and relaxation. The meandering walkway can be accessed by the public without passing through the private work or living areas. It is conceived as a continuation of the Spree riverbank walk, as set out by the citizens' initiative "Spreeufer für alle" (Spree riverbank for all).

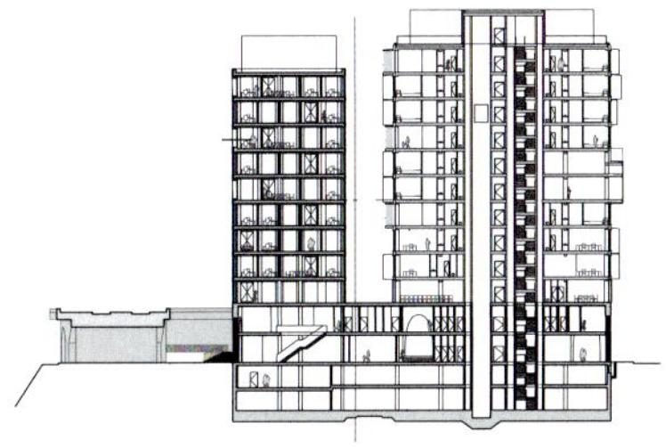

Section

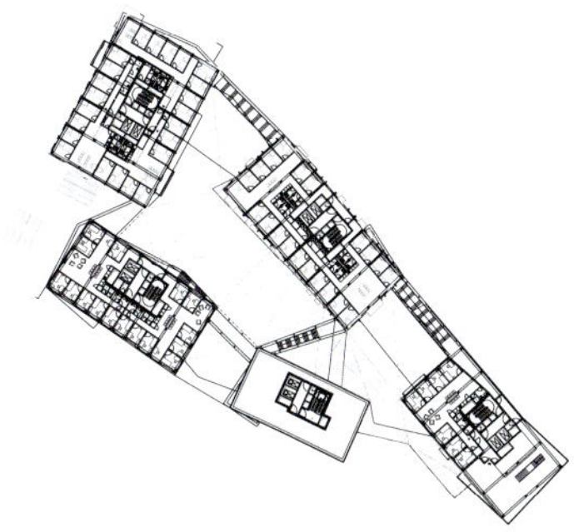

Tenth floor plan

Second floor plan

Separate towers create a sense of openness.

By opening the site and much of the building to the public, it interweaves public circulation into a private development. In contrast to the solid, durable nature of the plinth, the towers embody lightness and variability through their wooden frontage. Wood is both a renewable material and part of the history of the site, formerly home to the riverside timber market.
The floor plans and the façades of the towers both follow a modular design principle, enabling them to be individually modified and adapted.

The Eckwerk project manipulates the natural tendencies of socio-economic change within the urban matrix, proving the viability of creating new working environments and affordable housing in otherwise expensive areas.

KFW CREATIVE LAB

Project: Office, new work environments, new construction
Location: Berlin, Germany
Client: KfW Bank
Year: 2018

Creative laboratory of the KfW Campus

The cubic volume is divided into two stories and a roof terrace.

Tasked with designing a new space for the KfW Campus, a creative laboratory dedicated to addressing the future demands of the KfW Bank, GRAFT proposed the addition of two stories to the company's current location near the Gendarmenmarkt in the center of Berlin. This new creative lab is conceived as a clearly recognizable, accessible place of inspiration within the city block.

Hidden from view in the existing building's inner courtyard, this innovative platform will provide expansive views over the rooftops of Berlin, offering free rein to ideas and inspiration.

As an expression of KfW's corporate culture, GRAFT developed a design that is open, transparent and at the same time functional.

GRAFT's design envisages a simple cubic volume divided into two stories and a roof terrace. The lower floor will feature a kitchen and a bar, as well as a flexible multifunctional space that can be modified according to its intended use—whether exhibitions, readings, workshops, cooperative work or even just relaxing. By widening the stairs leading to the upper floor, the space will be transformed into a mini auditorium, while the top floor itself, the *bel étage*, will offer breathtaking views over Berlin and enable a variety of representative and functional uses face-to-face with Schinkel's Konzerthaus, the French Cathedral, Brandenburg Gate and other iconic symbols of the city. Above it, a roof terrace will also serve as a communal garden.

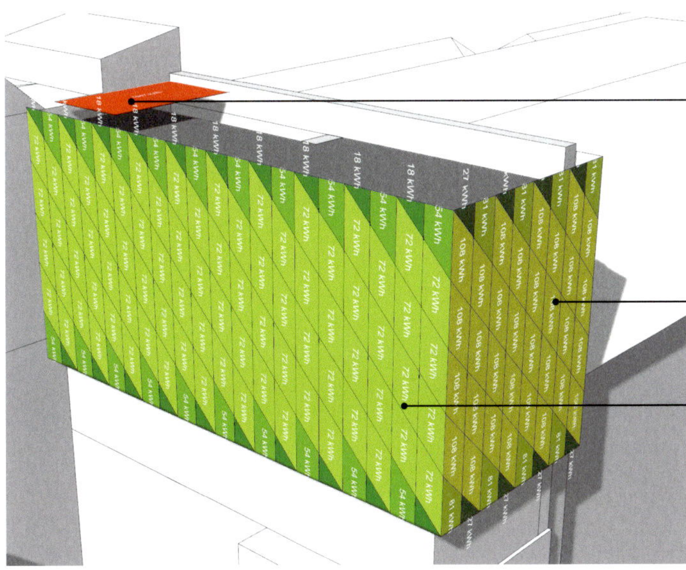

Photovoltaic study (kWh/ per year)

Interior with open staircase and creative space

Particular attention is given to the façade: It will consist of maneuverable panels that can be individually programmed across both floors, able to respond to the position of the sun and the amount of shade needed. In this way, the heat input and the resulting cooling or heating energy needed can be significantly reduced. The façade will produce electricity using photovoltaics and a solar tracking system that continually orients the panels to the optimal position relative to the sun, thus guaranteeing the best possible efficiency.

As a result, the new extension not only covers its own energy requirements, but also contributes to the overall energy balance of the whole complex. Through its adaptive façade, the appearance of the creative lab changes according to the time of day and its ascribed use, creating a kind of visual narrative and becoming a built symbol to KfW's corporate philosophy.

Open façade with photovoltaics

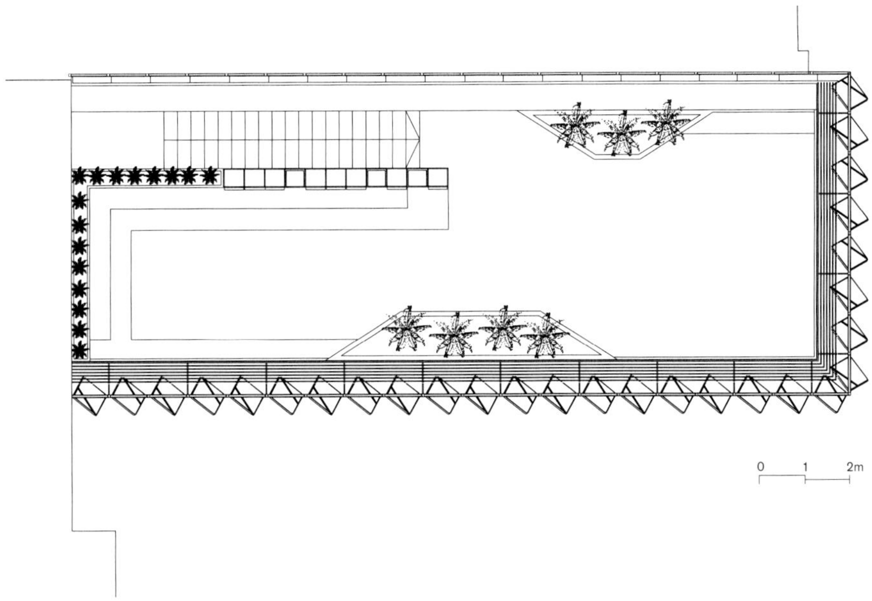

Rooftop floor plan

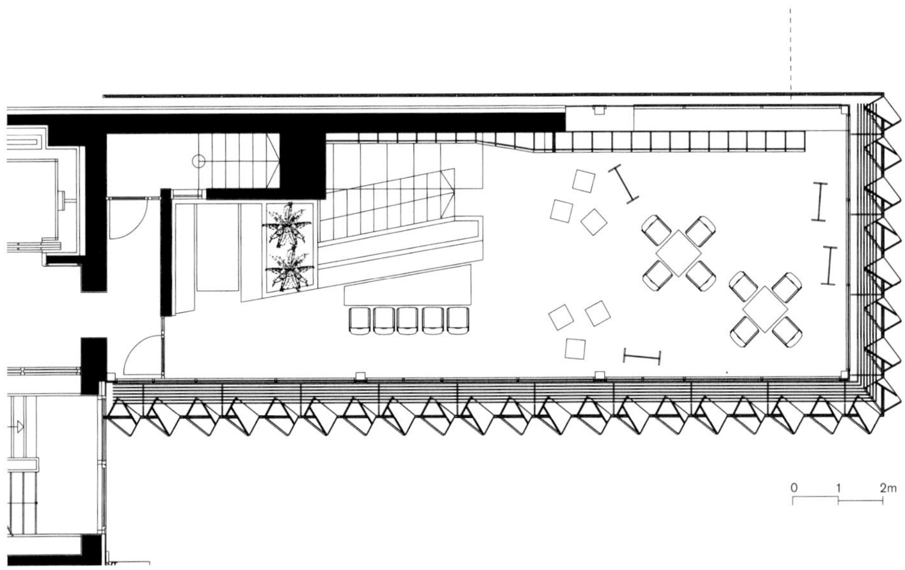

Seventh floor plan

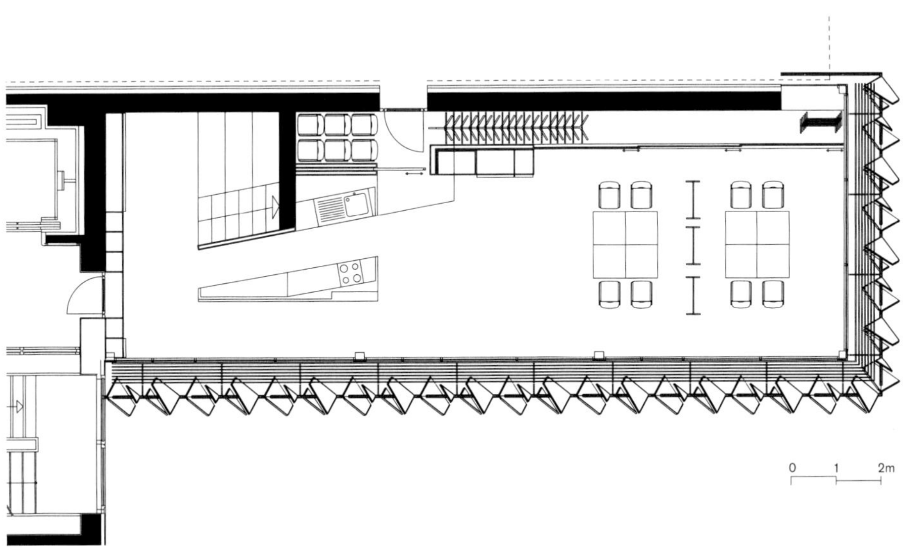

Sixth floor plan

RITTERSTRASSE— CLOUD SPACE

Project: Office, retail, new work, co-working, competition design
Location: Berlin, Germany
Client: Kurth Göttingen, Berlin, Ritter 16–18 GmbH und Co. KG
Year: 2018
Size: 8,000m²

Participating in a 2018 competition to design an office building in the Berlin district of Kreuzberg, GRAFT proposed a concept that incorporates new theories of working environments. The design features a flexible building plan to meet the needs of 21st-century office formats, creating various zones with an emphasis on efficiency and functionality.

With its T-shaped floor plan, the proposal rounds off a prominent urban ensemble in Berlin-Kreuzberg. Its main façade, along the street side of the plot, makes a bold urban gesture, appearing to usher the outdoor space into the communal areas in the building's interior.

Rounded entrance towards Ritterstrasse

Open, multifunctional space

Atrium with staircase and large seating area

The flexible spatial units of the building's three arms are oriented in such a way that, together with the central "cloud space," they allow a huge degree of variability in the sizes of the areas available for rent. Linking them to a collective space, which takes in the balconies, the ground floor and the usable roof area, each unit is afforded an increased potential for work and an additional recreational value.

The building opens onto Ritterstrasse with a generously proportioned rounded entrance, harmoniously balancing out its vertical dimensions. Employees and visitors are received by an open, multifunctional space that can be used for events, readings and exhibitions. Next to this reception area, the ground floor is linked to the first floor by a staircase that doubles as a large seating area. The foyer also marks the beginning of the cloud space, which extends three-dimensionally through the building, connecting the different working environments, flexible functional units, informal meeting spaces, quiet areas and break-out zones, creating numerous opportunities for encounters and knowledge production.

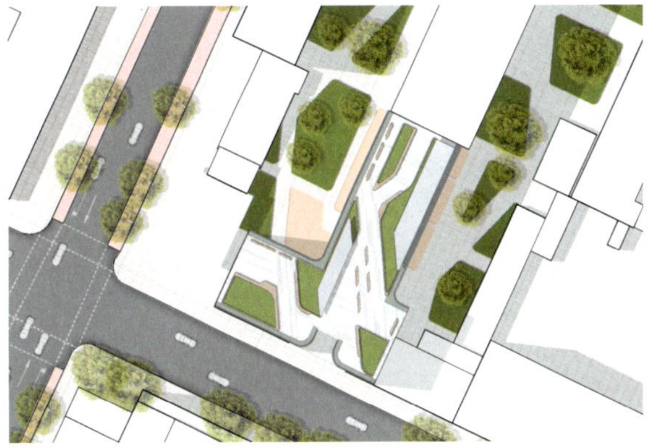

Site plan

The ambiguity of interior and exterior space is a theme that runs consistently through the entire building, highlighted in its courtyards, balconies and other threshold spaces. A roof terrace, balconies and flexible balconets offer the potential for outdoor working, interaction, inspiration and relaxation, while the courtyard will become a green oasis in the heart of Kreuzberg.

Courtyard

SIEMENSSTADT 2.0

Project: Master plan, mixed use, office, residential, retail, leisure, mobility, competition design
Location: Berlin, Germany
Client: Siemens AG
Year: 2019

Green axis

GRAFT's master plan "Siemens Werk Stadt" for the Siemensstadt quarter in Berlin is characterized by its highly developed, future-oriented design. It envisages transforming the original Siemensstadt into a space for learning and for an open urban society in general, one that incorporates the distinctive network structure of the former Siemens factory grounds with its surrounding neighborhood.

The integrated concept of the master plan proposes a sustainable, self-sufficient urban quarter marked by density and diversity, while managing to maintain a human scale: Green spaces, social amenities and residential buildings are harmoniously arranged around a central, highly visible technology cluster.

The design tackles the challenge of approaching a factory complex, formerly cut off from its surroundings, by creating two prominent axes—northsouth and eastwest—that extend beyond the factory site itself and form a direct connection with the well-established city quarter nearby.

The Siemens Werk Stadt has been conceived as a heterogenous urban ensemble in which the existing administrative and production facilities will be largely retained, complemented by a few new buildings and independent, innovative systems for energy, waste and mobility.

Due to their central location at the intersection of these two axes, the switch halls and tower will retain their prominent status as urban landmarks. The old administrative building will form the heart of the master plan and aim to represent and reflect Berlin's demographic diversity: Alongside a kindergarten, a youth center and an intergenerational house, the building will also accommodate a private university and an exhibition space. This "augmented agora" seeks to expand the catchment area of Siemensstadt and provide relief for social amenities in neighboring districts.

The new Siemens Werk Stadt will incorporate the latest technical and social innovations. In contrast to the existing Siemensstadt, where work, research, living and manufacturing were strictly separated due to their different requirements regarding noise and pollution, today's quiet, low-emission transport and production technologies make it possible to merge these different typologies.

Green axis crossing the former production labs

Many of the companies that will establish new offices in the Siemens Werk Stadt work in the fields of mobility, energy, AI and healthcare. The New Work hall, for example, will offer flexible office units in the form of containers, an indoor green avenue, a food court and an administrative center, while the factory tower opposite will be completely stripped and used as a multifunctional "hypershelf." By spatially interweaving laboratories, manufacturing areas and office spaces, the design allows the creation of hybrid architectures that unlock a wide range of synergy effects.

Robotic lab

Site plan

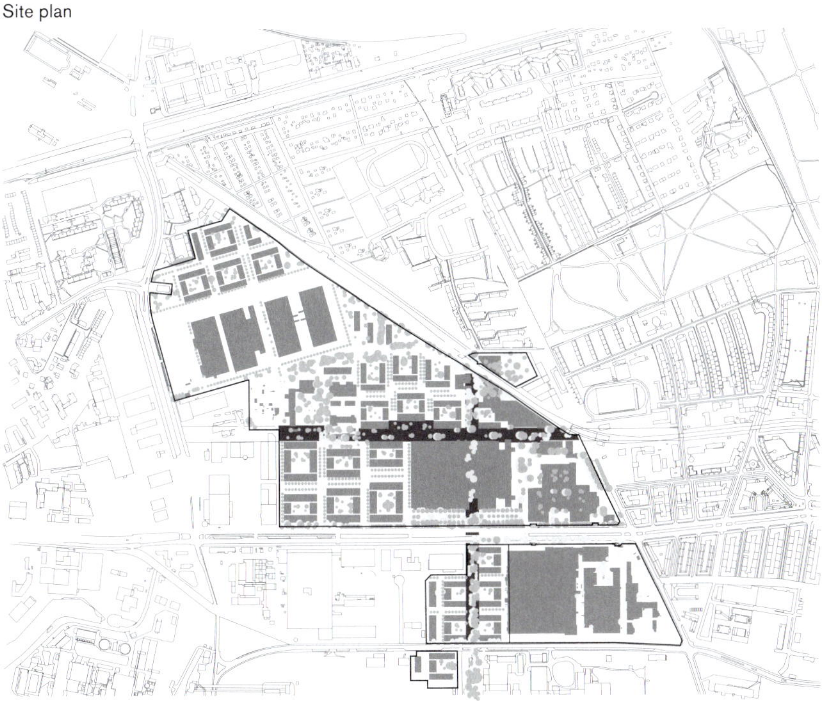

The most striking piece of hybrid architecture is the only planned new building: The Siemens Lab, which will function as an automated manufacturing facility and a welcome center featuring offices and a restaurant with panoramic views. Internally, the design affords visual relationships between automated production halls and PC-based workspaces. Externally, at 47 meters, the building will help generate the identity of the location while simultaneously creating a sense of transparency—its diverse functions will be visible when viewed from the adjoining square.

1 5 3

The Siemens Werk Stadt is best accessed via its green axes by foot, by bike or by self-driving car. To achieve this, the existing access road will be extended by two intersecting axes inaccessible to cars with conventional combustion engines. The green axes will connect the Siemens Werk Stadt to the adjacent green spaces and create a large, linear recreational area.

It will also pass through the former switch hall, whose lively ground floor area will blur the boundaries of inside and outside. The switch hall will thus become an attractive, flexible functional space for addressing future scenarios in the fields of energy, mobility and artificial intelligence—an Electropolis 2.0.

Mobility axis

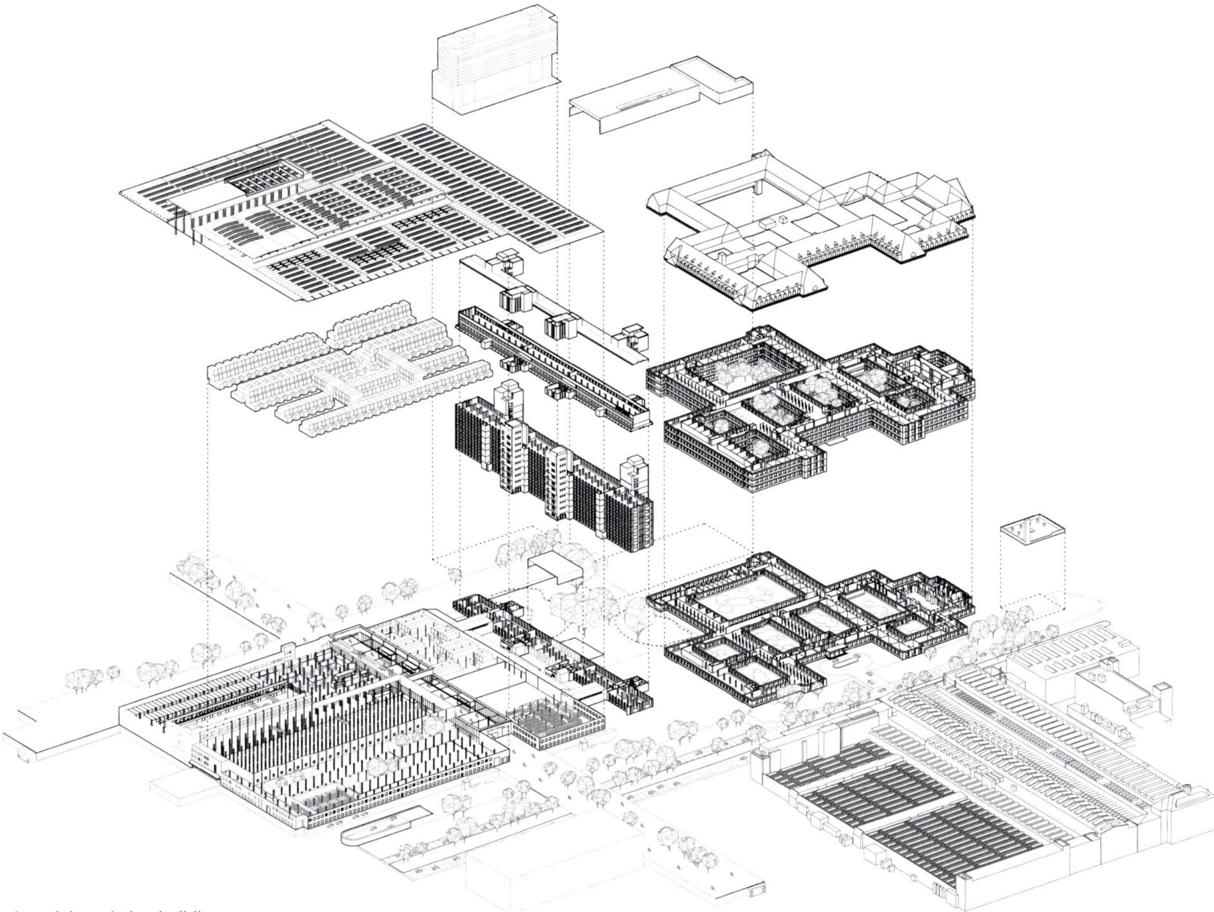

Conversion of the existing buildings

Tech lab corridor

In the east–west direction, the green axis is crossed by the factory axis, which is exclusively dedicated to new GPS-controlled forms of mobility. The factory axis will serve as a (sub)urban public space that promotes the compatibility of living and working through emission-free mobility.

Along the axis, projections and recesses of the blocks create wider sections, enhancing their quality as recreational environments. A large tunnel under the factory axis enables quick and easy technical upgradeability of the section, which will serve as a laboratory for testing the newest types of mobility systems.

WRIEZENER KARREE

Project: Office, retail, new work
Location: Berlin, Germany
Client: TLG IMMOBILIEN AG
Year: 2019 – 2023
Size: 37,000m² (GFA)

GRAFT was commissioned as a general planner to develop an innovative new work office campus on the site of Berlin's former Wriezener Bahnhof railway station.

Northeast view towards the office building

R
K

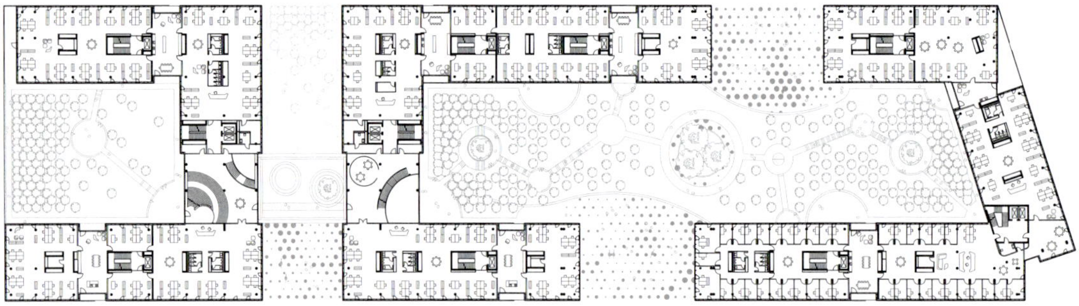

First floor plan

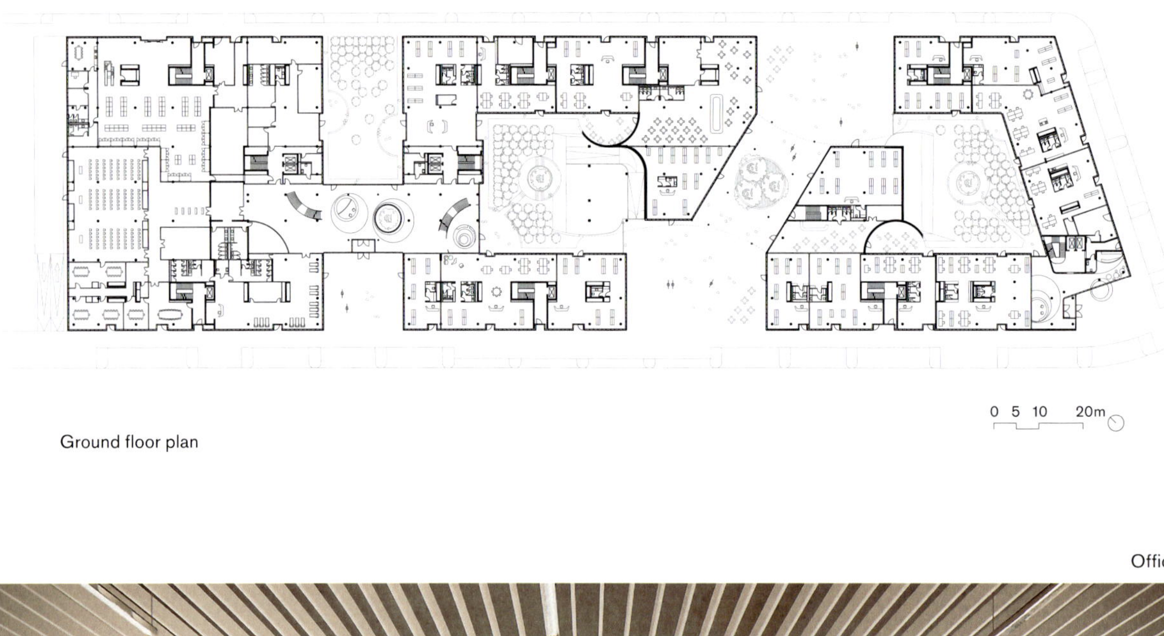

Ground floor plan

Office space

Lobby café

During the GDR era, the residential buildings that had survived World War II were demolished and the area was redeveloped for commercial use, with the last tenant being a large-scale industrial furniture store. Today, most people know the site because of its prominent neighbor, the internationally renowned techno club Berghain.

Now, the area is set to become the site of a new urban quarter. The Wriezener Karree will be the first block in the development and thus crucial for identity generation. Planned mainly to be an office building, it will feature an additional mix of small-scale businesses on the ground floor, consisting of small retail units, gastronomy, supermarkets and sports facilities. These amenities will lend a new urban identity to the wider neighborhood, which until now had a preurban, commercial feel.

Amenity space

GRAFT divided the desired program volume into three buildings on the roughly 14,200m² plot. A diagonal passage between two city squares will create a public thoroughfare and link the site to the adjoining neighborhood. This passageway will form a connection between the Ostbahnhof train station—a main regional infrastructure hub—and the iconic Berghain building and its surrounding green space.

A series of publicly owned plazas and privately donated public spaces will create a new urban choreography, forming the "backbone" of the new quarter and ultimately connecting the area with the vibrant neighborhood of Friedrichshain to the north.

On the first block to be developed, a green landscape will unite the three buildings, creating a lush urban oasis in their inner courtyards—in an environment still heavily influenced by industrial and commercial uses. A landscaped bridge will cross the diagonally intersecting "broadway" and create an exciting floating garden above street level. The large circular opening above this passage seeks to let in light and create visual connections.

In line with the revolution of workplace behavior in the New Work generation, the main goal was to create innovative environments with a focus on flexibility. To break down the large urban volume to a human scale, GRAFT divided the program into individual "working neighborhoods," making the buildings appear as a collage of stacked houses and reducing the visual impact on the surroundings. The individual units can be deciphered as forms of personalized identity per cubic volume and reference playful and organic narratives on this former train yard site.

Lobby

View from the landscaped bridge towards the office building

Amenity space

The intentionally inexact arrangements of the neighborhood building blocks create areas of "in between," where special communal functions and collaborative programs of the working campus are located.

Green courtyard

Amenity space for lectures and presentations

Lobby

Green landscaped bridge

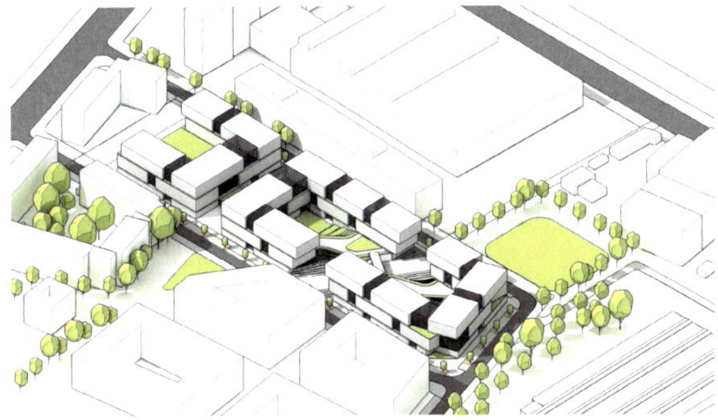

Isometric view of the "working neighborhoods"

These empty spaces are places of encounter within the fabric of this complex, allowing for movement and participation, communication and interaction. Each office unit has its own private void. They create meeting points, informal spaces for communication and serve as connecting elements between the floors and units.

The appearance of the stacked boxes references the scale of *Gründerzeit* parcellation, relating to the narrative of the site's former industrial character, and has a rigorous and effective organizational structure. In contrast, the voids are lighter and more artistic in their design, thus conveying the inner life to the outside.

As well as the focus on innovative working environments and user comfort, great importance is attached to sustainability: A coordinated energy concept was developed in collaboration with climate engineers from Transsolar, and high-level LEED certification is being sought.

To address the topic of mobility, the project envisages a separate underground bicycle lane. With attractive, prioritized access for cyclists, independent of car traffic, the design will promote the use of bicycles as a means of transport among future users.

Seven-story extension providing office spaces

Isonometric view: Extra story and new side wing for Bayerhaus

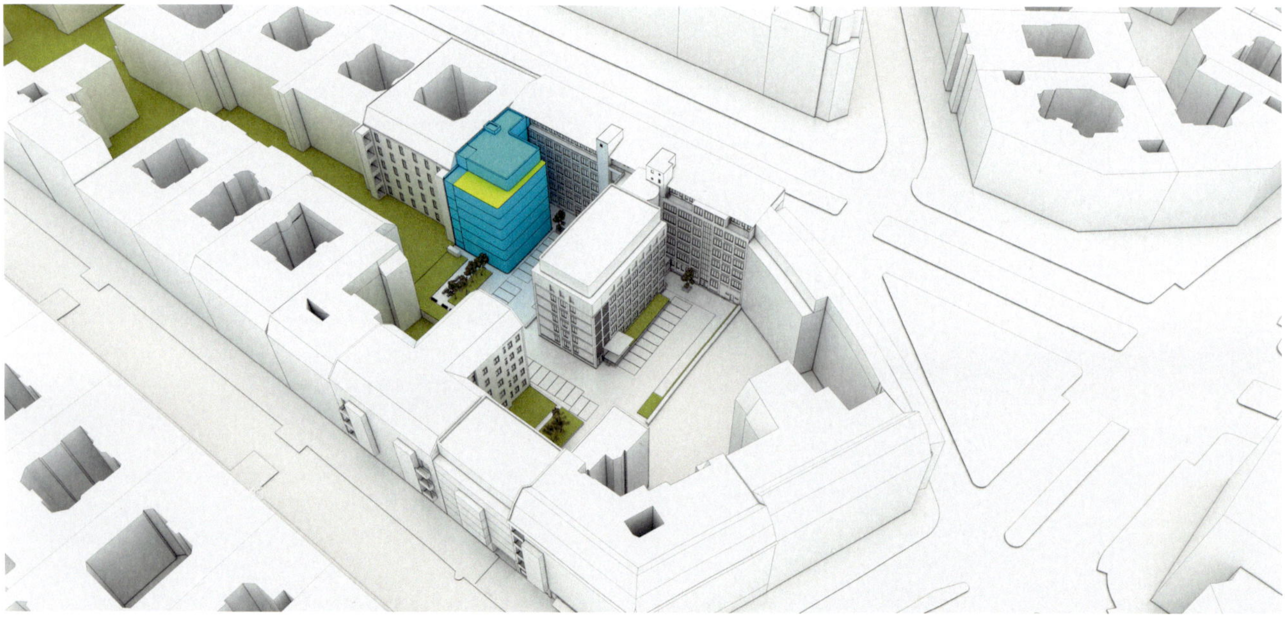

BAYERHAUS

Project: Office, retail, residential, refurbishment, new construction
Location: Berlin, Germany
Year: 2017 – 2022
Status: Under construction
Size: 6,000m² (GFA)

New extension of the listed Bayerhaus

The Bayerhaus, a seven-story office block built as the administrative center of the Bayer pharmaceutical company in the early 1950s, was one of the first post-World War II buildings to be erected in West Berlin.

With its elegant, reinforced concrete grid façade and stylish interior, the building, considered one of Berlin's most beautiful at the time, is among the most impressive symbols of a new architectural direction in postwar Berlin.

The Bayerhaus is now set to receive an extra story and a new side wing. In addition, the façade facing the rear yard, which was cladded with fiber cement plates in the 1980s, will be removed and re-rendered, restoring its original appearance, with its grid-like relief and large window openings.

To the rear, the building will receive a seven-story extension, providing office space that can be used independently or in addition to the space available in the existing building. Large windows, a highly flexible floor plan and state-of-the-art technology form the basis for the creation of a contemporary working environment in the building's interior. The room-high glazing elements, with a uniform grid pattern and alternating casement windows, will ensure optimal natural lighting and ventilation.

Taking up the history and elegance of the original Bayerhaus, the architectural language of the extension will lend the ensemble a new appearance and function. The modest organic forms of the existing building are expressed in the consistent application of characteristic historical details throughout the extension, such as rounded corners and the use of particular materials.

The vertical and horizontal elements of the new glass façade adopt the color scheme and well-balanced proportions of the original building, right down to the smallest detail. With its delicate, tailor-made façade profiles in different shades of brass and the minimalist safety rails that echo the formal language of the existing building, the new extension helps to reactivate the identity of the original, heritage-protected Bayerhaus.

Historic photo of the Bayerhaus lobby

The Bayerhaus lobby today

Window detail

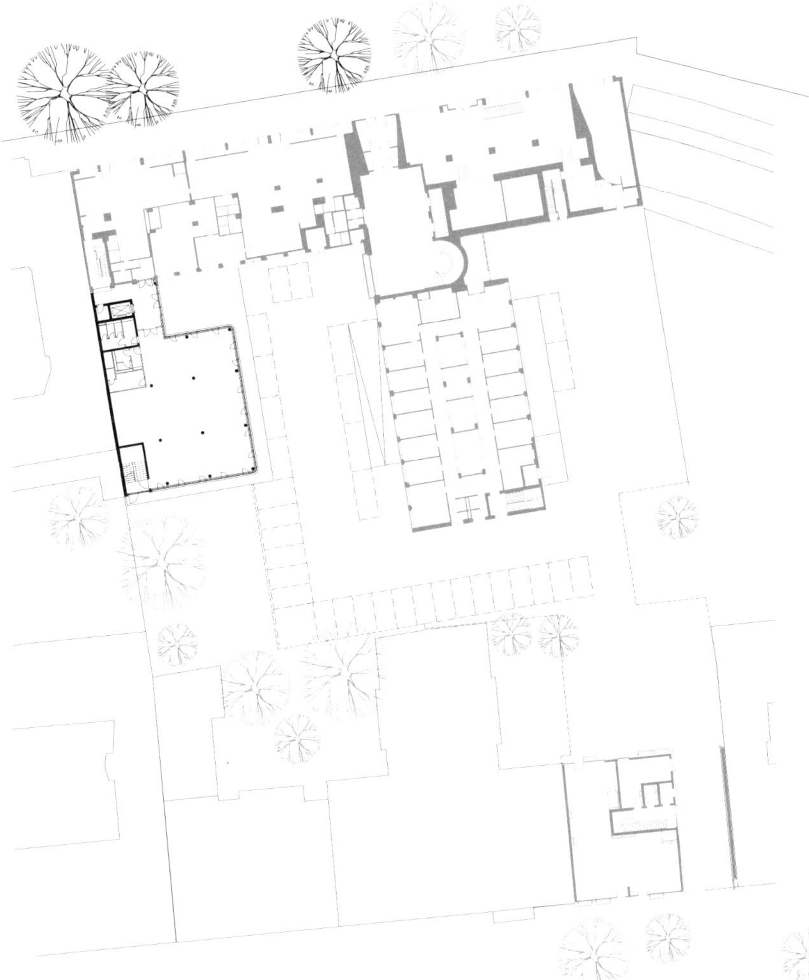

Ground floor plan

Standard floor plan

Section

EISWERK

Project: Office, residential, commercial
Location: Berlin, Germany
Client: Trockland
Year: 2017 – 2022
Status: Under construction

Perspective from the River Spree

GRAFT was commissioned to convert and redevelop a former ice factory on the banks of the River Spree in the Mitte district of Berlin. Located close to the Ostbahnhof train station, the development features a new residential building with commercial units on the ground floor and an additional commercial building with underground parking facilities.

The historic Kühlhaus including roof extension

Lobby in the new building

The factory is part of an industrial area that stretches from the River Spree to Köpenicker Strasse. Home to lumberyards and lumber markets in the 18th century, it was later bought by the Norddeutsche Eiswerke A.G. (North German Ice Works Company), who constructed a residential and industrial complex with two courtyards on the street side of the plot—and which is now a listed building.

The existing residential building along Köpenicker Strasse will be renovated and partially converted into smaller units and brought in line with current housing standards.

With a focus on retaining its original industrial character, the former cooling house will be converted into a commercial building with two office units on each floor. Devised as spaces for group working, each office will be equipped with a kitchenette and a lounge area.

Further office space will be created in a new building that spans two volumes, offering flexible layouts and adaptable as individual and group offices. The entrance and reception areas to these offices will be situated on the ground floor—along with a restaurant and other commercial, cultural and exhibition spaces.

Lobby in the new building

The historic Kesselhaus (left), Kühlhaus (center) with roof extension and new construction (right)

Isometric view

A second new building will close the current gap on Köpenicker Strasse, adding a front building and side wing to the existing cross-building. This will create a total of 34 apartments and two additional commercial units.

With the Eiswerk, GRAFT is creating a modern, inner-city quarter that complements the existing building stock and revitalizes the area around the former ice factory while paying heed to its long history.

Ground floor plan

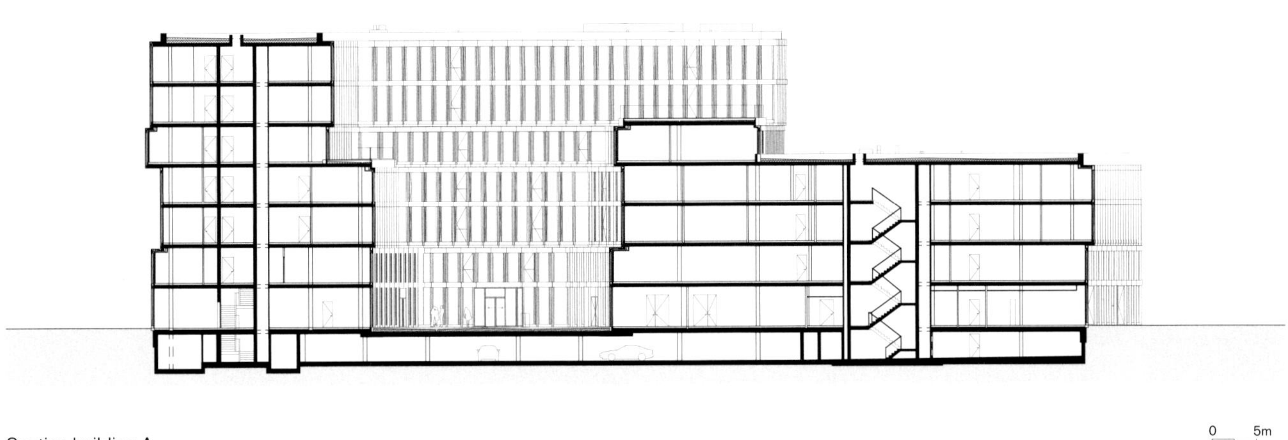

Section building A

The art nouveau façade of the historic Admiralspalast with new construction

ADMIRALSPALAST

Project: Office building, new construction, refurbishment
Location: Berlin, Germany
Year: 2017 – 2021
Status: Under construction
Size: 9,600m² (GFA)

The roof of the Admiralspalast was used as a public bath. Historic photo: “Admirals Bad, Russisch-Römische Bäder,” 1938

Section new planning

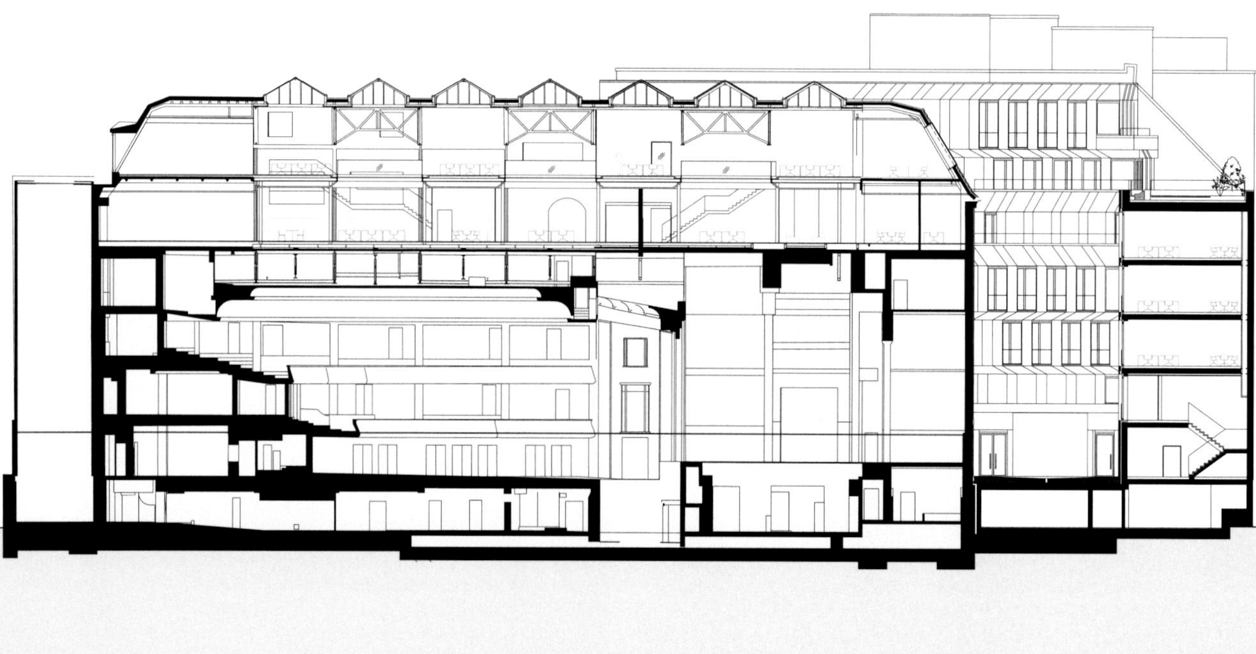

Historic photo of the entrance hall: "Vorraum zu den Bädern," 1912

The former women's bathing area will be transformed into office spaces. The listed mosaic basin will be displayed under a walkable glass floor. Historic photo: "Bassinhalle im Damenbad," ca. 1920

GRAFT was commissioned for the renovation and expansion of the Admiralspalast, a prestigious, historically listed building complex located between Friedrichstrasse and Planckstrasse in Berlin-Mitte.

The new building is being constructed as an extension of the Admiralspalast and the previously unused roof area above the main event space. Its design takes up the elaborate formal language of the Admiralspalast in an abstract manner, with the folded horizontal and vertical bands of the façade creating a dynamic plasticity that is amplified towards the corner of the building.

The new building will serve as the functional expansion of the venue, providing a redesigned delivery area, a side stage, artists' dressing rooms and storage areas on the first and second floors, as well as separate office rental space on the upper floors.

More office space will be created in the expanded roof area, which will be connected to the usable space in the new building via a newly designed floor plan. A new gallery level will be added to the usable roof areas, creating a two-story space with a room height of eight meters.

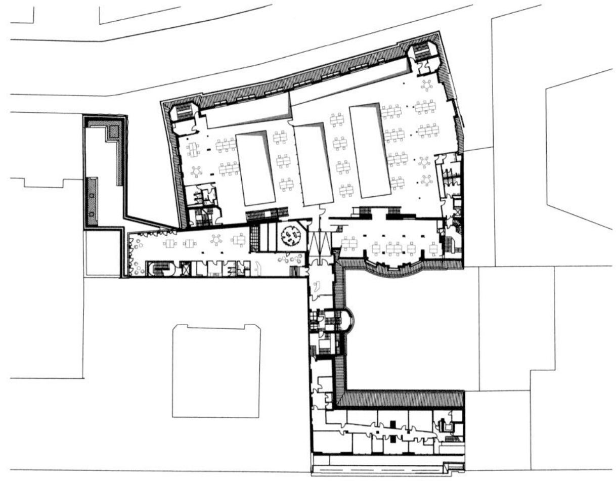

Fifth floor plan

0 2 4m

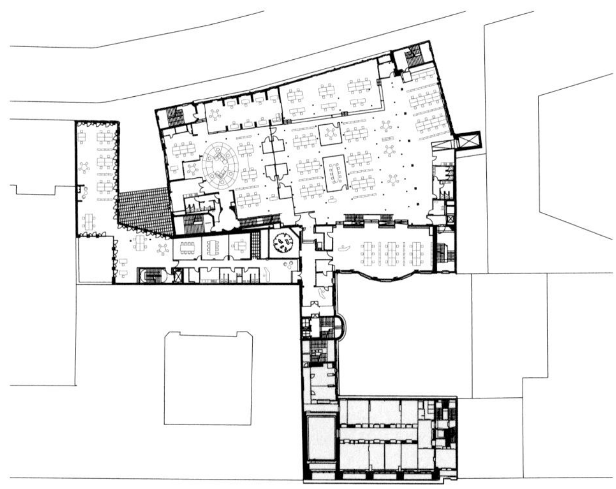

Fourth floor plan

0 2 4m

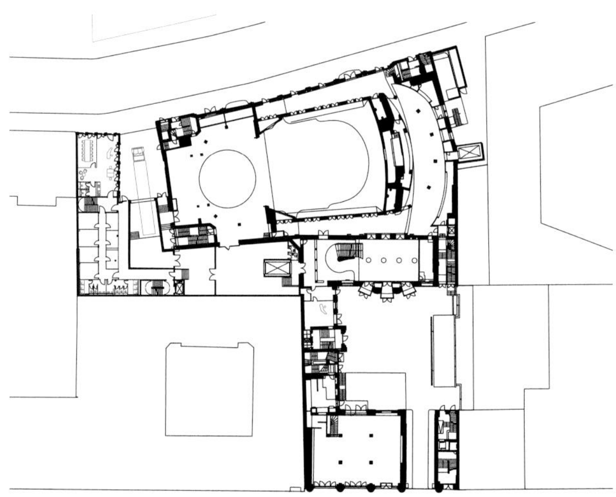

Ground floor plan

0 2 4m

View of the façade towards Planckstrasse

Re-activated skylights in the former public bath, now transformed into office spaces

After renovation, the historic steel support structure of the roof will form a defining element of the predominantly open-plan office space, while the skylights, which have been clad for decades, will be re-glazed and once more serve as a source of lighting.

After opening in 1910, the roof of the Admiralspalast was used as a public bath, with separate sections for men and women. Of these lavishly decorated baths, only the mosaics surrounding the women's pool have survived. The new building will incorporate these preserved mosaics, displaying them under a walkable glass floor.

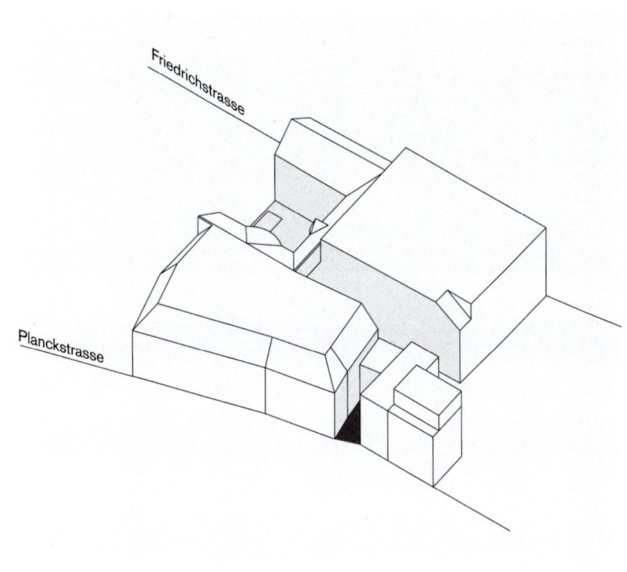

Existing buildings

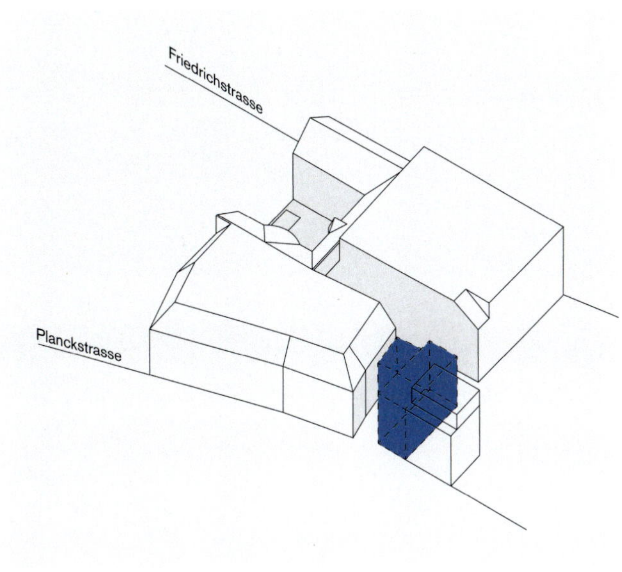

Demolition of the former Garderobenhaus

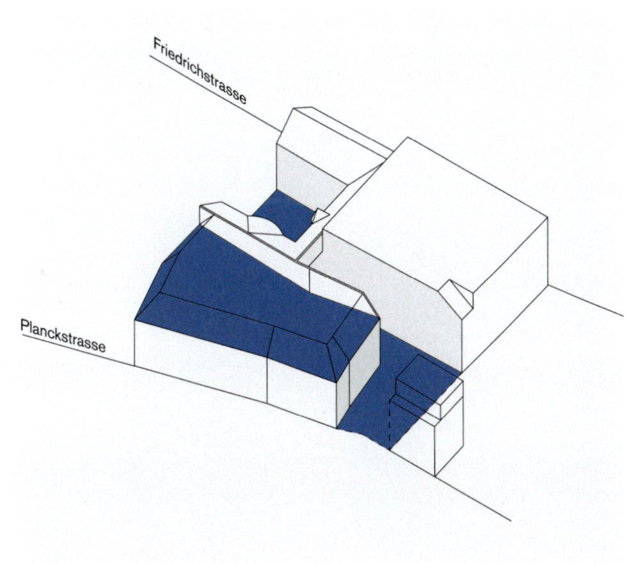

Activation of the building plots

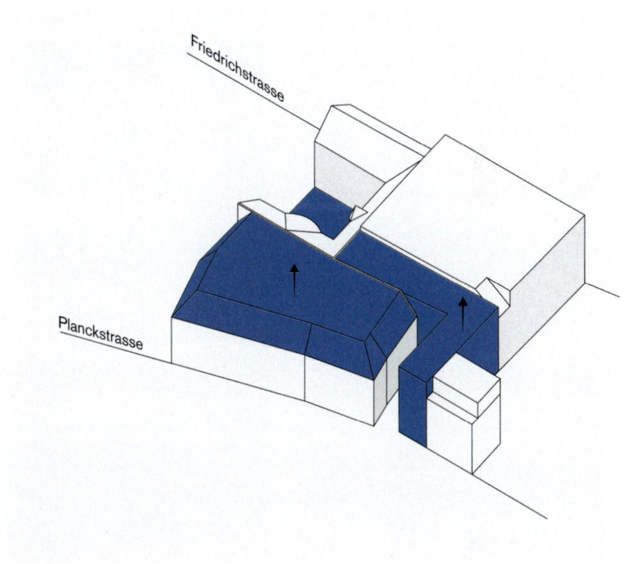

Increasing the volume

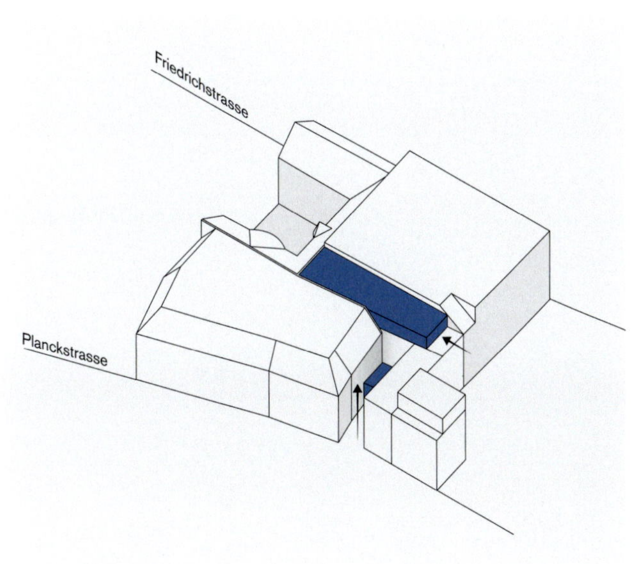

Volume transformation

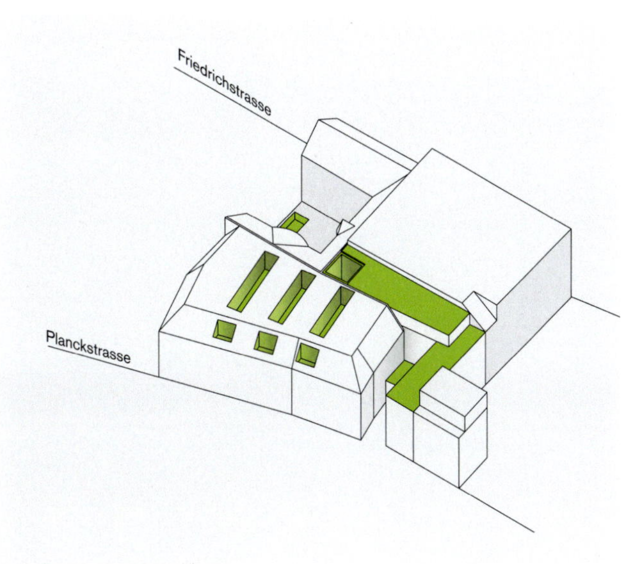

Green roofs and courtyards

BRANDING

FUTURE BRANDING

A CONVERSATION WITH NIKOLAUS HAFERMAAS AND RICO ZOCHER

The methodology of GRAFT's architectural practice is deeply rooted in a hybrid design approach. With a founding principle of *grafting* different realities and crossing boundaries between disciplines, their inclusive approach dovetails naturally with strategic branding tasks. In 2014, the agency GRAFT Brandlab was established to complement GRAFT's creative endeavor of devising spaces and experiences beyond the traditional boundaries of the architectural profession. Nikolaus Hafermaas and Rico Zocher joined GRAFT Brandlab as a new dual leadership in 2020, focusing on progressive brand innovation concepts for digital and analog media as well as multidimensional immersive spaces.

The following dialog elaborates on how different typologies and disciplines mutually inform each other and how branding is a tool with a public impact.

GRAFT What are the key elements of brand identity and how would you align them with each other?

RICO ZOCHER There are different models out there that are helpful when organizing a strategic brand platform. The ones we use most frequently contain market and consumer insights, a brand promise, values, tonality and a positioning statement. But there are also additional elements that define a brand, such as a mission statement and/or a vision. Lately, everyone has been striving to define their brand purpose. All these elements are used to establish the identity of a brand.

BRANDS THAT DON'T MOVE TOWARDS DIVERSITY AND INCLUSION WILL END UP DEAD IN THE WATER.

I would always recommend a strategic approach. When you are defining a brand strategy, it's essential not just to rely on words but to dig deep and use imagery and projective methods that explore the true meaning behind certain words or phrases. In this early phase of the branding process, the aim is to get beyond the conscious awareness of words in order to affect the emotional drivers. This means you have to explore the true meaning of a certain expression, value or phrase, and only when that is understood can it become a building block of a strategic foundation for a whole design system that can then be applied in digital and analog brand environments.

NIKOLAUS HAFERMAAS Once the core of a brand is defined, you start applying design methods to orchestrate every possible touchpoint between you and the people that make up your brand. As well as your employees, these are also people who form part of your brand through identification and association. What does it sound like? What does it look like? What does it feel like? What is the attitude of the people representing the brand to the public? All of these things are part of a brand identity.

GRAFT This touches on the realm of theatrical and performative expression, asking questions about the atmosphere, the feeling and the emotional quality of a space. It's very important to differentiate between the individual identities that are reflected in a brand and the collective identities that are reflected in spatial environments. The transitions between branding, corporate communications, advertising and spatial branding design are becoming more fluid every day. And that is also manifested in the built environments of brands.

HAFERMAAS The instruments at our disposal to make a brand come to life are becoming broader and more versatile, equipping us with the means to create more fluid and dynamic systems to communicate a brand. In the collaboration between GRAFT Architects and GRAFT Brandlab, we can work hand in hand with the physically built environment, but GRAFT Brandlab addresses the other layers that go beyond the static architecture. If you take a look at branding from a time perspective, you are managing different pace layers, which quickly reveals extremes: On the one hand, you have time spans of decades, deriving from the time it takes to create a building and the assumption of its life span. On the other hand, you have brand articulations that are in the realm of short-lived media campaigns. In between those two extremes, you have exhibitions, "mediatectures" and interior design experiences. All of these expressions work on a different time trajectory. As multidisciplinary branding specialists we have the opportunity to really address each of these pace layers individually and as an orchestrated whole.

GRAFT It's true, the built envelope, the core and shell of a building, lasts much longer than its interior, which over time responds better to brand values associated with flexibility, intelligence, smartness or changeability and adaptability. When it comes to customer journeys and retail, we are able

BRANDING ALLOWS US TO BROADEN OUR MEDIUMS OF EXPRESSION. WE CAN CREATE A COHERENT MESSAGE THROUGH A VARIATION OF INSTRUMENTS IN THE ORCHESTRA OF ARCHITECTURE.

to change the built environment every other year and adapt it to the dynamics of the brand strategy. And we are able to react even faster with the integration of media technology into interior design; with mediatecture we're able to change the environment and its atmosphere dramatically in the blink of an eye.

ZOCHER Indeed, but all these channels and measures have to speak a certain coherent language that is connected to the brand so they can effectively communicate as one entity. They have to be based on a common idea, which is, of course, the brand itself. The brand itself has to become the "glue" that holds all these channels and communication measures together.

GRAFT For us as architects, this new awareness of different layers of communication really has created a much larger canvas on which architecture can exercise its professional qualities. It's about scenography and creating narratives, about communicating the architectural navigation of ideas, emotions and a sense of aesthetics. For this reason, brand architecture—especially the partnership between GRAFT Architects and GRAFT Brandlab—suits our strategic creative objectives extremely well. Branding allows us to broaden our mediums of expression. We can create a coherent message through a variation of instruments in the orchestra of architecture. We embrace architecture as something that allows us to navigate three- or four-dimensionally between experiences. It's obvious that with the digital, architecture has left the built environment to evolve into something beyond physical presence. The narrative of spatial branding has entered a global domain, and we're able to navigate and design this domain more seamlessly than ever.

Seamless integration of media and architecture: DAZZLE is a permanent public artwork commissioned for San Diego International Airport's Rental Car Center. Artist team Ueberall International (Nikolaus Hafermaas, David Delgado, Dan Goods, and Jeano Erforth) conceived this site-specific design that brings the façade structure to life. The artwork features more than 2,000 tiles of a material similar to the technology found in handheld e-readers but adapted for an architectural scale. The artwork features custom, dynamic animations.

HAFERMAAS I agree. This seamlessness is a big, if not the biggest, opportunity I see from a designer's perspective, because the fusion of physical space with dynamic media goes beyond the ubiquitous screens that we are seeing right now. I firmly believe that the next step will be the abandonment of these screens in favor of media that is seamlessly embedded into our physical environment, on a human and architectural—and even communal—scale. We won't have to decide between inanimate physical objects and dynamic media any more and there won't be any devices between us as physical bodies and our experience of media. It will become one. Once we get rid of these VR goggles that separate people from each other, we're going to have a new, entirely different social experience that will allow us to immerse ourselves in shared digital experiences. This is where we will see the greatest advances, both in the realm of architecture and branding.

GRAFT Let's elaborate a little on the terminology of seamlessness. The retail market in particular creates awareness for new products, ideas and values through online branding. When the audience finally gets the opportunity to have a physical experience by entering the built environment of a brand, they already have a certain expectation, and that needs to be coherent with what has been communicated digitally. As architects, we have to anticipate that expectation or come up with a process of effectively managing expectations in commercial architecture. Since we spoke of ubiquitous branding and our overexposure to screens, how far away are we from a future where these processes are ubiquitously embedded in the built environment and how biased will the algorithms that deliver the content be? We are well aware that social media algorithms are criticized for being too streamlined with regard to gender or race.

HAFERMAAS If you look at these aspects from a positive point of view, you can see that large parts of society are becoming smarter and much more media-savvy. People's detectors have been fine-tuned and they're no longer as easily fooled as they were with a mass medium like television. This is a positive development. Along with this new mass awareness, you can see that successful brands now have to be inclusive and diverse. We've long left the era in which one size fitted all. Today, the expectation is that products should cater to the specific needs and wants of the individual, no matter how non-mainstream these might be. You have to meet everyone's expectation that they'll be invited to participate.

ZOCHER To be honest, I think we're already there. At GRAFT Brandlab, we have clients who are active in the field of generative designs that respond to the states of mind of their users. I believe we will be seeing many more of these hyper-personalized design solutions in the very near future.

HAFERMAAS I can only reemphasize that. I think brands that don't move towards diversity and inclusion will end up dead in the water. I don't believe that any brand will be excluded from that general trend. Users indeed become the brand if the brand is smart about inviting them in. Customers can be affiliated with a brand through active participation, through co-creation or through customization of their specific experiences. Each user becomes a participant, a specific and sometimes highly individual facet of a brand.

GRAFT We saw that in the brand environments and retail spaces we designed for Mercedes-Benz, where media technology is used extensively. Why did Mercedes-Benz as a brand put so much emphasis on that? The interactive retail design enabled them to react quickly to their clients, to be responsive and customize the space with respect to the customer. The whole idea is that the space opens up to being informed by the clients themselves. In a few years, we'll find out whether this is manipulative or a creative tool for people to interact with. We're going to see the way different brands use media technology within this spectrum, and we're also going to see which applications and strategies are more successful. We hope that this is a step toward democratizing accessibility and the possibility of interacting with space—a mission we at GRAFT have believed in from the very first day.

HAFERMAAS The seamlessness of this experience lies within the blending of digital and physical space, creating new intuitive interfaces. That brings me to my favorite topic, mediatecture, by which I mean the seamless embedding of media into physical space; media becomes architecture. Mediatecture becomes a stepping stone for how we perceive environments around us in a dynamic way. We will also see the advent of new terms such as ambient media, gentle media and non-disruptive media. We will have interfaces that become invisible and highly intuitive. And most importantly, the immersive media experiences that we currently encounter in virtual reality, for example, will become shared immersive experiences. If we can transform something that is currently just used for a nice visual effect into something that actually provides meaning and the opportunity for shared immersive interaction, then we're on the next level of experience.

GRAFT Another new aspect in this realm is the influence of artificial intelligence on the design process. What developments do you expect to see here?

ZOCHER The way brands communicate is already hugely influenced by AI and smart data. Not only by sending the right message to the most favorable target through the most suitable channel at the right moment, but also by using AI to generate designs that take into account places, situations, audiences or even individual preferences and moods.
AI calls for the development of design systems that are easy to understand and apply. Design automation will provide more consistency and efficiency. And that's very important for the companies we're working for, as it enables them to become more active and involved in the design development process. One of our aims is to provide tools and materials to our clients so they can use AI systems to manage their brands more efficiently.

HAFERMAAS AI is a tool, a process and an outcome at the same time. For one thing, it's a new design tool; it's also a new experience paradigm. As a tool, AI helps with generative design, and that will help us to create highly customized design solutions, meaning user experiences that are individualized and responsive and offer opportunities for participation and individual expression. Using algorithms to optimize design solutions will enable us to develop smarter solutions and create endless iterations that can be easily customized. As an experience, AI can help make the invisible visible, the intangible tangible. We're surrounded by data, but how much of that data is actually useful information? AI can help us filter through the overabundance of data—and that's an extremely powerful tool.

GRAFT This transdisciplinary collaboration with you is interesting for us because AI hasn't really played a role for us as architects. The whole industry is still very much stuck in the mid-20th century. It will take a long time for AI to gain ground in architectural planning methodologies and even longer for it to be adopted by the construction industry. But it will surely happen. Another subject that has become more prevalent in public discussions about urban and architectural design is the issue of participation. Do you think that brands are also becoming more democratic in this regard? They will have to listen more carefully to the customer, but also become open to influences from their own employees, as well as those from the market and the public.

ZOCHER It's a fact that customers are better informed and more critical than ever. This is even more true for the well-educated and urban audiences. I remember recently, Siemens became the subject of public discussions after they chose to conclude a contract with an Australian coal mine. This happened at a time when everyone was talking about climate change and the role that coal and fossil fuels play in it. While public image is opening up to new opportunities today, it can end up posing a devastating threat in the future. As a brand you have to be very, very careful about where you go, what you say, who you talk to and what you do.

HAFERMAAS Yes, it's a big challenge: Can you actually live up to the claims you make as a brand? Are you authentic in the sense of really aligning your actions with how you portray yourself? And as we've seen so many governmental failures in recent times, I think it's fair to say that people look towards brands to take on much greater responsibility. As well as expecting brands to sell products, people also expect them to be part of a solution towards a more sustainable world.

GRAFT It's interesting that some of these big names, whether product brands or their offshoots, like IBM and Bill Gates, have become crucial players in the international solution-finding process. And whether it's fake or not, we as

Mediatecture for Mercedes-Benz: A customized interior using LED walls

BRANDS CAN PLAY AN IMPORTANT ROLE BECAUSE THEY HAVE THE ABILITY TO UNITE PEOPLE BEHIND SHARED IDEAS, CULTURES AND DREAMS. AND THAT'S WHAT MAKES BRANDS EXTREMELY POWERFUL.

brand designers and architects need to find ways to help our clients to make a positive impact. I think we can all agree that climate consciousness, low-impact lifestyles and so on are already well-established as consumer expectations, and consumers expect those topics to be addressed. At the moment, we're experiencing the Covid-19 pandemic; this could play a big role in shaping new customer expectations.

HAFERMAAS It's difficult to predict the full extent of the economic and social impact of the current crisis at this point, but I think it will certainly force everyone—and I mean everyone: Organizations, individuals, nations—to reassess their business priorities and strive for smarter solutions with less impact on the environment and global connectivity. My hope is that we will see a new level of adaptiveness and resilience coming out of this. There will certainly be, at least for a while, very different patterns of consumption. We will see how long this lasts, or whether at some point we will just start pretending that nothing happened.

ZOCHER To be honest, I'm not sure if this crisis will have a long-term effect. I would, of course, love to keep seeing Italians singing on their balconies, and I would also like to keep the reduced carbon footprints but, quite frankly, I'm not very optimistic about that. I don't think humankind will change and we will simply return to old habits after the crisis. We will consume and buy even more in order to make up for the hardship. I also think that mainstream politicians and business leaders don't really have an interest in debating a new consumer consciousness. On top of this, I believe that the main goal will be to stimulate economic growth to balance government debt and to push stock markets back up to the next all-time high. I deeply hope that I will be proven wrong.

GRAFT But it's also possible that things will change for the better. We might see an increased motivation to make cities and states more resilient to such a crisis and numerous attempts to realize this. Healthcare standards will find their way onto the agenda of international debates and funding programs. Societies will entertain greater autonomy in times of crisis, private individuals will think about backup plans, digitization will be addressed, along with retail and delivery rituals. Talking to colleagues in South Korea, it was interesting to hear how easily they switched to staying at home and getting everything delivered, because the whole industry is used to superfast last-mile delivery. You get your groceries, medicine—whatever you want—just by pressing a button. And this, in combination with one of the world's best healthcare systems, proved to be the best setup for putting a halt to a challenge like the corona pandemic.

HAFERMAAS There was a term introduced by Nassim Nicholas Taleb in 2012: Antifragility. He came up with that term towards the end of the banking crisis in 2008, when he said the common notion of robust being the opposite of fragile was wrong. Robustness means stiffness. Antifragility is actually the property of a system to increase its ability to thrive and become stronger as a result of stresses, shocks, noise, mistakes and faults. These difficult situations result in it becoming better as a system. I think that's an interesting way of looking at what's happening right now. I hope you're going to be proven wrong, Rico; I hope that by undergoing this extreme stress test, the system will improve as a result.

GRAFT You've painted very different pictures of what the world might look like after this crisis. One predicted a completely new awareness of the fragility of our world, whereas Rico thinks that we're going to experience an all-time consumption high. And the third possible outcome was a boost to digitization and the emergence of new markets. How do you think brands can contribute to shaping these respective futures?

HAFERMAAS Well, brands are looked upon as providers not only of goods and services, but also of orientation and meaning. That sounds kind of weird, but some brands have become quasi-religions. People are willing to associate themselves with certain brands. With that comes an incredible amount of responsibility, but if you're aware of these powers, brands can really go deep into what kind of stance to take on major global problems.

ZOCHER Brands can play an important role because they have the ability to unite people behind shared ideas, cultures and dreams. And that's what makes brands extremely powerful.

GRAFT True, but consumers also have a very ambivalent relationship towards brands, because although they might idealize them and treat them like a religion, they are aware of the damage a certain brand might do—harming the environment, not paying the taxes they should be paying, exploiting their workers and so on. Do you think that's going to change due to the fact that consumers are more informed? Because right now this doesn't actually seem to affect the supply channels or tax systems of any of the big corporations.

HAFERMAAS Hopefully it will become increasingly difficult for brands to get away with harmful behavior like that. And hopefully the tools for whistleblowing and rebelling against bad actors will become more accessible to larger parts of the population, the global population, so to speak.

GRAFT Branding is not just a tool for commercial purposes, but can also be used for public entities, institutions and communities. Do you have a favorite example of a commercial brand strategy being applied in a completely different context?

HAFERMAAS Here's an example that might be described as *branded activism*. Youmna Chamcham, born and raised in Beirut, Lebanon, is a former student of mine and a pioneer in the use of branded social media and branded activism. In 2012, she started a movement called Live Love Beirut. She was tired of being pitied for coming from Beirut, based on the widespread perception that Beirut is a war zone. She countered this negative image by saying that in reality Beirut is one of the most vibrant, beautiful places in the world with a thriving culture. She saw that the story of the super-inventive, smart and creative young people of Beirut was not being told. With her Instagram account Live Love Beirut, she encouraged peers in her hometown to use photography to paint a different picture of Beirut. The brand Live Love Beirut completely took off and even became the official tourism campaign for Lebanon a few years later. Now, the Live Love brand has about 50 affiliated cities and countries with 1.5 million followers and over 15,000 volunteers. She created a branded grassroots

Brand activism as exemplified by "Live Love"

Through its volunteer program, "Live Love" encourages young people to get together and see that by working hand in hand they can have an impact on the world around them—as here, cleaning a beach in Beirut.

social media movement that goes way beyond posting pretty pictures, but actually activates people for local cleanups, for example at times when Beirut's municipal services are temporarily impaired. Youmna is incredibly brand- and social media-savvy and great at organizing people for social activism.

GRAFT We love that example because there's a very clear underlying intention in the name. There's a clear motivation for people to support that message. And that brings me to a question of how brands have become umbrellas for collective values. How much do you think cities and even nations have to take care of their branding? There is clearly a need to control the outside narrative of a location so that it stays attractive for tourists and people in general, but also to create a magnet in the competitive global field of megalopolises.

HAFERMAAS Yes, branding a place that is so diverse and rich in so many aspects makes it almost impossible to actually brand it if you think of brands as a one-size-fits-all umbrella. This complexity makes it an astonishingly tempting task for me. I would love to take on Berlin, as it has now reached global recognition as a creative epicenter. At the same time, Berlin is still healing from all the historical disruptions it went through, and continues to change radically, becoming wealthier and

1974: "We, the Berliners, serve metropolitan cocktails." An early campaign to brand Berlin as a cosmopolitan city

more established. With all its economic growth, Berlin is in danger of losing some of its edge, which is the very substance that made it such an amazing brand over recent decades. I'd love to help tell this incredible story with all its ambivalences, complexities, struggles and opportunities.

ZOCHER I agree. Destination branding has also played a big role in my career and I consider Berlin a highly interesting branding case. But if you asked me to choose a branding assignment, I would love to work for Lufthansa, as for me it's a truly iconic brand and I've always been fascinated by aviation. I was very impressed by the redesign of their visual appearance in 2018, and for everyone involved in that it must've been a once-in-a-lifetime experience.

HAFERMAAS Well, you might get your chance, because airlines will have to reevaluate their brands and entire strategies on the heels of the current crisis. They might not necessarily call it branding, but there's going to be a lot of rethinking that has to be done. The clichéd image of traveling abroad and enjoying the company of other people all rings very hollow given the current situation. Once we get through this, there will be a great deal of work on the horizon, as virtually every brand will need to be recalibrated.

Karl Charal (1928): Berlin's very first marketing campaign poster: "Everyone should go to Berlin one day."

2009: "Be street, be catwalk, be Berlin." City marketing poster during the "Be Berlin" campaign. *(The campaign features two alumni of the notorious Rütli School who succeeded in launching their own fashion label, RÜTLI WEAR.)*

2018: GRAFT's monument championing Berlin's spirit of freedom stands in front of the entrance to Berlin Central Station. 25 meters long and 2.5 meters tall, the monument takes the form of the "*Be Berlin*" campaign hashtag #FREIHEITBERLIN.

Rico Zocher was born and raised in Meissen, Germany. He studied business administration with a major in international marketing and international management in Dresden and Lille, France. He began his career at Hugo Boss in New York City before starting at MetaDesign, Berlin, in 2003, where he worked in various positions until 2013. Following his position as head of unit at MetaDesign, he switched to the client side and became head of marketing and sales at Direct Line Insurance AG (now Verti Insurance).

In 2016, he went back to the agency side and started at Superunion Germany (formerly known as Brand Union). As managing director, he was responsible for their operations in Hamburg as well as coordinating their business development activities in Hamburg, Berlin and Munich.

Between 2003 and 2017 he lived in Berlin; he now lives in Bielefeld.

Nikolaus Hafermaas graduated from Berlin University of the Arts with a degree in visual communication, later earning an Executive MBA at the Berlin School of Creative Leadership.

Early in his career, he joined Triad Berlin, soon becoming chief creative officer and principal partner. He designed large-scale exhibitions and experiences for Expo 2000 in Hanover and Expo.02 in Switzerland.

In 2004, he joined ArtCenter College of Design in Pasadena, California, serving for 14 years as dean and department chair of graduate and undergraduate graphic design, revolutionizing the design curriculum by fusing print and packaging, motion and interaction design into transmedia design.

While in LA, he founded Ueberall International, an artist platform that conceives and produces award-winning mediatecture installations.

Since returning to Berlin in 2018, he has continued his academic affiliation as professor and executive director of the ArtCenter Berlin satellite studio, where he fosters future-forward global collaborations and transdisciplinary projects.

INTERNATIONAL RETAIL DESIGN FOR MERCEDES-BENZ

Project: Brand architecture, retail, brand identity
Location: Worldwide
Client: Daimler AG
Year: Pilots since 2016, roll-out since 2017
Status: 1st place two-stage competition, completions worldwide

Car dealership in Budapest, Hungary
Typology: Car dealership international, new construction

The world's first retail outlets featuring Mercedes-Benz's new brand identity can already be seen in car dealerships in Hong Kong, Beijing, Budapest and Istanbul. For three years, GRAFT has been working on concept development and engineering, creating design guidelines and planning tools that can be implemented at sales and service locations around the world.

**THE ARCHITECTURAL IDEA:
THE DUALITY OF TOPOGRAPHY AND SKY**

The architecture is designed to provide an optimal setting for the brand and its products. The guiding principle is the duality of a dark floorscape and a silver-white roofline—topography and sky. These colors reference two main facets of the Mercedes-Benz brand: Emotional dynamism and technical intelligence. They create a clearly ordered space with upper and lower limits. At the same time, an outer skin, which is as transparent and minimalist as possible, emphasizes the fluid transition between interior and exterior; for Mercedes-Benz, the whole world becomes a showroom.

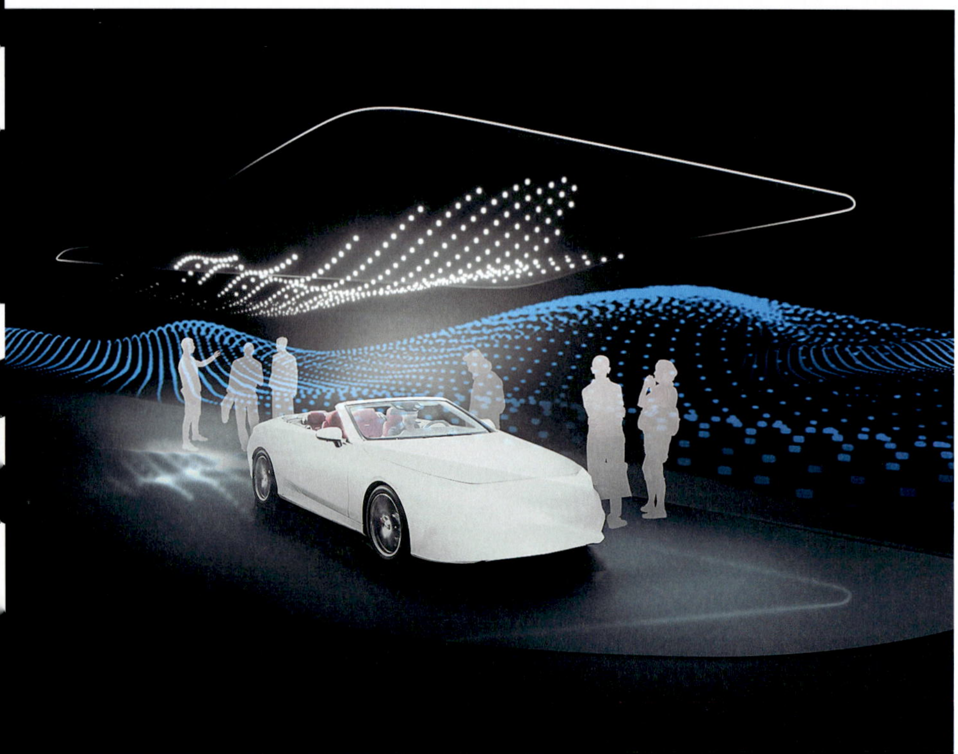

**THE PRODUCT STAGING IDEA:
CONCENTRATING THE BRAND EXPERIENCE**

The tension between topography and sky creates an environment that concentrates the brand experience: An endless horizon forms a stage for displaying the vehicle and a platform for interaction.

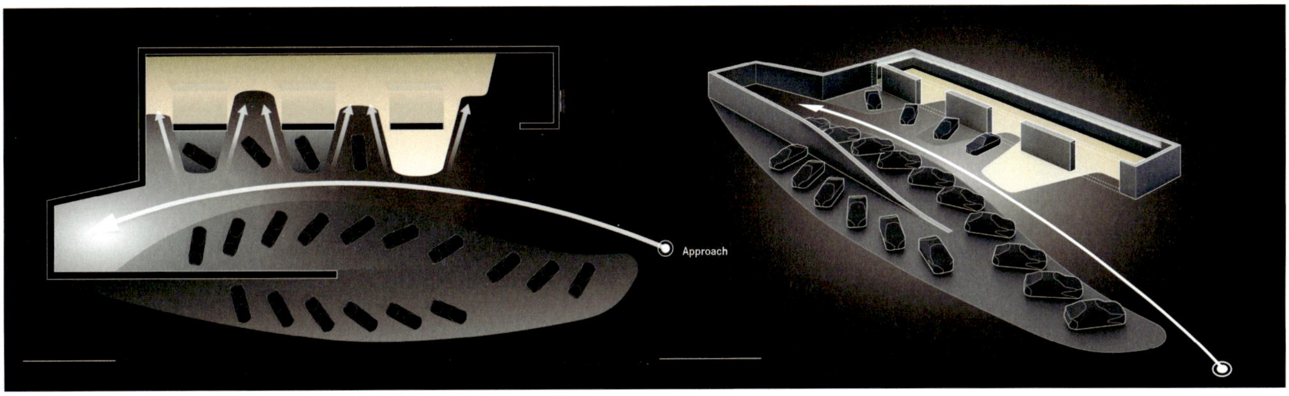

Radical scenography change that integrates and interweaves presentation and consultancy areas, as well as the brand's physical presence with the virtual potential of a media horizon.

This enables an adaptive approach and an personalized customer journey: The intuitive route takes the form of a main walkway and a network of individual paths between the touchpoints.

A zonal pattern and openings between the black wall elements highlight transitions between the main zones.

The main route begins on the outside, leads into the showroom in an arc along a dynamic vehicle display and ends at a highly staged location—ideally the vehicle handover. The layout of the vehicles along this route increases the visibility of every single model and enhances the dramatic effect of the journey through the showroom.

Vehicles are not arranged parallel to each other. The floor pattern accentuates the display areas through a darker floor color.

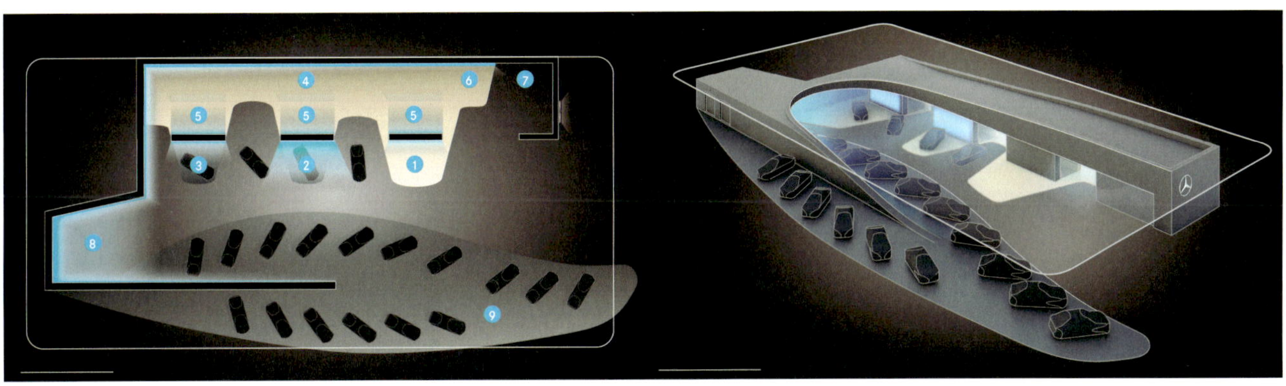

MEDIA SPACE

Media surfaces extend and animate the architecture. The seamless merging of the virtual with the physical creates a media space:

1. Welcome area: Multitouch high desk, wall screens for retail marketing
2. Main stage: Large media background (always on)
3. Sub stage: Large media background (always on)
4. Consulting area: Horizontal media band defining the boundary of the spaces (when activated)
5. Consulting rooms: Wall screens in the rear face of the wall elements (when activated)
6. Shop: Multitouch high desk, media surfaces in media horizon
7. Service lobby: Optional screen
8. Vehicle handover: Media wall
9. Service outbound: Optional screen (outdoor compatible)

TOPOGRAPHY AS MEDIA CARRIER

- All vertical surfaces that are part of the topography are able to house media elements
- The increased use of media for product presentation means there are fewer vehicles in the showroom than before but they are displayed in a higher-quality setting with virtual extensions
- Flexible, media-supported brand differentiation is possible within the vehicle display
- Media content is emotionally appealing, informative and seamlessly integrated into the architecture
- Screen bezels are never visible as media units are always integrated behind black glass elements and completely hidden when switched off

Customer service and vehicle areas are interwoven with flexible consulting areas.

Interior design of typology:
Car dealership international,
new construction in Budapest,
Hungary

The planning catalog ranges from façade specifications and roof design to the interior design of customer contact areas, including media integration and furniture design.

Together with the TRIAD creative agency from Berlin, GRAFT won a two-stage competition against renowned international competitors.

Car dealership in Bangkok, Thailand
Typology: Car dealership international, urban stacked format

Interior of car dealership in Bangkok, Thailand

Entrance of car dealership
in Bangkok, Thailand

The concept of a new, seamless customer experience with modular touchpoints—developed in close cooperation with Mercedes-Benz and TRIAD—responds to changing customer expectations both on- and offline.

Interior of car dealership in Bangkok, Thailand

Focused on developing a customer-oriented retail experience, GRAFT's striking architecture and high-quality interior design creates flowing transitions from exterior to interior.

Within the customer service area of a car dealership, vehicle presentation is interwoven with focused yet flexible consulting areas. Similarly, modular media elements can be incorporated into the interior fittings that shape the showroom, strengthening the combination of the real and virtual brand presence. This makes it possible to address and respond to the changing requirements of different target groups and successively and adaptively incorporate them into diverse spatial environments.

The resulting scenography creates numerous opportunities to interact with the Mercedes-Benz brand at different levels.

PRIMUS

GLA

In addition to developing the concept and elaborating design guidelines, GRAFT has also been Mercedes-Benz's lead planner since 2017, responsible for supporting the roll-out of the brand's new identity on the German market.

This can already be experienced in Mercedes-Benz dealerships around Germany, including Böblingen, Berlin, Kaufbeuren and Darmstadt.

Car dealership in Heilbronn, Germany
Typology: Car dealership international, conversion

Mercedes-Benz
smart

The Hague, Netherlands

Uhingen, Germany

Budapest, Hungary

Hong Kong, China

Vienne, France

The Hague, Netherlands

Budapest, Hungary

Budapest, Hungary

Heilbronn, Germany

Mulhouse, France

Istanbul, Turkey

Trier, Germany

The Hague, Netherlands

Hong Kong, China

Dartford, United Kingdom

Budapest, Hungary

The Hague, Netherlands

Dartford, United Kingdom

Hong Kong, China

Heilbronn, Germany

Bangkok, Thailand

Menden, Germany

Leipzig, Germany

Dartford, United Kingdom

Istanbul, Turkey

RETAIL DESIGN FOR MERCEDES-BENZ BY GRAFT

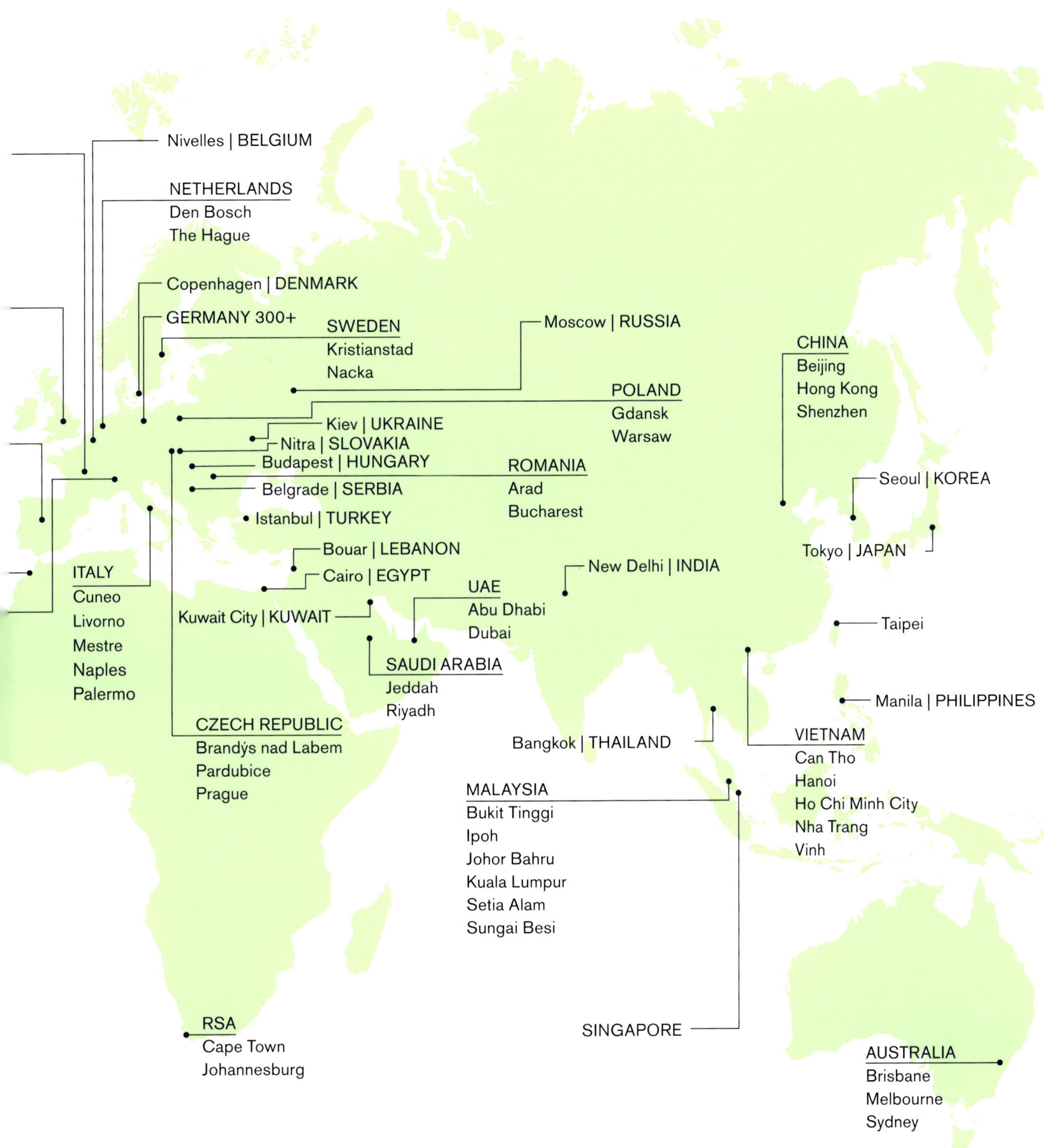
Nivelles | BELGIUM
NETHERLANDS
Den Bosch
The Hague
Copenhagen | DENMARK
GERMANY 300+
SWEDEN
Kristianstad
Nacka
Moscow | RUSSIA
POLAND
Gdansk
Warsaw
Kiev | UKRAINE
Nitra | SLOVAKIA
Budapest | HUNGARY
ROMANIA
Arad
Bucharest
Belgrade | SERBIA
Istanbul | TURKEY
Bouar | LEBANON
Cairo | EGYPT
ITALY
Cuneo
Livorno
Mestre
Naples
Palermo
Kuwait City | KUWAIT
UAE
Abu Dhabi
Dubai
SAUDI ARABIA
Jeddah
Riyadh
New Delhi | INDIA
CZECH REPUBLIC
Brandýs nad Labem
Pardubice
Prague
CHINA
Beijing
Hong Kong
Shenzhen
Seoul | KOREA
Tokyo | JAPAN
Taipei
Manila | PHILIPPINES
Bangkok | THAILAND
VIETNAM
Can Tho
Hanoi
Ho Chi Minh City
Nha Trang
Vinh
MALAYSIA
Bukit Tinggi
Ipoh
Johor Bahru
Kuala Lumpur
Setia Alam
Sungai Besi
SINGAPORE
RSA
Cape Town
Johannesburg
AUSTRALIA
Brisbane
Melbourne
Sydney

Mercedes and Maybach trade fair stand

MERCEDES & MAYBACH CAR SHOW AMI

Project: Commercial, trade fair stand
Location: Leipzig, Germany
Client: DaimlerChrysler AG
Year: 2006
Status: Completed
Size: 1,487m^2

GRAFT's stand design for Mercedes and Maybach sought to embody the brands' prestige and self-confidence and marked a radical new approach to their commercial exhibition design. Its large, free-flowing forms replaced the small-scale fragmentation usually found in trade fair stand construction.

Central to the design, and clearly visible from all distances and angles, is the undulating skyscape that seems to float above the display area.

This representation of the sky, which connects the Mercedes and Maybach stands, creates an atmosphere of expanse and lightness—a breath of fresh air.

The structure's lines and formal vocabulary are inspired by the contours typical of the Mercedes brand, while drawings and graphic elements of Mercedes vehicles provide inspiration for the skyscape and the design of the wall elements. Thus, the visual language and general design principles of the brand are reflected in the stand's floor plan, its contoured ceiling and the vertical wall sections.

All functional spaces are integrated in the rear wall of the stand: The store, meeting room and office areas are all positioned at varying angles relative to the presentation area and separated from it. The openings they create transform the lines of the stand into a frame for viewing the vehicles on display.

As far as was possible, the techniques used in constructing the stand were based on production methods used in car manufacturing. Through serial production and the development of modular dimensions, this untypical exhibition stand concept was made both feasible and economically viable.

Visitors to the Mercedes & Maybach Car Show

Undulating skyscape at the Mercedes and Maybach trade fair stand

The KU64 dental clinic

KU64 DENTAL CLINIC & KIDS CLUB

Project: Healthcare, commercial
Location: Berlin, Germany
Client: Dr. med. dent. Stephan Ziegler
Year: 2005, 2010 & 2011
Status: Completed

There are few environments with more negative associations than dental clinics.

The hygienic, sterile atmosphere, the obligatory "white color palette" and the distinctive smell are usually connected with a feeling of physical and psychological discomfort. With this in mind, we should be striving for a radical new understanding of both hospitals and dental clinics—moving away from negative reactions towards an atmosphere of well-being and relaxation.

Treatment room at the KU64 dental clinic

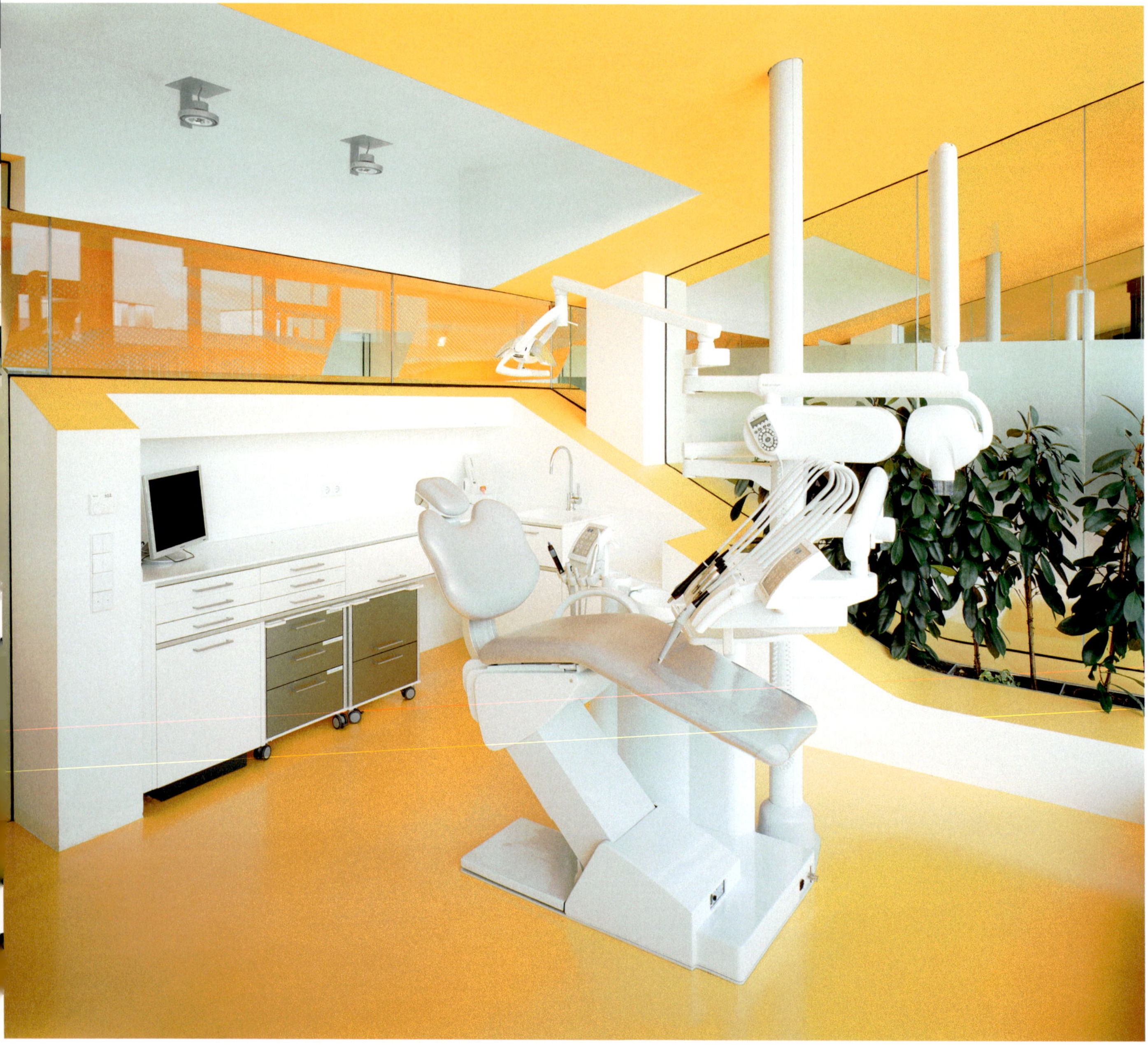

Entrance to the KU64 dental spa

Dental spa

The waiting area integrates experiences of beauty, health and wellness.

The aim of this project was to enable patients to forget about their fears and relax in ways they would typically experience in a spa, café, restaurant or hotel. Why not embellish the reality of a dental clinic with experiences of beauty, health and wellness?

A visit to the dentist could be seen as a journey of well-being that balances potentially distressing medical treatment by such services as consultation, preventive checkups, beauty therapy, dental care and alternative practices.

Waiting area at the KU64 dental clinic

Hallway of KU64 dental clinic

Reception at the kids club

New extension

Hallway at the kids club

View into the underwater-themed kinderdentist clinic

KINDERDENTIST

Project: Healthcare
Location: Berlin, Germany
Client: Dr. med. dent. A. Mokabberi
Year: 2008 & 2015
Status: Completed

When children visit the dentist, they are usually greeted by a cold, white, sterile world that bears no relationship to the playful environments they revel in.

A twelve-foot wave in blue tones welcomes children to the kinderdentist.

The Mokabberi dental clinic, specializing in the treatment of children, redefines this experience in their branch office in Berlin's Prenzlauer Berg district, offering young visitors an imaginative space with the qualities of an indoor playground. GRAFT devised an underwater world that captures children's imagination and encourages them to enjoy themselves. A twelve-foot wave in vibrant blue tones welcomes visitors into the building. It unites the upper and lower levels of the clinic, guiding patients into the reception room below and providing views into the treatment rooms above.

The extension ...

... with new waiting area

The decorative architectural and spatial elements all emphasize the impression of an underwater experience. Pixelated schools of fish swim across the walls between treatment rooms, while the silver upholstery in the waiting rooms calls to mind submarines. From arrival to waiting through to treatment, a visit is orchestrated as a playful experience.

As such, the practice cultivates a positive attitude towards visiting the dentist from an early age. In 2015, GRAFT designed and planned the extension of the original space.

The extension of the original space

Playful spatial elements redefine the experience at the dentist.

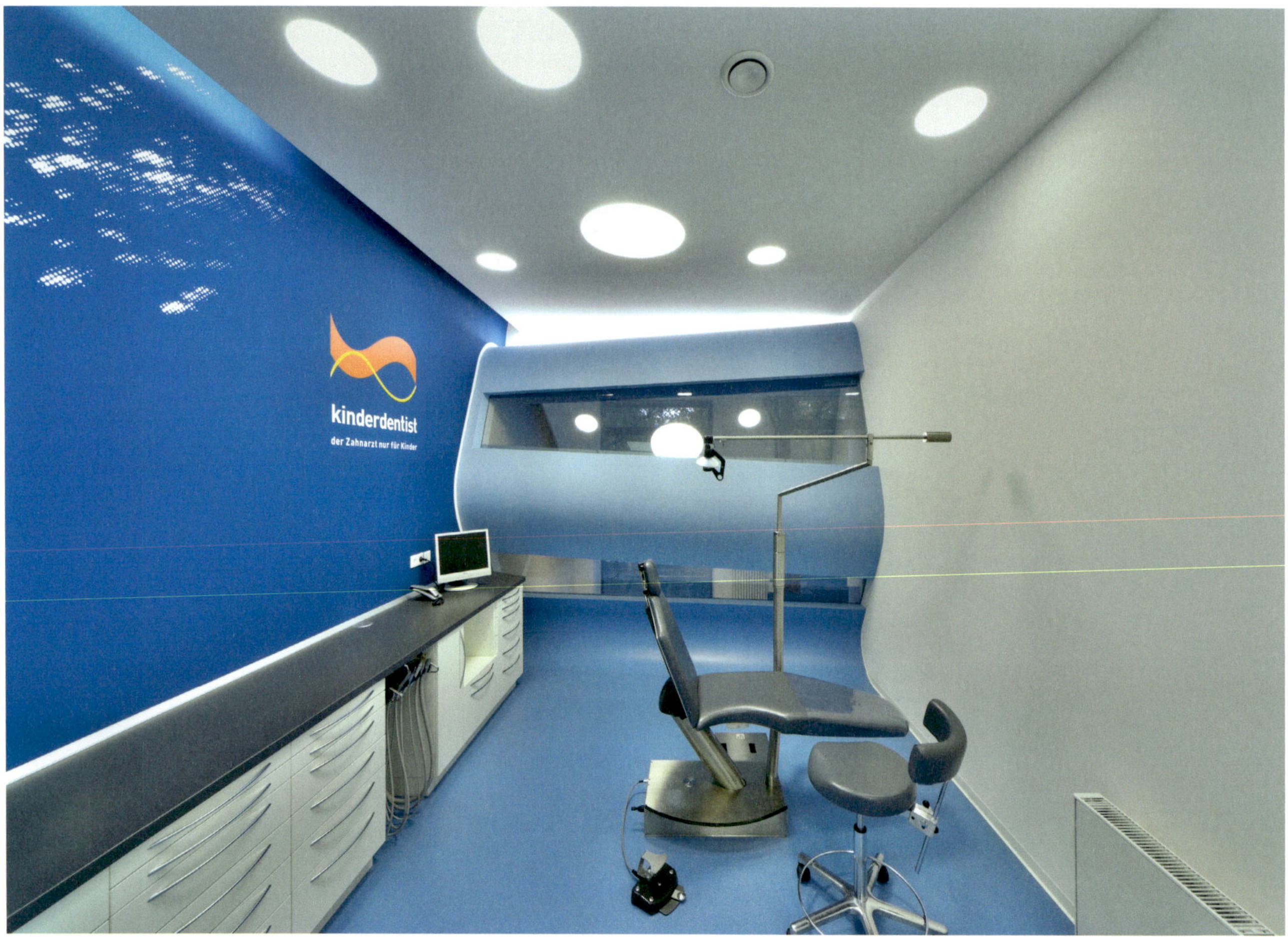

The wave element unites the different levels of the clinic.

BRLO BRWHOUSE

Project: Mobile brewery, container architecture
Location: Berlin, Germany
Client: Braukunst Berlin GmbH
Year: 2016
Status: Completed
Size: 892m²

Situated in Berlin's "Urbane Mitte," between the eastern and western parts of the city's Park am Gleisdreieck, GRAFT designed and planned the BRLO BRWHOUSE mobile brewery and beer garden.

Notable for its modular container architecture, the building combines a restaurant, bar and event space with a craft brewery and administration areas.

The BRLO craft brewery at the Park am Gleisdreieck

GRAFT created a freestanding structure using shipping containers, similar to the two PLATOON Kunsthalle container buildings opened in Seoul in 2009 and in Berlin in 2012.

The prefabricated containers were individually tailored according to their function and arranged to form a mobile base for the young local brewing company BRLO. The building is designed for temporary use over a period of three to five years, and can easily be dismantled and reconstructed at another location as and when needed.

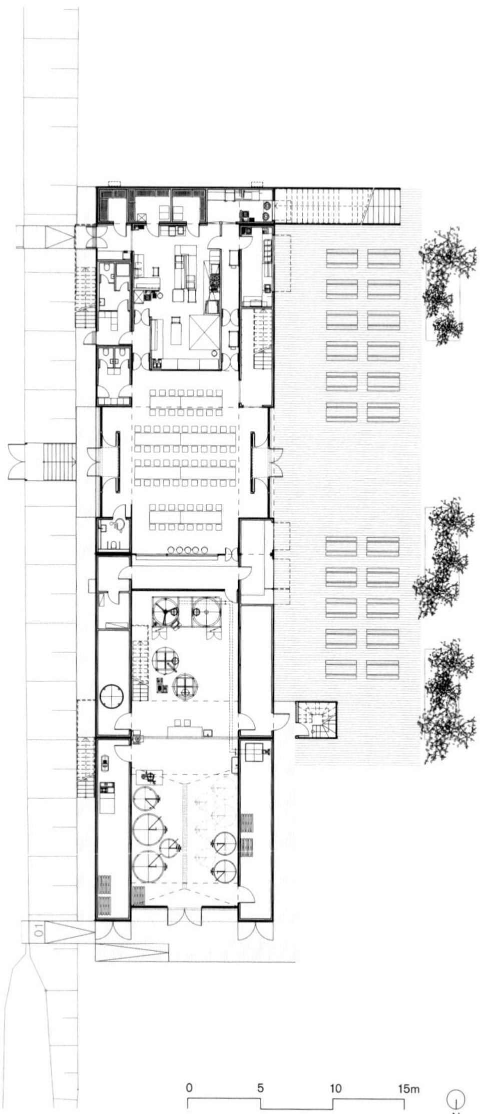

Ground floor plan

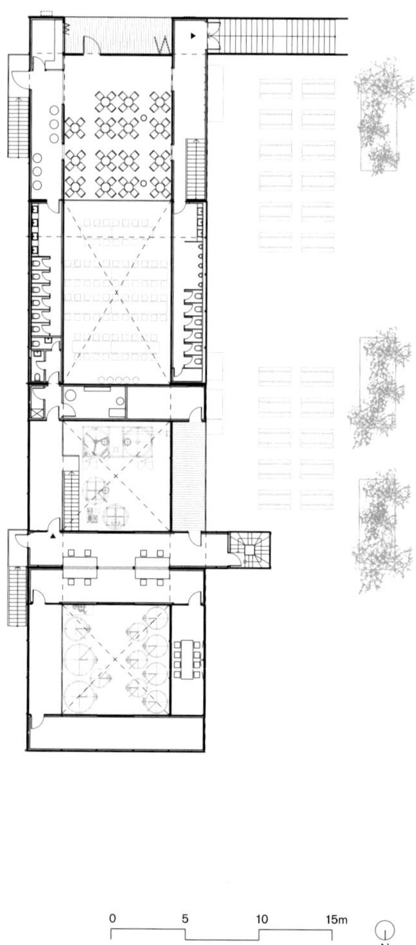

First floor plan

Craft brewery and beer garden

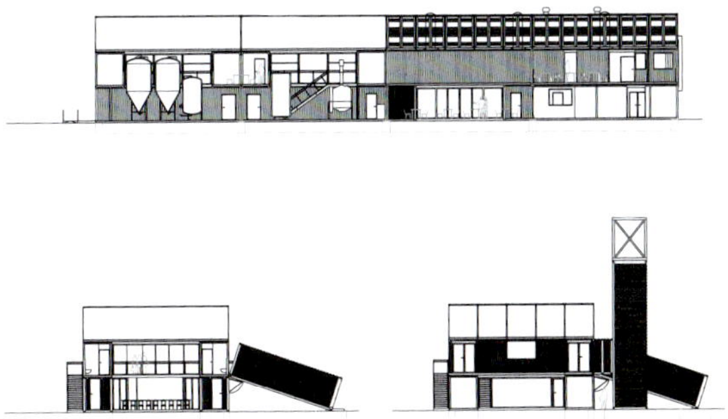

Sections

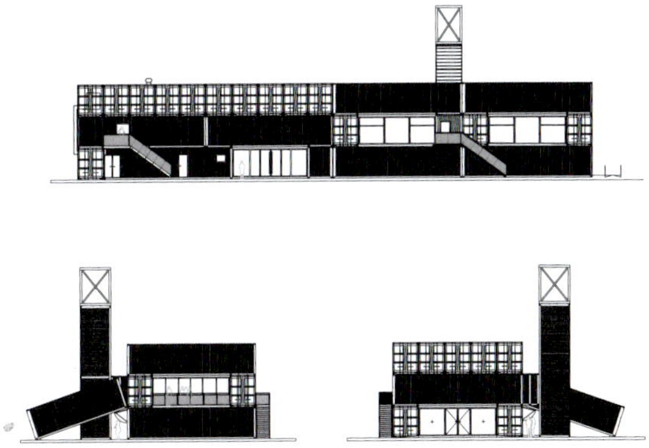

Elevations

0 5 10 15m

2 3 3

Four containers long and three containers high, the block provides about 892m^2 of floor space, enough to accommodate the brewing equipment and provide space for guests, events and offices. To the west, a vertically placed container houses a staircase that serves as the entrance to the office spaces. A second, inclined container at the building's western end provides outside access to a gallery level.

The utilitarian character of the container architecture is emphasized by its anthracite color.

The container architecture houses a brewery, a restaurant and office spaces.

Beer garden in front of the BRLO brewery

BRŁO

BRŁO

Outdoor area in front of the BRLO brewery

FRANKFURT REGIONALS

Project: Retail
Location: Frankfurt International Airport, Germany
Client: Gebr. Heinemann, Hamburg
Year: 2010 & 2012
Status: Completed
Size: 40m²

Heinemann duty free shop at terminal 2 of Frankfurt International Airport

ULTRA SMOOTH,
PERFECT FOR SHARING.

With over eleven million hectares of forest, Germany is one of Europe's most densely wooded countries—and a number of highly unusual trees have taken root at the Heinemann duty free shops at Frankfurt International Airport.

Heinemann duty free shop at Frankfurt International Airport

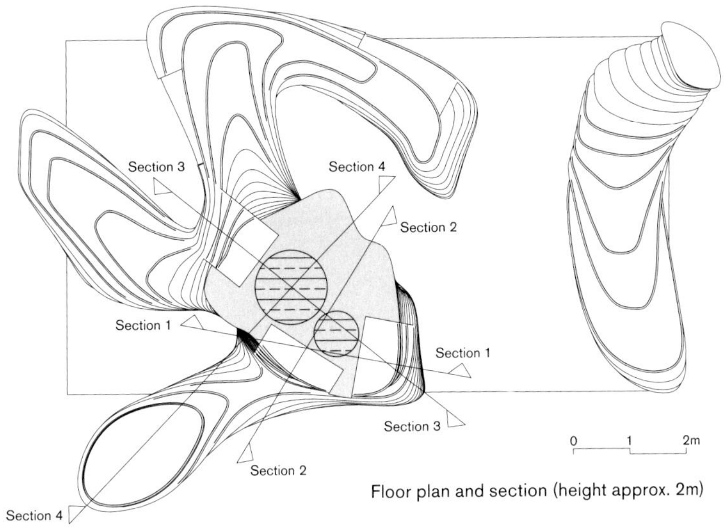

Floor plan and section (height approx. 2m)

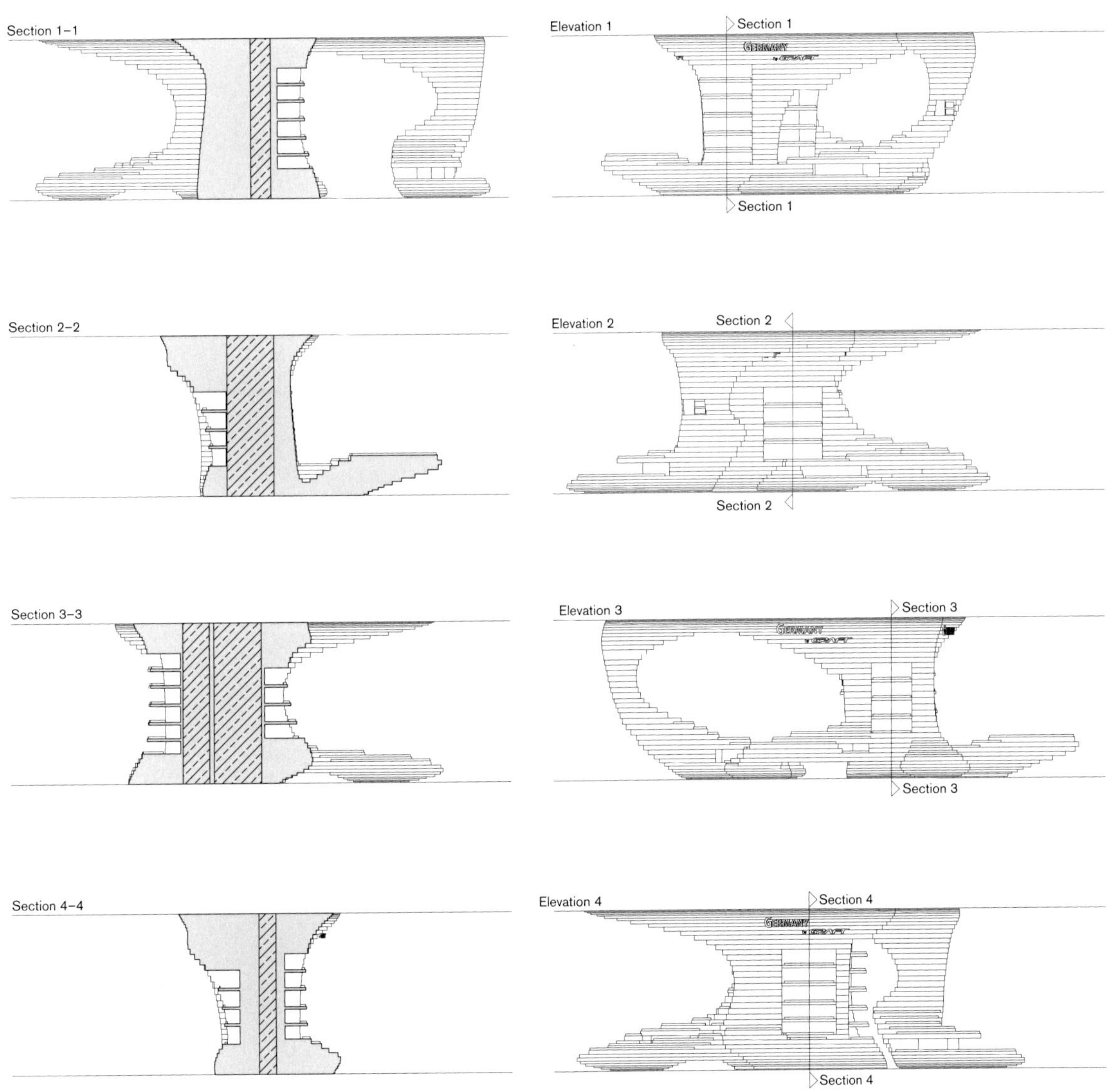

Sections and elevations

Tree sculptures made of stacked layers of oak

GRAFT designed forest-themed installations for the "Made in Germany" regional specialty areas of three different Heinemann duty free shops: Dynamic tree sculptures made of stacked layers of oak that serve as eye-catching centerpieces for shoppers.

With this modern interpretation of the forest, GRAFT has created an open and fluid space, a clearing in which passengers can pause for a while amid the hustle and bustle of the airport terminal.

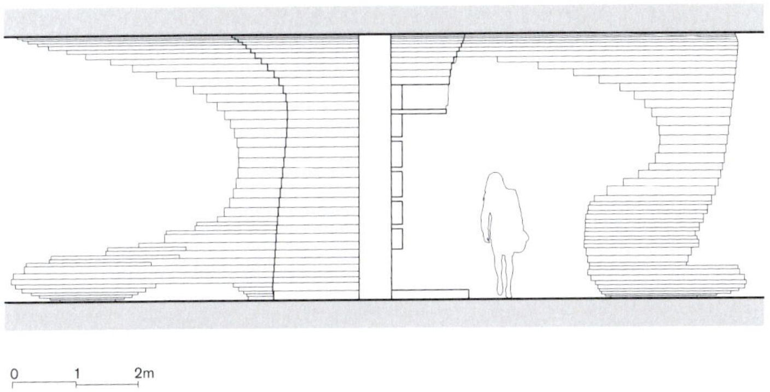

Section

Heinemann duty free at Frankfurt International Airport

2

4

3

OPTICON HAMBURG

Project: Retail, commercial
Location: Hamburg, Germany
Client: Hamburg Eyewear ON GmbH
Status: Completed
Year: 2007

Product display within interactive design elements

GRAFT's design for an optician's boutique store in Hamburg creates a holistic customer experience that merges interactive design elements with product display.

The concept merges spatial boundaries with functional elements. A sculptural wall incorporating shelves, showcases and storage cupboards winds its way around the entire store, transitioning into the mirrored wall at the rear. The highly dynamic space offers an array of different presentation options, making the extensive product range—over 2,100 pairs of glasses displayed in alternating constellations—into an integral part of the store's design.

Large pieces of custom-built furniture are interspersed throughout the interior, their vivid colors and velvet coverings nestling into the space's natural niches.

They offer customers the opportunity to linger a while, take in the surroundings and interact with each other, fostering an atmosphere of homeliness.

Interior with vivid colors and velvet coverings

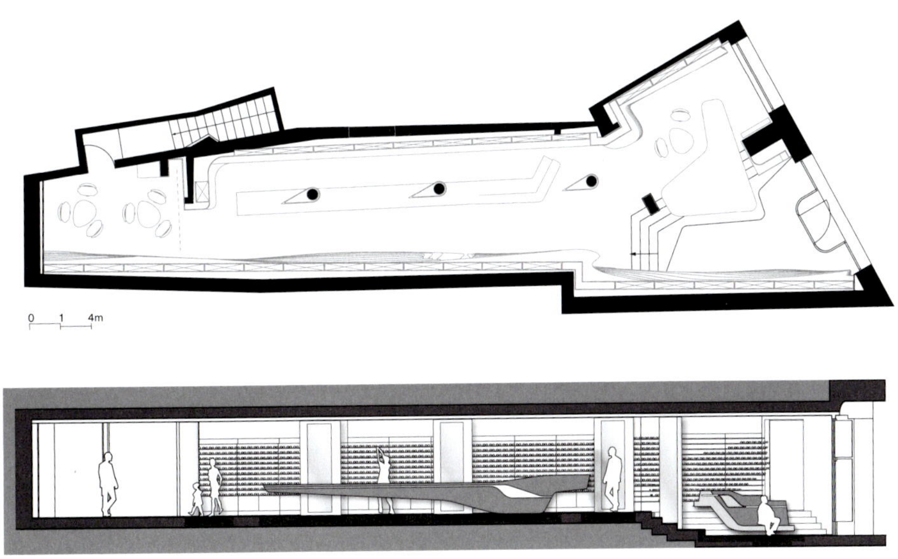

Floor plan and section

ERIC PARIS SALON

Project: Beauty and body care, retail
Location: Beijing, China
Client: Eric Paris Salon
Status: Completed
Year: 2008
Size: 580m^2 (GFA)

A sinuous, flowing staircase connects the two spaces at Eric Paris Salon.

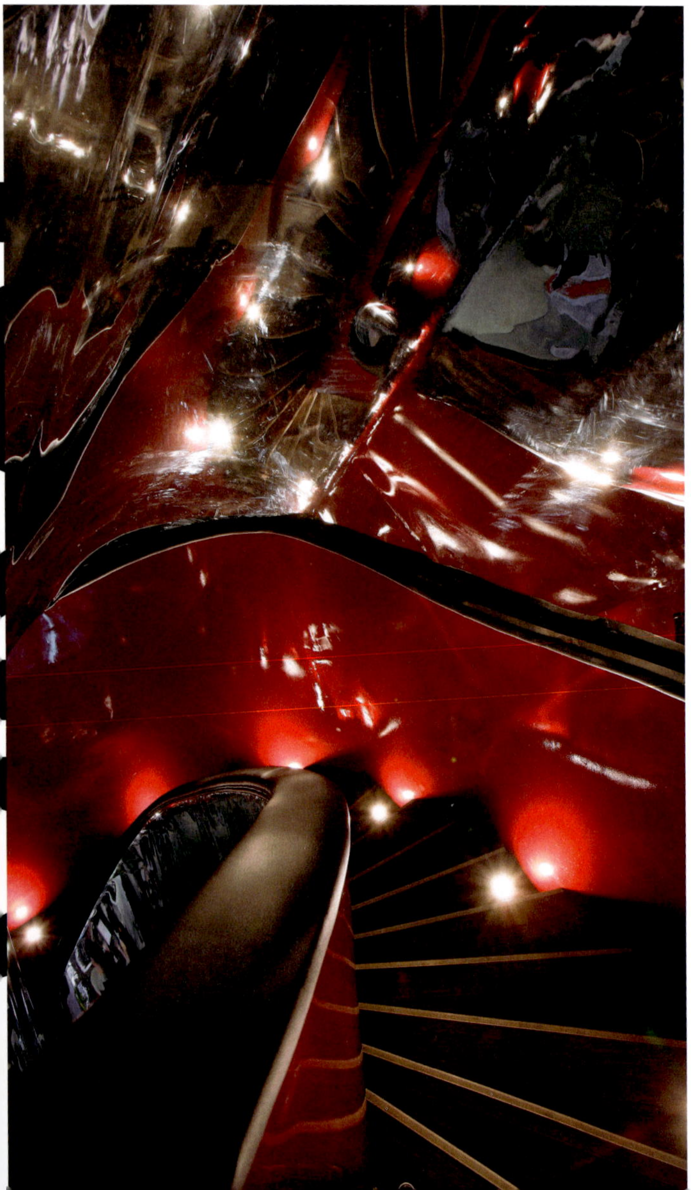

Reception area

The remodel of Eric Paris Salon in Beijing began with the need for a connecting element between the newly acquired second-floor space for new haircutting stations and the existing entrance, reception and retail areas on the ground floor.

Treatment stations

Open treatment area

Treatment stations

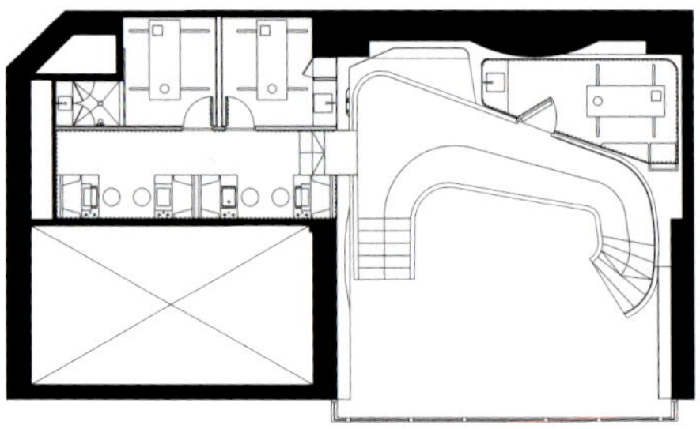

0 1 2m

Mezzanine floor plan

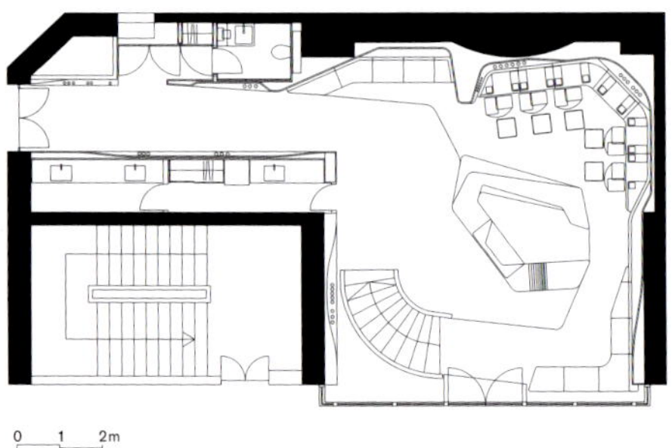

0 1 2m

First floor plan

GRAFT introduced a sinuous, flowing staircase that links the two spaces and creates a "vertical catwalk." It becomes a central feature from which the different functional areas branch off.

Manicure and pedicure stations are set to one side as galleries, where customers can wander by and watch others having treatments, while hidden rooms clad with padded, patterned leather feature custom-designed massage tables.

As the staircase ascends, it morphs into the wall paneling and loops over to enclose a corridor before peeling upwards to the second floor—its spiraling form accentuated by the polished metal cladding. Its inner wall echoes the sensuous boldness of red nail polish; the exterior mirrors customers in abstract patterns as they return from their beauty treatments.

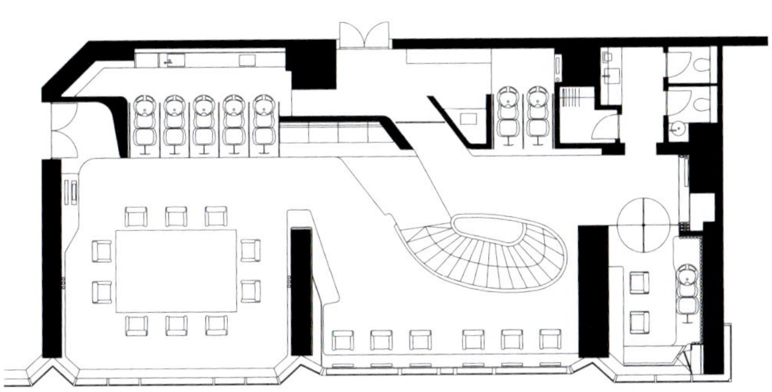

Second floor plan

Movable display units in
DC Shoes shop, New York City

DC SHOES SOHO NY

Project: Retail
Location: New York, NY, USA
Client: Quicksilver
Year: 2004
Status: Completed

DC Shoes, a shoe and clothing company based in Southern California, quickly achieved cult status among the international skating community. Founders Ken Block and Damon Way celebrated technical innovation as well as a particular sensibility associated with the skating counterculture; the success of their products has much to do with their being identified as synonymous with these values.

GRAFT was asked to aid in developing the brand's retail identity by designing their flagship store in the fashionable SoHo district of New York City. GRAFT's spatial concept offers customers a unique and innovative space that exemplifies the company's values. The architectural concept is based on the principles of flexibility, suspended motion and technical innovation.

All products are presented on movable display units suspended from the ceiling, meaning the space can be reorganized to allow different presentations and host events. The color palette is limited to black and white, DC's signature colors, emphasizing the products on display. Nothing in the space touches the floor; instead the products are suspended in mid-air as if in motion—an homage to the gravity-defying maneuvers performed by skaters. This idea breaks with the conventional retail rule of "putting the product on the floor."

Black and white interior design derived from the brand's signature colors.

Entrance to DC Shoes in SoHo, New York City

Movable display units

DC
109

SCI-FI CHANNEL STAND

Project: Exhibition design, commercial
Location: San Diego, CA, USA
Client: NBC Universal Television Network; Sci-Fi channel USA
Year: 2005
Status: Completed

GRAFT won the competition to create an imaginative and innovative exhibition stand for showcasing the NBC Universal Television Network's Sci-Fi channel brand. As an identifiable icon of the sci-fi world, the aim of the stand was to attract consumers and engage them with the channel's identity and programming.

The continuous sculptural form of the Sci-Fi channel stand

HAPPY TREE FRIENDS

The freestanding trade fair unit incorporates furniture and multimedia elements.

Visitors to the Sci-Fi channel stand

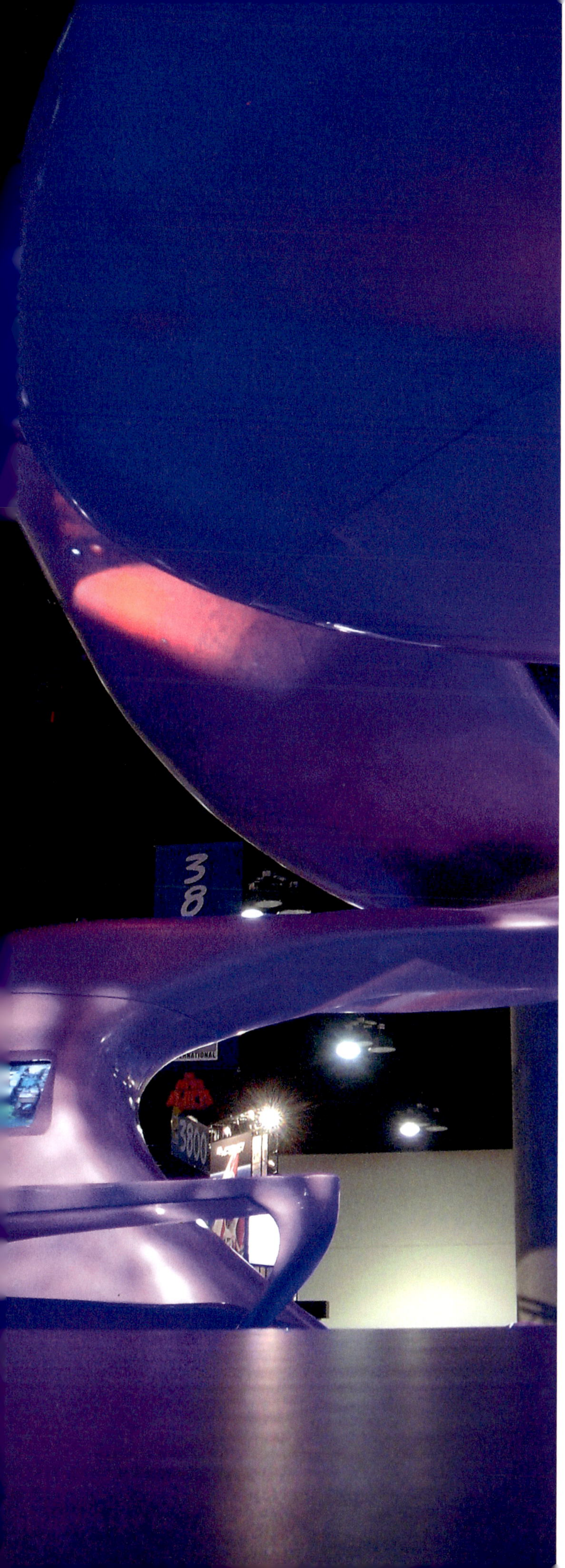

As a departure from traditional exhibition design, in which space is defined through the classic architectural expression of wall, floor and ceiling, the Sci-Fi channel exhibition stand grafted these tectonic features into a continuous sculptural form that allocated zones of occupancy while simultaneously satisfying specific functional requirements.

The stand thus became a freestanding, autonomous object in which furniture, audio, video and multimedia elements were incorporated, projected upon and disseminated from its performative, modulated fiberglass skin.

Multimedia elements

URBAN HEROES

Project: Brand identity, interior design, brand guidelines
Location: Hamburg, Germany
Client: Undisclosed
Year: 2016
Status: Completed

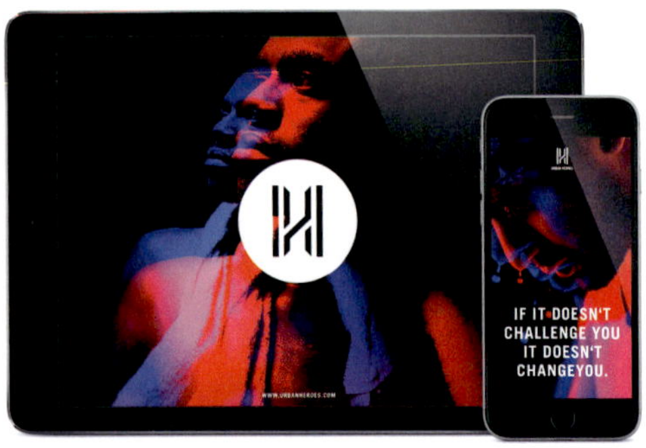

New brand identity for URBAN HEROES

In 2015, GRAFT Brandlab was approached by an ambitious London investor who wanted to establish a new fitness studio brand with a concept entirely new to Germany: A combination of nightclub and fitness studio offering training, where stressed managers can efficiently burn off energy. GRAFT Brandlab assisted with the market positioning and brand strategy as well as the development of a new brand identity and interior guidelines for the company's fitness boutiques in Germany. The result is a unique brand expression, specifically tailored to the product and aimed at a distinct client base. After opening the first studio in Hamburg in 2016, further locations in Frankfurt am Main, Munich and Berlin are currently in planning.

GRAFT Brandlab developed a unique brand position and designed the brand's identity hand in hand with a distinctive interior design signature, creating an instantly recognizable brand experience that appeals to the core target group.

The interior captures the essence of the brand: URBAN HEROES customers experience dynamic, high-intensity interval training in a stimulating environment that mixes modern industrial design with elements of underground club culture.

The overall mood is dark and rough yet elegant, with raw, industrial materials set in contrast against more refined, luxurious details.

Designed to stand out in a sea of mainstream fitness, URBAN HEROES' bold and memorable "H" logo serves as a strong icon that promotes identification with the URBAN HEROES community and spirit. Manuals for both brand and interior design offer a comprehensive set of guidelines for achieving consistent branding across all disciplines.

Interior design for URBAN HEROES

Distinctive interior design

Recognizable brand experience

Visitors to the VW SHIFT exhibition

VW SHIFT

Project: Exhibition design
Location: Berlin, Germany
Client: Volkswagen Group
Year: 2017
Status: Completed
Collaborators: Archimedes Exhibitions, Rat für Ruhm und Ehre

Following the Volkswagen emissions scandal, the Volkswagen Group presented an exhibition about sustainability at its DRIVE Forum in Berlin. After winning the call for proposals, GRAFT Brandlab was commissioned to realize the exhibition with its “SHIFT” concept, which asked questions and shed light on the topic of sustainability from both internal and external perspectives:

How do autonomous vehicles affect the appearance of our cities? How can the Volkswagen Group ensure fair and sustainable supply chains? What are different products really made of?

Another key topic is the recognition of and the call for personal responsibility regarding sustainability. A central mirror installation in the entrance area draws attention to the stance that it is ultimately personal purchasing decisions that have the greatest impact on our future. Interactive exhibits illustrate interrelationships and reveal new paths.

The VW SHIFT exhibition at the DRIVE Forum in Berlin

HYUNDAI

Project: Commercial, trade fair stand, car show booth
Location: Geneva, Switzerland
Client: Hyundai
Year: 2020
Status: Completed

Looking to refine its brand strategy to express its commitment to doing the right thing for people and society, Hyundai launched "Progress for humanity," a scheme that places emphasis on human-centered storytelling.

To represent this new company philosophy at trade fairs, GRAFT Brandlab was commissioned to implement their "Treasured Moments" concept, which is about making meaningful experiences possible by embracing the beauty and wonder of life.

Trade show designed with Hyundai's new Experience Guideline

Creating new formats for exterior application

Implementation of Hyundai's "Treasured Moments" concept

The design uses circular, organic forms to convey the impulsiveness of life and create a spatial expression that highlights treasured moments.

Based on a generative design approach, the concept ensures maximum adaptability and flexibility for application in various different contexts.

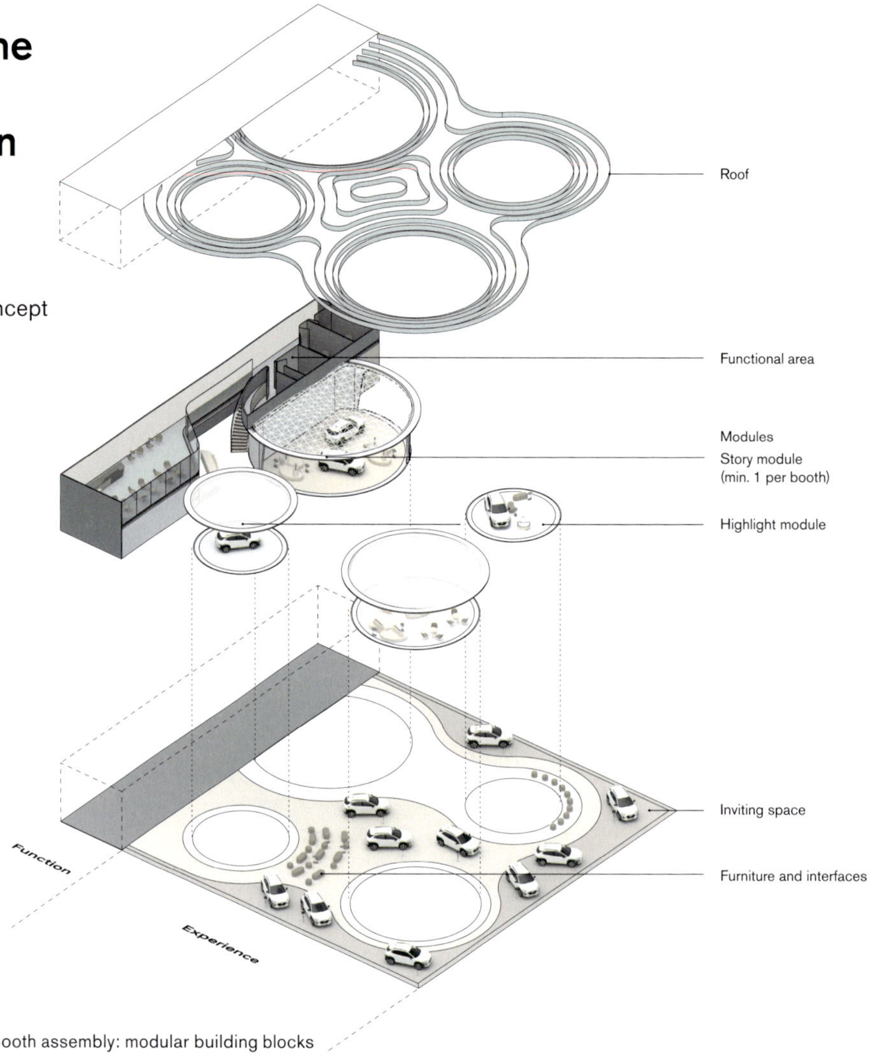

Booth assembly: modular building blocks

Experiential spaces created using the "Treasured Moment" principles

Realization of Hyundai's trade fair stand at the Geneva International Motor Show

URBAN CULTURE

REMAKING URBAN CULTURE

A CONVERSATION WITH PETER CACHOLA SCHMAL

With offices on three different continents spanning numerous time zones, for GRAFT, coexisting identities are not a reality to struggle with, but the ideal premise for fostering ideas that break new ground. Architecture—especially on the scale of urban planning—is a powerful tool for representing multiple, partly overlapping identities with the necessary complexity. GRAFT's designs are cultural expressions that derive from a multitude of identities. In such a context, diversity and pluralism are not only abstract concepts but valuable assets for creating a resilient, multifaceted identity. Can this idea of urban space thrive within the narrow conception of the European city? To what extent can architecture contribute to cultural or social identity? GRAFT explored these and other questions with Peter Cachola Schmal, director of the Deutsches Architekturmuseum in Frankfurt.

GRAFT Peter Cachola Schmal, GRAFT and the Deutsches Architekturmuseum (DAM) have both had the opportunity to realize their visions at the German Pavilion at the Biennale Architettura di Venezia, either as curator or general commissioner.

In 2018, with UNBUILDING WALLS, we responded to contemporary debates on nationalism, protectionism and isolationism. That year, the Wall had been gone for the same amount of time as it had stood: 28 years. Together with Marianne Birthler, we took this temporal parallel as a starting point for examining the effects of division and the process of healing on architecture and the urban environment. The former border zone, an unprecedented void in the midst of an often-dense urban space, is now home to an extremely heterogeneous mixture of architectural typologies, whose identity is the source of a very ambivalent debate. With your 2016 concept "Making Heimat. Germany, Arrival Country," DAM addressed the notion of *Heimat*[1] and its spatial significance. At the time, Deutschlandfunk [radio station] quoted you as saying: "*Heimat* doesn't need to be beautiful." The concept of *Heimat* is closely linked to the idea of identity. In your opinion, what factors create identity when it comes to architecture?

PETER CACHOLA SCHMAL In my opinion, the new-found popularity of the word identity, especially in relation to people, is quite strange. In a social context, it's a matter that primarily concerns the appreciation and recognition of minorities. In architecture, however, the question of identity follows a different pattern, one associated with mathematics and logic: Is this building identical with the building next to it? If the sum of its qualities is the same as the sum of the qualities of the other, then yes. Does this mean that architecture can have an identity? And according to what criteria?

1 Translator's note: In German, *Heimat* roughly means "home," "homeland" or "home country." But the term has connotations that link it to German culture, society and—through history—German nationalism. With this in mind, the English word "home" doesn't do justice to the original concept.

EVERY BUILDING, EVERY STRUCTURE, HAS A DISTINCT IDENTITY, IN A WAY THAT IS UNIQUE AND CAN'T BE EXACTLY REPRODUCED.

Biennale Architettura di Venezia 2018, German Pavilion, UNBUILDING WALLS, curated by GRAFT and Marianne Birthler; see p. 336

Biennale Architettura di Venezia 2016, German Pavilion, "Making Heimat," curated by Peter Cachola Schmal, Anna Scheuermann and Oliver Elser

Yes, every building, every structure, has a distinct identity, in a way that is unique and can't be exactly reproduced. Even serial products can't be replicated exactly, as was demonstrated by the architecture of the Soviet Union and the GDR—standardized building types also underwent changes according to their respective sites. In the 100 series there were at least 350 special cases, and even modular combinations didn't change this. Accordingly, architecture is the creation of a unique product. This, by the way, actually makes an architect's work more difficult, as they can rarely take advantage of serial production. In this sense, they aren't "repeat offenders" but creators of unique products—although visual self-similarities aren't excluded from even the most distinctive design signatures.

But it is much more difficult to prove whether the identity of a building goes beyond a mere product identity—i.e., is it socially or culturally recognizable? Trying to ascribe specific characteristics relating to epochs or political systems only works to a very limited extent: Associating certain characteristics with the term "Nazi architecture," for example, ignores the fact that there were similar design phenomena present in the UK and the USA in the 1930s. What's the difference between them and the buildings in Berlin? Setting out to determine whether a building has a democratic or fascist identity on the basis of its floor plan, a certain elevation or a photograph simply doesn't work.

Heimat2 (2015): When large numbers of refugees arrived in Germany in 2015, GRAFT founded Heimat2 to help overcome the structural housing shortage for refugees.

GRAFT Such precise ascriptions might sometimes prove to be difficult, but we understood the quote more as an invitation to view the concept of *Heimat*—which can also be interpreted as an architectural idea—in a more open sense. Identity has only become such a readily used term recently because the self-evidence and dominance of an individual or collective "self" seems to have been shaken. In Germany, the struggle for interpretational authority raised its head again after reunification. In the increasingly strident political debates, the negotiation of these concepts is primarily carried out using criteria of exclusion. How do you explain the growing need to assign a political identity to creative ideas?

SCHMAL *Heimat* is still a controversial topic—and sadly it has ended up in the domain of the right wing again. And with our exhibition in the German Pavilion we wanted to reclaim it by saying that, above all, *Heimat* is a positively loaded concept that encompasses much more than the dominant associations that equate it with the rural village. In Germany, we now have *Heimat* ministries that mainly deal with the development of rural areas and agricultural issues. But to me, this is a very one-sided definition. Right-wing political forces weave a similar narrative of this idealized German village—and for them it's a place where no foreigners live.

In "Making Heimat," we defined the concept in a fundamentally different way. At the time, architects and politicians were creating a new *Heimat* for the newly arrived refugees in so-called "arrival cities"—or more accurately, neighborhoods. But there were political groups that didn't want these new people to settle there. Their strategy was to begin using the essentially positive concept of *Heimat* against these "others," which they have been doing with relative success ever since. Interestingly, positive associations with one's own idea of *Heimat* are almost always completely detached from such narratives. Currently at the Deutsches Architekturmuseum, we are showing an exhibition about a trade union-led housing corporation called Neue Heimat. In it, we focus on peripheral residential developments of the 1960s and 1970s, which became *Heimat* for many people. A large number of people who grew up in these places said that life in a car-free zone, where there was a lot of greenery and traffic was separated from living, was not bad at all.

GRAFT When the new refugee debate began in 2015, we wondered how we could make a contribution as architects. After reading a number of studies on low-cost construction, container architecture and easy-build temporary solutions, we founded a company that offered to work as a project developer producing modular buildings at a very reasonable price. We called it Heimat 2, as we believe that people can have more than one *Heimat*.

The term *Heimat*, which you also view as a concept with positive associations, can also be imbued with heterogeneity and diversity—instead of surrendering it to others to use as a way to exclude. As architects and makers of exhibitions, this is an area in which we can really make a difference.

German Unity Flag (GRAFT in collaboration with Art+COM). In 2008, GRAFT developed a proposal for the Monument to Freedom and Unity: A pixel swarm in the three colors of the German flag that would float weightlessly above the country. Based on early drone technology, the flag would be an interactive flying object controlled by participatory online voting—the real-time travel path of the intelligent drone swarm would be influenced by democratic demand. Like a large ceiling over an urban plaza, broken up into smaller groups or individually returning to the ground to recharge, the individual drones and their temporary configurations would become a mental map of the complexity of our collective identity.

SCHMAL True. But if architecture is supposed to create identity, the question is: How can urban planning create identity? In the public debate in Germany, there is currently a consensus regarding the principles that underlie the European city.

To some extent, this is based on the fear of even alluding to the idea of a German nation as a reference of identity. Where is the German architect representing Germany in the international architectural discourse? German architecture no longer exists, there aren't any dominant father figures any more—Ludwig Mies van der Rohe und Walter Gropius were a long time ago. On the one hand, this gives rise to the European or global perspective, but on the other it results in a desire for local identities.

GRAFT We don't see this as a major problem: An identity based on the idea of having learned from a terrible catastrophe and instead using a European or global perspective as a reference point is something we welcome. We consciously broke from the European discourse in the mid-1990s and immersed ourselves in the debates taking place at universities in the USA. There, you could sense an optimistic rivalry of opinions between Columbia and SCI-Arc, one that openly celebrated difference and was far removed from the uniformity and style debates surrounding competitions taking place after German reunification. The architectural innovations and academic contributions that came from the USA in this period weren't as heavily based on a processing of history; instead they reveled in intellectual odysseys into deconstructivism and the beginnings of digitization. When we opened our second office in Berlin in 2001, as enthusiastic Europeans we wanted to bring some of this intellectual flexibility with us to Germany. We thought that this way of examining the past would hopefully lead to the acceptance of inquisitive positions, a responsible appreciation of history and a reciprocal, democratic respect.

IN THESE TIMES OF INCREASED IDENTITY POLITICS, WE HAVE WITNESSED AN INCREASE IN THE DESIRE FOR HOMOGENIZATION, AND THAT IDENTITY CREATION IS USED AS AN ARGUMENT FOR THE SEPARATION FROM OTHER POTENTIAL IDENTITIES.

SCHMAL That might be right. That's why we are quite staunch Europeans and prefer to talk about the European city. Using this as a point of identification, however, has consequences regarding content. On top of this, as architects we have to ask ourselves what we did wrong for architecture to have been universally considered as flawed, lacking in compassion and inhuman since the 1960s. Did the architectural community draw up plans with no regard for people? There's just no interest in new urban development projects nowadays. Wherever it is in Germany, city quarters don't just find their detractors in the press. The criticism often runs along the same lines: "Soulless, lifeless, boring, boxy." With larger projects there is always a danger that they'll be prevented by citizens' initiatives. The turn towards historical reconstruction isn't formed in a vacuum, it comes explicitly from a rejection of contemporary architecture. That's why, by setting themselves against contemporary architecture, reconstruction projects currently have more chance of being built.

Berlin, 2019: Two façades of the newly reconstructed Berlin Palace

Art Cloud (GRAFT), 2016: To fill the void left by the Berlin Palace and the Palast der Republik, GRAFT proposed an art haven for the young and vibrant art scene in Berlin.

GRAFT In such debates, we allow ourselves to be too easily drawn into a simple right–wrong, either–or argument. Of course, there was some terrible architecture in the 1960s and 1970s, the extremely functional and pragmatic spaces that didn't allow interactional gray zones and left nothing to chance. But there was also some fantastic architecture that dared to experiment, for example with their transitions from the natural to the built environment. The same applies for the so-called European city, too. The qualities that were being described were clear and coherent: The conception of a city as more like an interior, a theatrical space, a stage. Either way, architecture is also a process of experimentation and replacement of that which has proved unsuccessful. The play of the city is rewritten in every epoch.

If we were to declare one guiding principle to be a dogma, however, and therefore leave out many of the aspects that make up the quality of this ideal—i.e., coincidence and heterogeneity—then we end up, as has been proved, with one of these unpopular urban quarters you just described. A place that, at the push of a button, as it were, is supposed to elicit a feeling of aspiration, one that doesn't materialize when the building is experienced in its concrete form.

According to our experience as designers and planners of projects in many different cultures, we have to say farewell to dogmatic approaches.

THE NEW, INVISIBLE CITY THAT EVERYONE LIKES BECAUSE YOU CAN'T SEE IT: IS THAT WHAT THE ARCHITECTURE OF THE 21ST CENTURY WILL ULTIMATELY BE VIEWED AS? ARCHITECTURE THAT CAN'T PROVOKE OR CAUSE CONTROVERSY BECAUSE IT'S NO LONGER VISIBLE?

SCHMAL With "Making Heimat," we tried to break down and reformulate the political hypotheses of Doug Saunders and apply them to architecture and urban planning. Our approach was that an "arrival city" can work if it is small in scale and at ground level. Even within a larger structure like Manhattan, due to their relatively small dimensions and the possibility of operating retail outlets and businesses on the ground floor, the classic immigrant quarters like Little Italy and Chinatown were able to thrive. Immigrant neighborhoods today are quite different. They are often located in residential developments from the 1970s and, partly due to the urban landscapes we just addressed, have become spaces associated with fear. There is no critical mass of people at ground level, too few people strolling around to generate a sense of social control, meaning that at night it becomes an undesirable place to be if you're on your own—especially as a woman.

Some cities have recognized this problem and have transformed these 1970s developments accordingly. In the Netherlands, for example, a few cities have applied the logic of urban space present in the early 1900s to these areas, introducing studios, stores, more pedestrians and thus a much higher density and more social control. After being given completely new urban identities, these restructured quarters now work much better.

GRAFT These are interesting insights. In these times of increased identity politics, however, we have witnessed an increase in the desire for homogenization, and that identity creation is used as an argument for the separation from other potential identities. Using Berlin as an example, after the Wall came down, there were discussions about which model the rebuilding of the city should be based on. After the breach of civilization during the Nazi dictatorship, the destruction caused by World War II, a second dictatorship—which also carried out large-scale urban development—the main question was about forming a new urban identity. Eventually, the idea of a homogenization of the city based on the model of the Wilhelminian period aggressively asserted itself. Of course, even we like some of the high-quality spaces that this model gave rise to, but these construction kit blocks also repeated a lot of old ideas and proposed the not-quite-suitable as the solution for new problems. It was a missed opportunity that this identity came to be seen as the only formula and was applied wholesale across the entire city. In some places, the filling in of urban gaps was extremely successful, but wherever this principle was reapplied clone-like onto a generic grid, a lot of things went wrong. This kind of dogma isn't able to react to a specific genius loci, to a socially heterogeneous urban community, to the challenges of urban–rural topologies. In addition, the plot sizes were sometimes very problematic. The scenographies, the lines of sight and the spatial sequences are mostly lacking landmarks, and there's no programmatic or functional orientation. Proposing that a restored church should serve as the focus of a square and a classic creator of urban identity, for example, has hugely different connotations in a reunified Germany.

Through our international offices, our diverse projects around the world and being part of a collegial international debate, we know that, despite the presence of definitive master plans in many countries, there isn't a ban on alternative approaches or hybridization models. There are also a lot of successful urban spaces that don't pursue such an explicit goal at all. In Germany, too, society has developed into a complex network of identity layers with a great deal of territorial overlap. The reduction of our identity radii due to corona-induced quarantine measures has brought home the importance of a diverse, multilayered and pluralistic urban environment to many people. In the context of contemporary society, the desire for

THE NEXT BIG CHALLENGE FOR OUR CITIES WILL BE IN THE IMPLEMENTATION OF NEW CONCEPTS OF MOBILITY AND DIGITIZATION, WHICH WILL HAVE A HUGE IMPACT ON THE IDENTITY OF PUBLIC SPACE.

a single set of guidelines that makes everyone happy seems increasingly misplaced. A pluralistic, democratic approach acknowledges that there might be majority opinions—even for reconstruction projects like the Berlin City Palace or Frankfurt's old town—but at the same time provides scope for differentiated spatial collages that contain the expressions of different identities.

Architects and politicians alike are faced with a certain type of social challenge, such as the creation of affordable housing, (re)densification, land ownership, etc. In my opinion, the hotly debated public discussions and questions about large-scale reconstructions that are mostly supposedly aiming to remedy urban centers, make no contribution to this at all.

SCHMAL Besides this possible trend towards older, undamaged images, there is another development: The notion that Europe is turning into a kind of museum for the world—an idea that implies there is something unalterable in its urban landscapes. Needless to say, Venice works in its role as an attraction—even though hardly anyone lives there any more. It has become a kind of open-air museum with restaurants.

At the Deutsches Architekturmuseum, many architects are now telling us that a lot of the new architecture in London and Zurich is no longer visible as it's being built underground. Invisible architecture to make sure the city remains as it is. On the one hand, they are referring to the private construction projects of wealthy property owners, such as movie theaters and swimming pools underneath Victorian row houses, or even more so in new-build projects. On the other hand, they also mean public buildings, such as museums of which only the entrance is visible, hardly giving away the fact that there is

4,000m² of exhibition space beneath, like the extension of the Städel Museum in Frankfurt. These projects are highly praised by some people. The new, invisible city that everyone likes because you can't see it: Is that what the architecture of the 21st century will ultimately be viewed as? Architecture that can't provoke or cause controversy because it's no longer visible?

GRAFT That's interesting. We examined similar phenomena as part of our Biennale contribution UNBUILDING WALLS about Potsdamer Platz. Apart from being known for its architecture, this large square was also famous for being a historic traffic intersection. In 1924, the first traffic lights in Germany were erected here; they were seen as necessary because people would simply drive through the square without regard—trams, buses, everything was a big mess. When the new Potsdamer Platz was created, nearly all of the approach routes were moved underground: Parking lot, commuter rail lines, subway—they all arrive in the basement. The phenomenon of the invisible is an extremely interesting topic in urban planning.

SCHMAL The next big challenge for our cities will be in the implementation of new concepts of mobility and digitization, which will have a huge impact on the identity of public space. Even in Germany, inner-city zones will probably be car-free in around ten to 15 years, which means that city centers will be very quiet and clean areas. But will there still be urban density? What kind of people will live there? What will happen to our public spaces? Will there be any real reason to go there? Or will our lives, far removed from the city center, be so well organized through remote working and efficient last-mile delivery that public life will happen somewhere else altogether? In addition to this, technological developments happen much more quickly than changes in planning culture. I think some innovations will simply overwhelm us. This is especially true of mobility, for instance the emergence of autonomous vehicles and the huge changes this will bring about in urban planning. Further issues arise in connection with advances in the field of digitization: How will our cities change if we order everything online and high-street stores disappear? When considered from these perspectives, the identity of the city of tomorrow is extremely interesting—and it's already being negotiated today.

When major project developers swarm into our inner-city areas today, they often copy a tried-and-tested Asian model: A large, multiuse concept in the form of a cluster of high-rise buildings, with cultural amenities, restaurants, leisure attractions, offices, hotels and also condos, with direct connections to public transport, few parking places, etc. But for most of them it remains unclear how these new quarters will be brought to life or how urban density will be created.

GRAFT We believe that there will be a great deal of highly disruptive effects that will appear on the way to reaching this state of the empty, green inner city. Besides the current pandemic and all its associated economic disruptions, in the future we will experience upheavals of a technological nature as well as those caused by new financial systems,

THE TOLERANCE AND PLURALISM OF DEMOCRACY ALSO NEEDS TO BE REFLECTED IN ACADEMIC DEBATES ON ARCHITECTURE AND MANIFESTED IN OUR BUILT ENVIRONMENT. HYBRIDIZATION PROCESSES IN CITIES HAVE ALSO PROVED TO BE VIABLE AND ROBUST. IN THIS RESPECT, WE ARE EXTREMELY OPTIMISTIC REGARDING THE FUTURE OF MULTIPLE, MIXED IDENTITIES.

Frankfurt, 2017: The newly reconstructed old town in front of the skyline of Frankfurt am Main

demographic developments and newly imposed rules for international migration on the back of Covid-19. These things will influence the identity of our cities in as yet unknown ways. But going back to the subject of reconstruction: Besides the fact that these idealized images are massively instrumentalized by right-wing political forces, critics often accuse the initiators of such projects of having a skewed or unrealistic sense of history.

SCHMAL Yes, that's definitely true. There was a big discussion surrounding the New Frankfurt Old Town: Did it invert the historical narrative and even "undo" the war by making it no longer perceivable in an urban sense? I don't see it this way, as the people who were responsible for the reconstruction did it in such a manner as to make the breaks visible. For example, a timbered house with an entrance leading to the subway—albeit against a backdrop of skyscrapers.

That's why I don't think the New Frankfurt Old Town tries to cover up history. It was also carried out with a huge amount of dedication, a great deal of money and an enormous attention to detail. Although it's only 0.7 hectares, it has, partly due to its extreme inner-city location, a significant impact on the city's identity. Which is really quite astonishing, as the Europaviertel, measuring 145 hectares, was constructed at the same time. But no one's really interested in that—but then again no one used to go for a walk on the grounds of the former goods depot where it was built.

GRAFT For us, it's not really a question of whether such reconstruction projects are fundamentally wrong. Like you, we think that they should be executed in an accomplished manner or have substantial value in terms of identity creation. The desire to promote them as a panacea for the most complex of problems, however, is presumptuous and intellectually hollow. We wish to see an open debate that maps out the differences of urban tectonics in a nuanced way and celebrates the coexistence of diverse identities in the urban realm. The tolerance and pluralism of democracy also needs to be reflected in academic debates on architecture and manifested in our built environment. Hybridization processes in cities have also proved to be viable and robust. In this respect, we are extremely optimistic regarding the future of multiple, mixed identities. Frankfurt, in particular, is a great example, with its panorama dominated by skyscrapers, something rather untypical for a German city. We find it quite fascinating that this city manages to do so much at once yet retain a certain serenity.

SCHMAL True, skyscrapers and timber frames almost sounds as optimistic as laptops and Lederhosen—the combining of opposites. Frankfurt's brand-new old town is a small, museum-like, slightly nostalgic area that has an almost cinematic logic—maybe it can also act as a break in the narrative of the city.

Frankfurt, 2019: The reconstructed historic city center of Frankfurt am Main

Peter Cachola Schmal has been the managing director of the Deutsches Architekturmuseum (DAM) in Frankfurt am Main since 2006, after working there for five years as a curator. The DAM sees itself as one of the leading platforms for architectural discourse in Germany and as an international partner within the context of the International Confederation of Architecture Museums, ICAM. The DAM presents up to 15 exhibitions annually, as well as organizing over 100 architecture events and more than 150 educational events. Peter Cachola Schmal has represented Germany twice at architecture biennales: The 15th Biennale Architettura di Venezia in 2016 and the VII International Architecture Biennale in São Paulo in 2007. He grew up as an expat in Pakistan and Indonesia, and studied architecture at the TU Darmstadt, where he also taught as assistant professor.

ICE STADIUM SCHIERKER FEUERSTEIN ARENA

Project: Reactivation of a historical ice stadium, new roof structure
Location: Wernigerode, Germany
Client: City of Wernigerode, Germany
Year: 2017
Status: Completed
Size: 2,400m^2

The unique roof construction of the multifunctional arena in the Harz Mountains

In Schierke, a district of Wernigerode in the Harz Mountains, GRAFT was commissioned to renovate a listed natural ice rink.

With its proposal for a unique roof construction, GRAFT won a 2013, Europe-wide architectural competition to renovate the city's ice rink. The competition brief outlined the need to transform the facility into a multifunctional arena capable of hosting sports and cultural events on a year-round basis. The structure's existing stone terraces and listed timber umpire's tower had to be retained and incorporated into the new design. Sanitary facilities, technical services, offices, changing rooms and restaurant facilities were to be housed in two ancillary buildings as part of the arena complex.

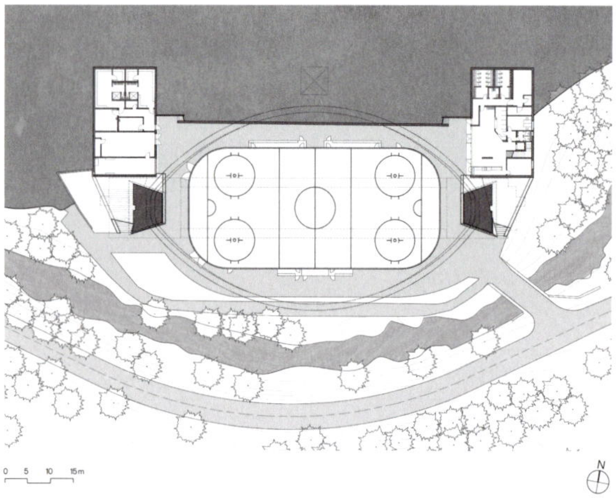

Ground floor plan

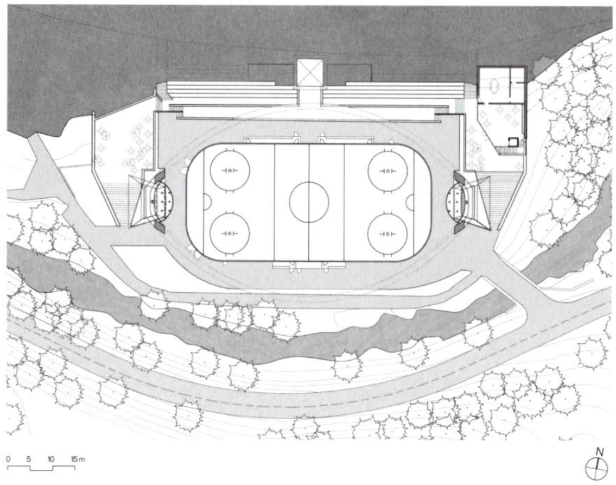

First floor plan

The ice rink in winter

GRAFT proposed a dramatic roof structure anchored at just two points, which provides protection from rain, snow and sunlight, but also frames the view of the mountains and sky beyond—its characteristic poise and elegance is indeed a response to the surrounding landscape.

Developed in collaboration with schlaich bergermann partner, the steel ring structure is spanned by a steel rope net covered with PTFE membrane totaling 2,400m^2.

Steel ring structure covered by a steel rope net with a PTFE membrane

The ice rink at night

With its transformation into a new, multifunctional arena, this former historic site has been turned into a year-round tourist attraction. In winter, it serves as a sheltered artificial ice rink, while in summer it is used as a venue for concerts and theatre productions or sports and health events.

Two new buildings to the east and west of the stadium host restaurant and café facilities along with other functions. By simultaneously acting as the footing blocks of the roof, these buildings also form part of the structure's overall composition. Embedded within the topography of the site, they are perceived as an integral part of the surroundings.

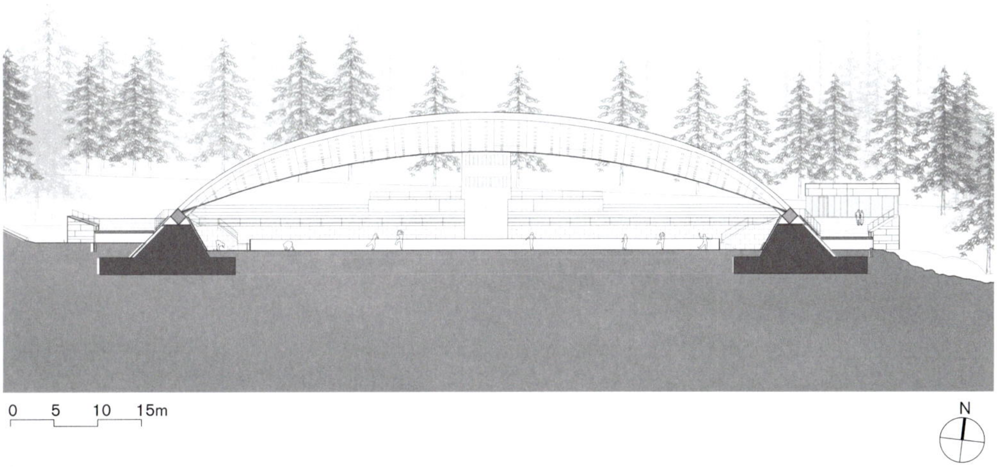

Section

Steel rope net with PTFE membrane

Dramatic roof structure
anchored at just two points

STRATIE

BECHSTEINHAUS

Project: Showroom, commercial, retail, refurbishment
Location: Berlin, Germany
Client: Undisclosed
Year: 2019 – ongoing

Passageway extending beyond the entrance portal

GRAFT's proposal for the BechsteinHaus in Berlin envisages a closure of the existing block development, establishing a new, representative headquarters with a dynamic entrance configuration and a newly created passageway.

The appeal of the company's new building will be emphasized by its accessibility via the newly redeveloped Franz-Liszt-Platz, whose formal gestures and attractive character help unlock urban potential and create a unique architectural identity. A passageway extending beyond the entrance portal invites visitors to explore the history of C. Bechstein against a backdrop that interweaves the old and the new building fabric.

BECHSTEIN
C.BECHSTEIN

Showroom of BechsteinHaus

Interior of BechsteinHaus

Conceived as the company's head office, the building will feature a showroom, a large music hall for 500 people, a smaller music hall for 50 people and administrative and museum areas.

Lofts for artists and musicians will be accommodated on the building's upper floor facing the green space at the rear, while the roof will be brought to life through the inclusion of areas for sitting and relaxing.
An integrated passage will enable a direct connection from the street to the art campus at Hamburger Bahnhof, as well as between the canal-side promenade and the greenway behind the existing building. The division of these two urban features—water and green space—will be broken down by the BechsteinHaus, contributing to the revitalization of this new inner-city quarter.

Made of red brick, the building's façade consciously takes up the materiality of the old building substance, while the transitions between open and closed vertical structures lend it a contemporary note. This contrast is most apparent in the entrance area, where the open façade design gives way to closed sections—behind which one of the music halls is located.

The BechsteinHaus seeks to realize the full potential of this current urban space in the Europacity development.

URBAN NATION MUSEUM

Project: Museum, exhibition space, refurbishment
Location: Berlin, Germany
Client: Stiftung Berliner Leben
Year: 2017
Status: Completed
Size: $500 m^2$ exhibition space

Elevation Zietenstrasse

Elevation Bülowstrasse

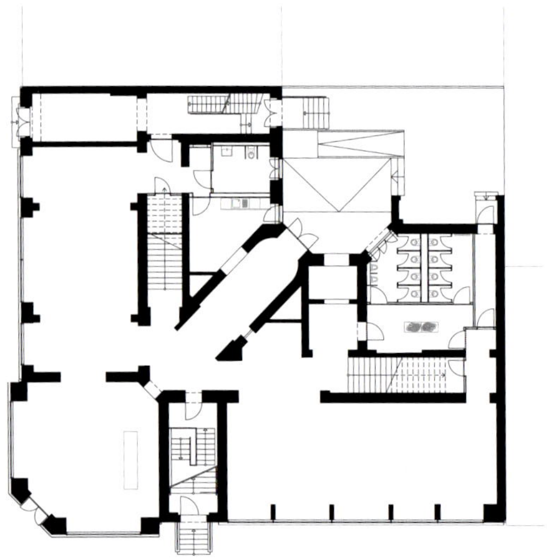

Ground floor plan

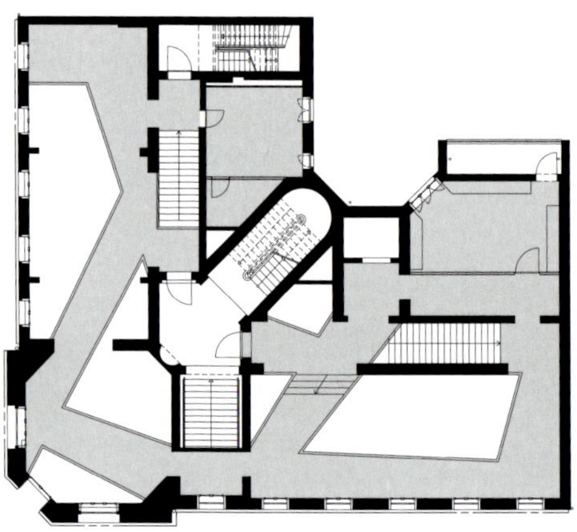

First floor plan

The Urban Nation Museum for Urban Contemporary Art—or Urban Nation Museum for short—is the first museum for urban art in Germany and is housed in a former residential building in the Schöneberg district of Berlin.

The modular façade sections serve as canvases.

The building itself becomes a work of art.

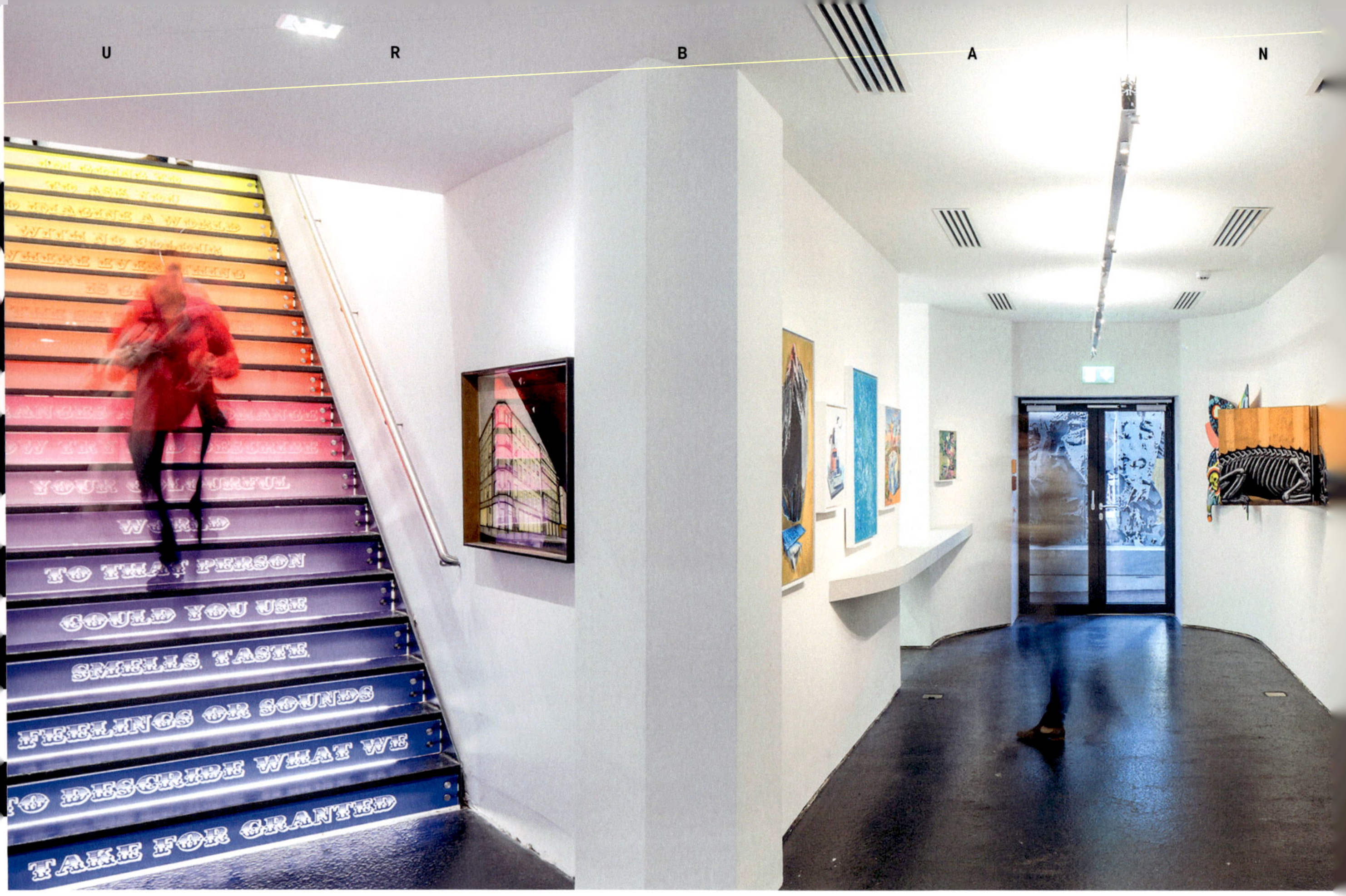

GRAFT's concept for the conversion of the building at the intersection of Bülowstrasse and Zietenstrasse envisaged turning the building itself into a work of art. This was achieved by constructing the façade from modular sections that serve as canvases for artists from around the world. These modular façade elements are frequently redesigned, replaced and subsequently added to the museum's collection as works of art.

Entering the building reveals a radical and unexpected space: Rooms branch off along different axes, over two or even three floors, creating a sense of height and depth. The anamorphic techniques of urban art permeate the realm of architecture, allowing them to enter new symbioses with each other.

A high line connects the exhibition spaces.

Ground floor interior

The internal walkway allows for the artworks to be explored from different perspectives.

The exhibition "UN-DERSTAND THE POWER OF ART AS A SOCIAL ARCHITECT" in fall 2018

The permanent exhibition "UN-DERSTAND THE POWER OF ART AS A SOCIAL ARCHITECT"

Entrance

The idea of the street finds continuation in the museum's interior: The exhibition spaces are connected by an internal walkway—a high line of sorts—making it possible to experience the different works of art up close and from afar.

The Urban Nation Museum also contains a library and twelve apartments for artists taking part in the Urban Nation artist residency program.

Urban Nation is an initiative of the Stiftung Berliner Leben, a foundation founded by the Gewobag housing association in 2013. Under its first director Yasha Young, the museum has gained a reputation as a platform for urban art that attract artists and visitors from around the world.

Opening night in summer 2017

GERMAN PAVILION EXPO DUBAI 2020

Project: Design of the German Pavilion for the Expo 2020 in Dubai
Location: Dubai, United Arab Emirates
Client: Kölnmesse GmbH
Year: 2018
Status: Competition finalist
Size: 7,400m²

The rational orthogonal space enclosed in a gridded scaffold structure

In 2018, GRAFT took part in the public tender for the design of the German Pavilion at the Expo 2020 in Dubai and made it onto the shortlist of finalists. The design focuses on sustainability, one of the three subthemes of the Expo 2020: Opportunity, Sustainability and Mobility.

The architecture of the German Pavilion expresses key characteristics of the nation—efficiency, technology, science and natural beauty—and relates them to the context of sustainability.

Inspired by the duality of Germany's innovative industries and scientific institutions, the decentralized system of cooperation across the country and the unique, rich landscape in which they lie, the design takes these aspects and represents them through two thematic spatial elements.

A rational, orthogonal space enclosed in a gridded scaffold structure houses the knowledge repositories, a series of nodal exhibitions interlinked in a decentralized network that visitors can move through freely. On six platforms, current and future major trends are presented as part of an interconnected, interactive and participatory exhibition concept. The exhibition is visible from all points of the pavilion and visitors can wander between the thematic areas, creating a flow of people and information transfer made visible by the architecture and its transparent structure.

Interactive art piece: Visual experiences of the visitors can be robotically engraved into a tree, which becomes a symbol of the exhibition's collective memory.

Section

At the heart of the pavilion is the emotional counterpoint to the rational knowledge repositories. This spacious, three-dimensional topography offers visitors the emotive sensations of expansive space, enclosure, and various vistas. The interior landscape is informed by an intuitive, emotional and even romantic response to the German landscape and is subjective, selective and atmospheric in nature. Linked to the rational, factual knowledge repository by an "interface" element, it is a variable space that sets up a stimulating tension with the rest of the pavilion.

Axonometrics

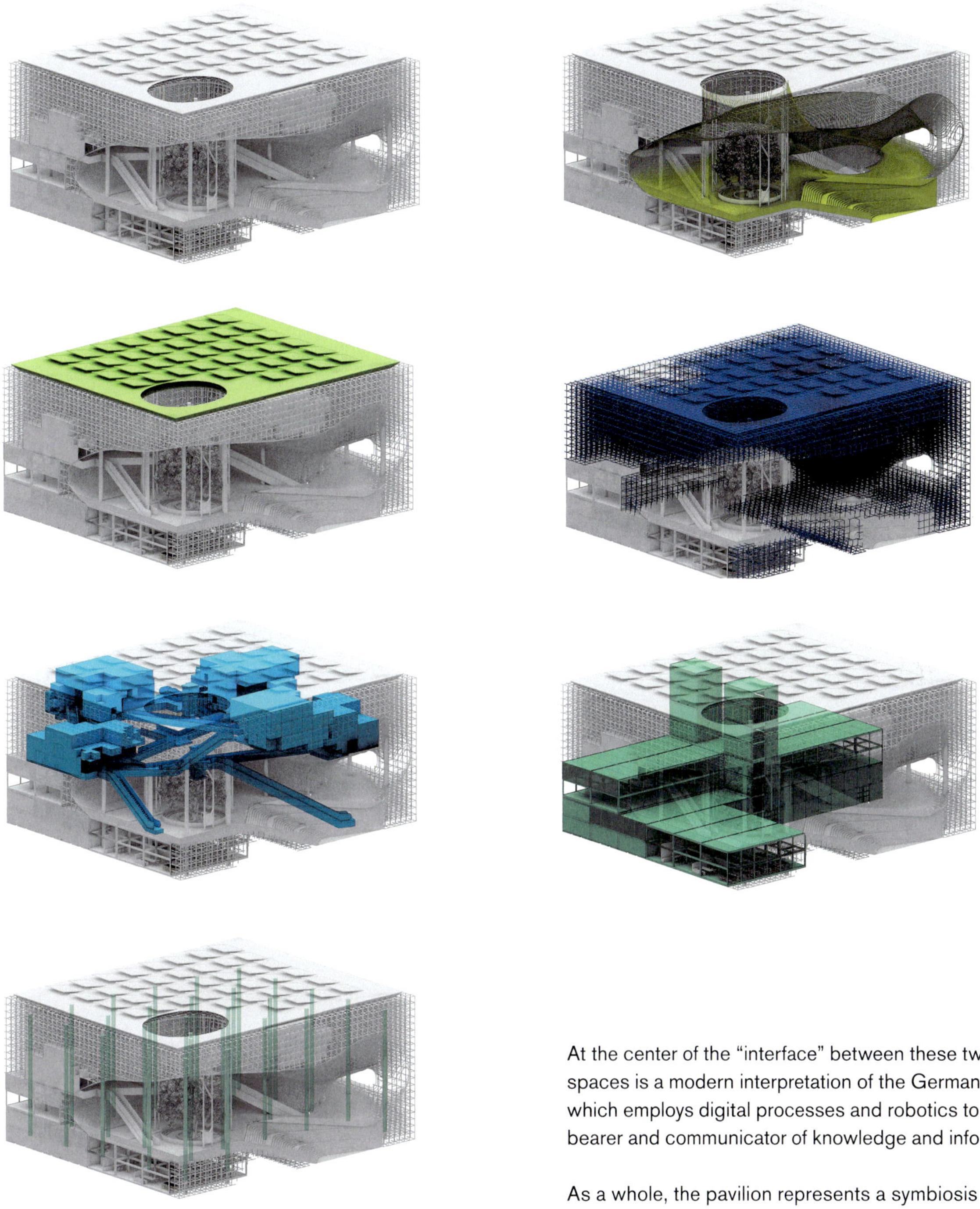

At the center of the “interface” between these two spaces is a modern interpretation of the German oak, which employs digital processes and robotics to act as a bearer and communicator of knowledge and information.

As a whole, the pavilion represents a symbiosis of core German qualities and presents them in a coherent overall concept.

As each individual element is made of a single material, the raw materials of the pavilion can be separated for later recycling. The entire pavilion can be dismantled after the Expo 2020 and reerected at another location in Germany or abroad. With a few modifications, the structure can also be rebuilt in an entirely different configuration, meaning it can respond to changing exhibition needs. The construction and assembly methods have been designed to ensure that all components and materials can be taken apart, separated and transferred into a second life cycle.

3
0
2

AQUI WINERY

Project: Winery, hospitality, retail
Location: Uco Valley, Mendoza, Argentina
Client: Ralf Wenzel, AQUI
Year: 2019 – ongoing

The AQUI winery in the foothills of the Andes Mountains

The Uco Valley in the province of Mendoza is located in the foothills of the majestic Andes Mountains. Wine produced in this region is considered among the best in Argentina.

In this context, GRAFT was commissioned to design a unique location dedicated to wine production, based on the AQUI brand's philosophy of bringing people together through wine. To underline this, the winery also offers guest accommodation developed around the idea of creating rituals for a community brought together by their passion for wine.

Taking inspiration from nature, the winery is shaped by the local surroundings—the rock formations of the High Andes, the sun's movement through the year and the views of the landscape. Using these features characteristic to Mendoza, GRAFT created four giant stones that embody specific rock geometries found in the high mountains.

They are arranged to frame a central plaza, in which the life of the winery is concentrated: Arrival and reception, harvest, tasting, wine festivals and celebrations. Shaped by the celestial movement of the sun, the stone volumes act like a calendar by reflecting the cycles of a year—just like a bottle of wine.

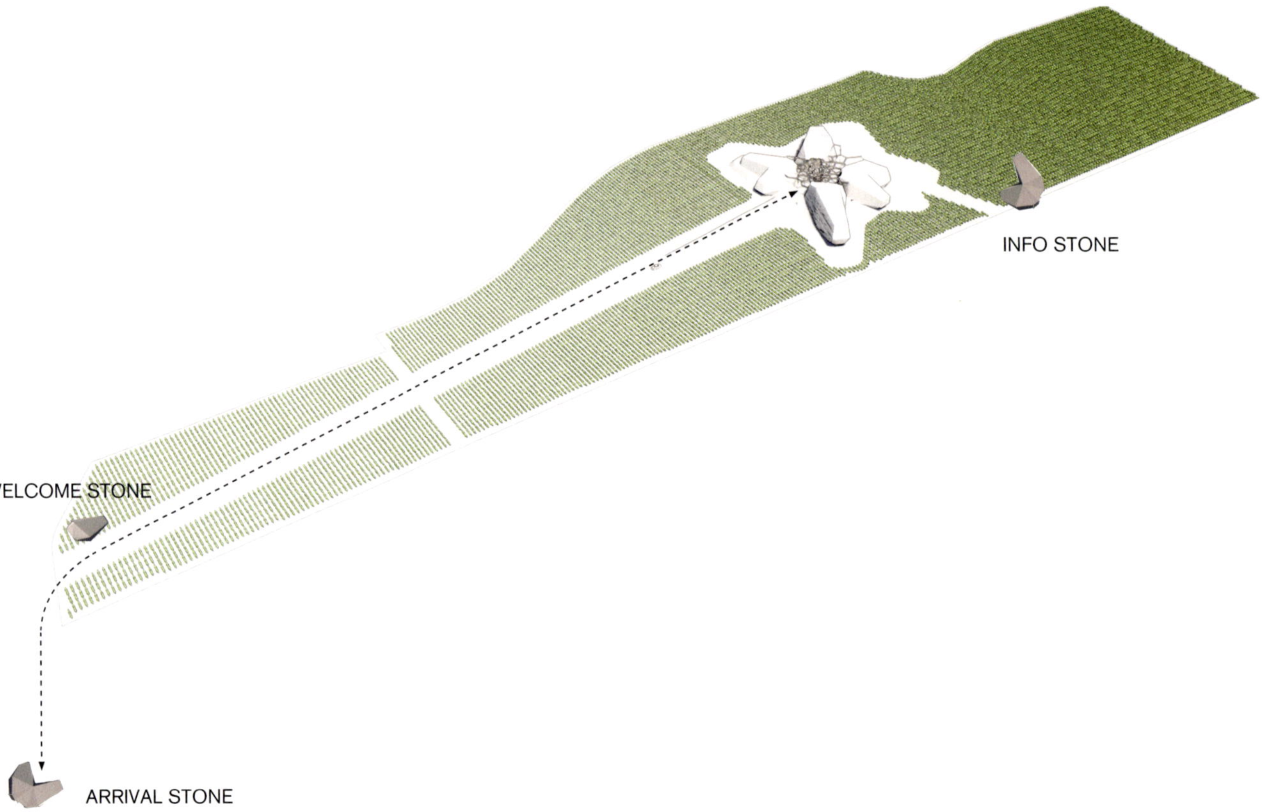

Site plan

The central plaza: A place for arrival, harvest, tasting and events

The design was inspired by the local surroundings.

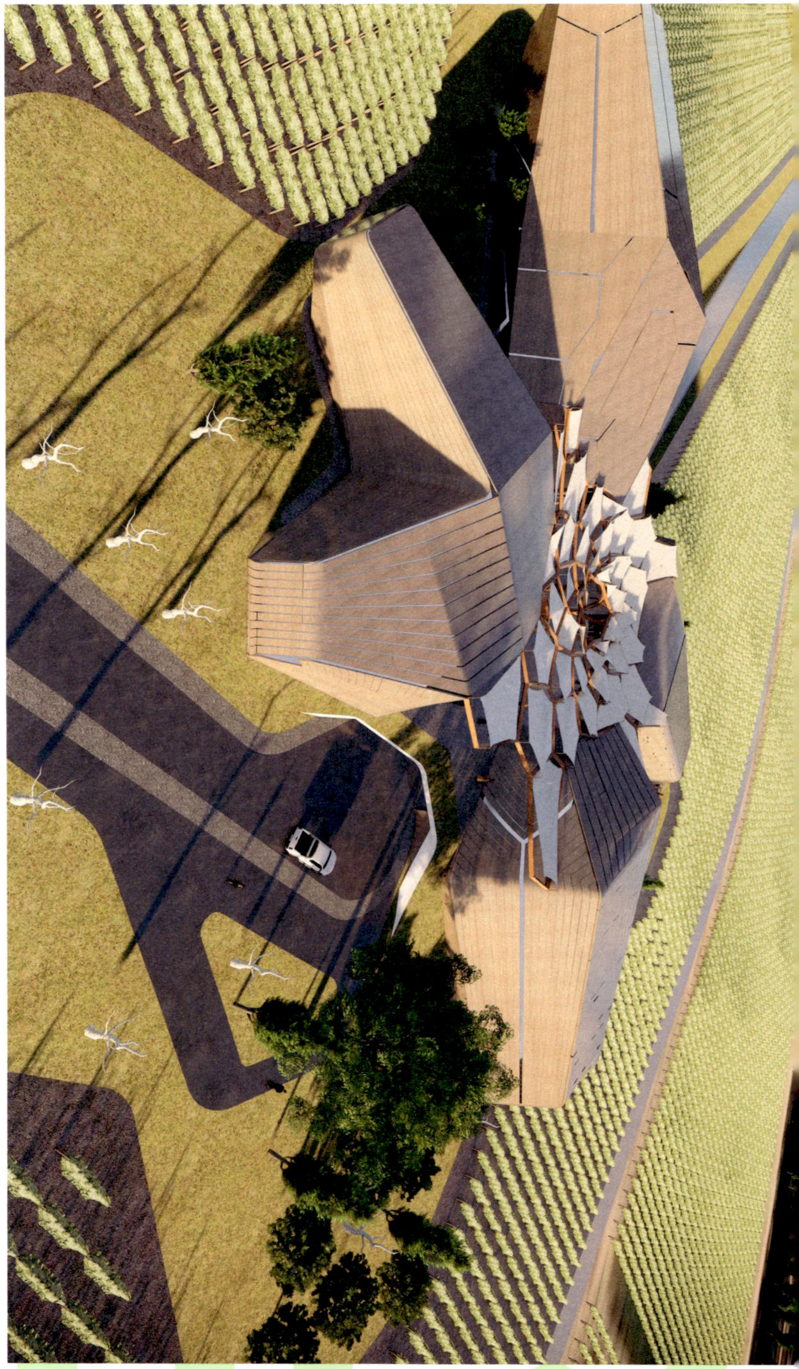

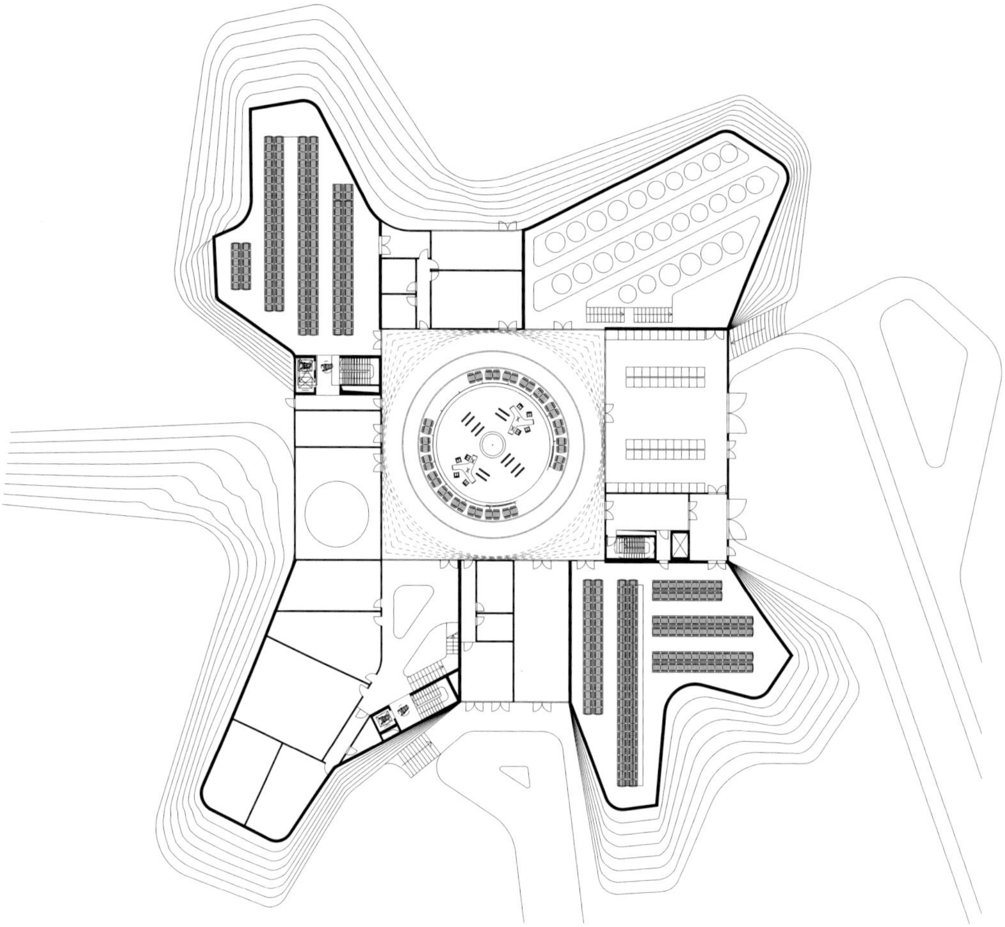

Basement floor plan

Organized over two levels in order to take advantage of gravity instead of using pumps, the winery has been developed using the idea of experimental circularity over that of rigid linear production.

This allows for interesting shortcuts and unusual juxtapositions in terms of both production and experience, enhancing creativity and innovation in approaching what is by far the most complex product humankind has ever invented: Wine.

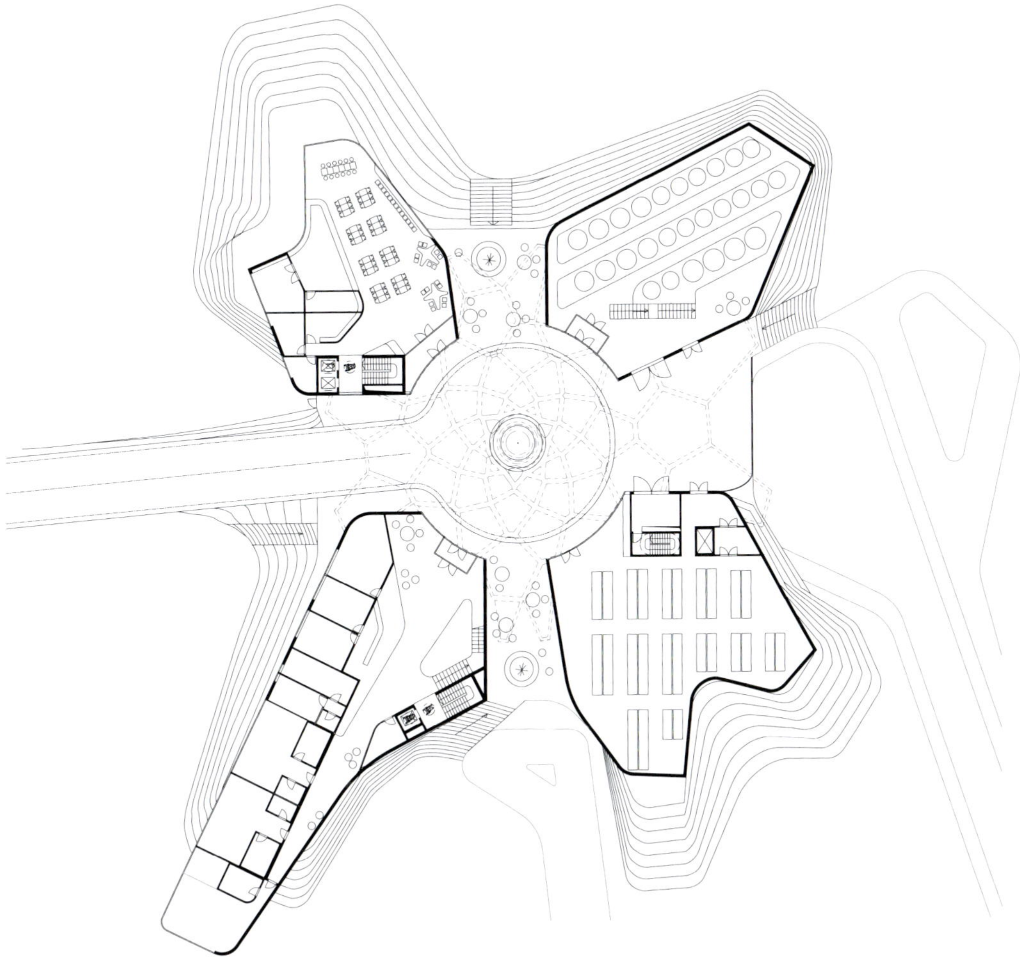

Ground floor plan

0 2 4 10m N

Section

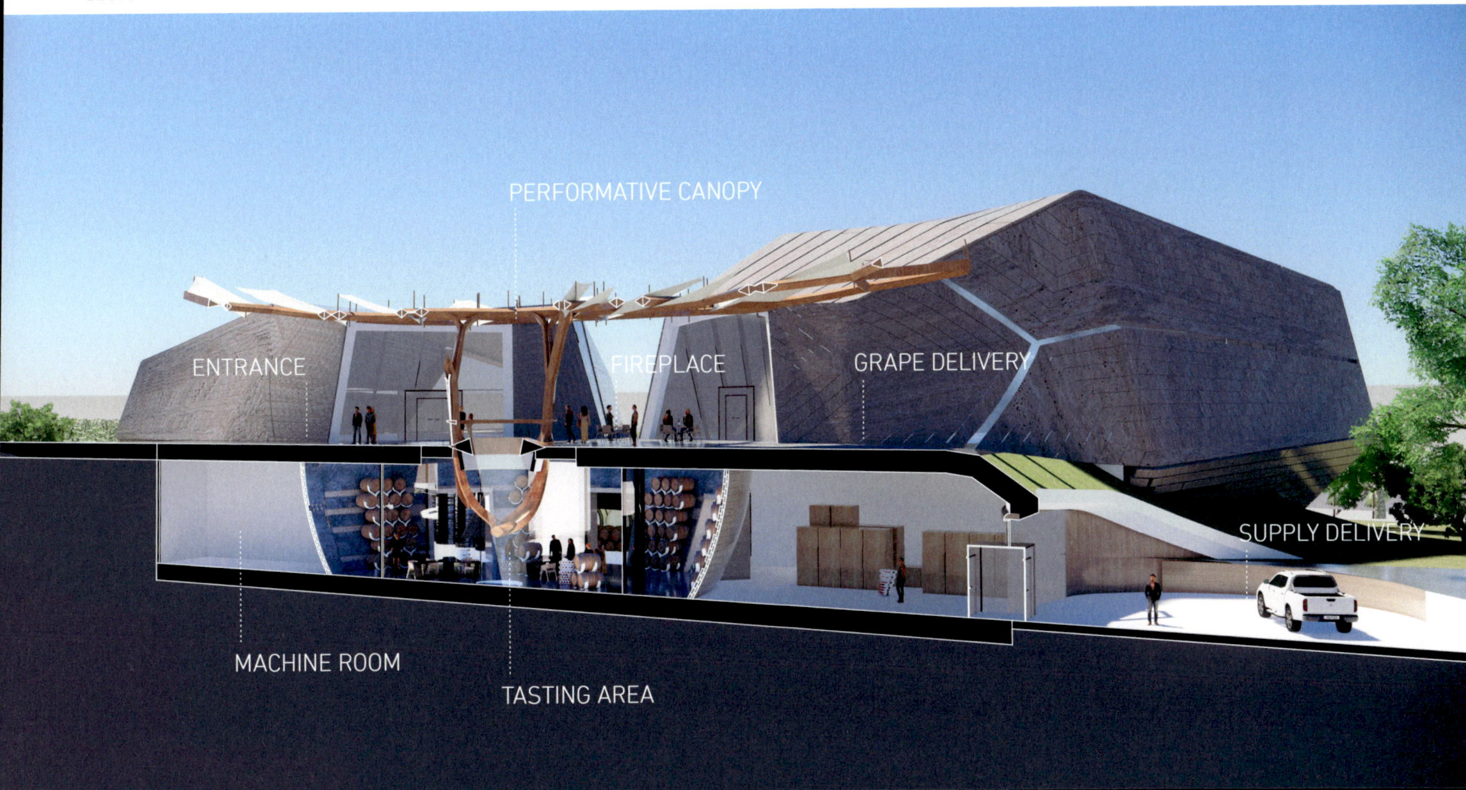

The former telephone exchange that was converted into the Kabbalah Centre Berlin

KABBALAH CENTRE BERLIN

Project: Cultural event and training space, refurbishment
Location: Berlin, Germany
Client: The Kabbalah Centre
Year: 2015
Status: Completed

BRICKS Berlin Schöneberg is an ensemble of buildings and courtyards located on the grounds of the former Postfuhramt (post office) near the Akazienkiez neighborhood of Berlin-Schöneberg. GRAFT has been commissioned to develop the complex into a unique residential and commercial quarter featuring a mixture of historical buildings and contemporary reconstruction.

The complex consists of three different courtyards and a public passage that blends perfectly into the vibrant heart of Schöneberg. Between the first and second courtyard, on the site of the listed Postfuhramt—built by Otto Spalding and Luis Ratzeburg in the early 20th century—is a richly decorated brick cross-building. Added at a later date, it features a spectacular, 7.5-meter-high hall on the third floor that was originally used as a telephone exchange. This became the new home of the Kabbalah Centre Berlin.

Visitors and guests enter the Kabbalah Centre through a spacious foyer, which offers views of the historic coffered ceiling. By freeing the high, rhythmically arched hall of all provisionally added features, an impressive sense of space is restored.

This is emphasized by the uncovering of the coffered ceiling, which allows the vast hall to be experienced to its full extent. Despite providing the necessary small rooms and intimate spaces, the aim of the design is to give an impression of the entire space and enable it to be experienced from different angles. To achieve this, a second level, which seems to float freely inside the hall, is partially integrated and accessible via spacious staircases at both ends. This mezzanine level offers visitors an unexpected close-up view of the coffered ceilings and provides numerous different perspectives of the main lower level. The design preserves the total ceiling height in the lecture hall and the entrance area of the Centre.

The historic coffered ceiling

The mezzanine level offers close-up views of the coffered ceiling.

Passing through the entrance area, with its generously proportioned staircase winding upwards, the visitor is led past the teaching rooms and office spaces directly into the large lecture hall—the apparent goal of the "path." An oversized mirror on the rear wall visually extends the space, reflecting the rhythm of the rounded arches. In the lecture hall, a second staircase leads to the upper level, which houses a gallery and kitchen able to accommodate large parties and dinner events for up to 100 guests. The large, historical windows afford unobstructed views of the two adjacent courtyards and Otto Spalding's architecture.

The architectural concept translates one of the central ideas of the teachings of Kabbalah: Gradual perception as spatial development along a path. Accordingly, the different uses and spatial qualities of the different areas—with both personal and public functions—create a scenography of perpetual movement and interaction.

The reception and presentation areas are given the largest room heights, while festive events and moments of collective celebration float lightly above with unobstructed views into the distance.

As all the rooms are interconnected, the training rooms and lecture hall are flexible in size and can be combined as needed by room-high curtains. The same concept is applied in the upper level, where curtains can be used to temporarily divide group areas into smaller spaces.

3 1 2

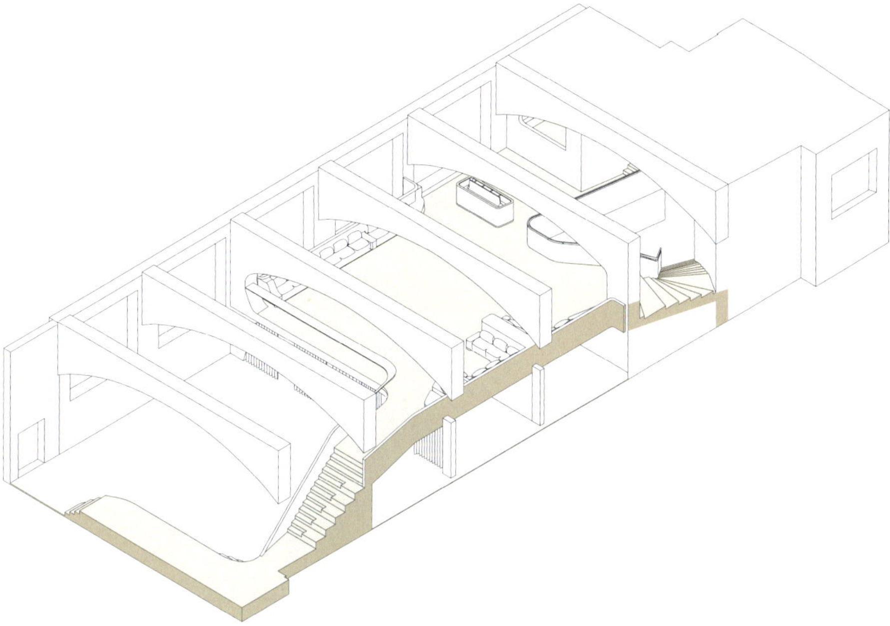

Axonometric diagram

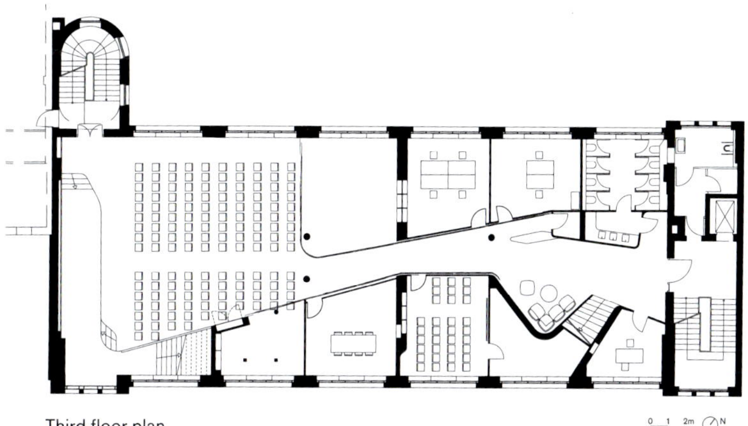

Third floor plan

Section

The consistent light color throughout the space is based on the white tones found in the color palette of the historic building materials. Only the renovated coffer ornamentation, with its orange and brown tones, stands in contrast to this, clearly indicating its origins at the turn of the 20th century. In this way, another gem of architectural history becomes mentally and physically attainable, made tangible through its new function and a new spatial interpretation.

1

3
1
5

RUSSIAN JEWISH MUSEUM

Project: Museum, adaptive reuse
Location: Moscow, Russia
Client: Federation of the Jewish Communities of Russia
Year: 2007
Status: Competition, 1st prize

The Russian Jewish Museum will inject a new lease of life into one of the most spectacular landmark buildings in Moscow, the Bakhmetevsky Bus Garage by Konstantin Melnikov.

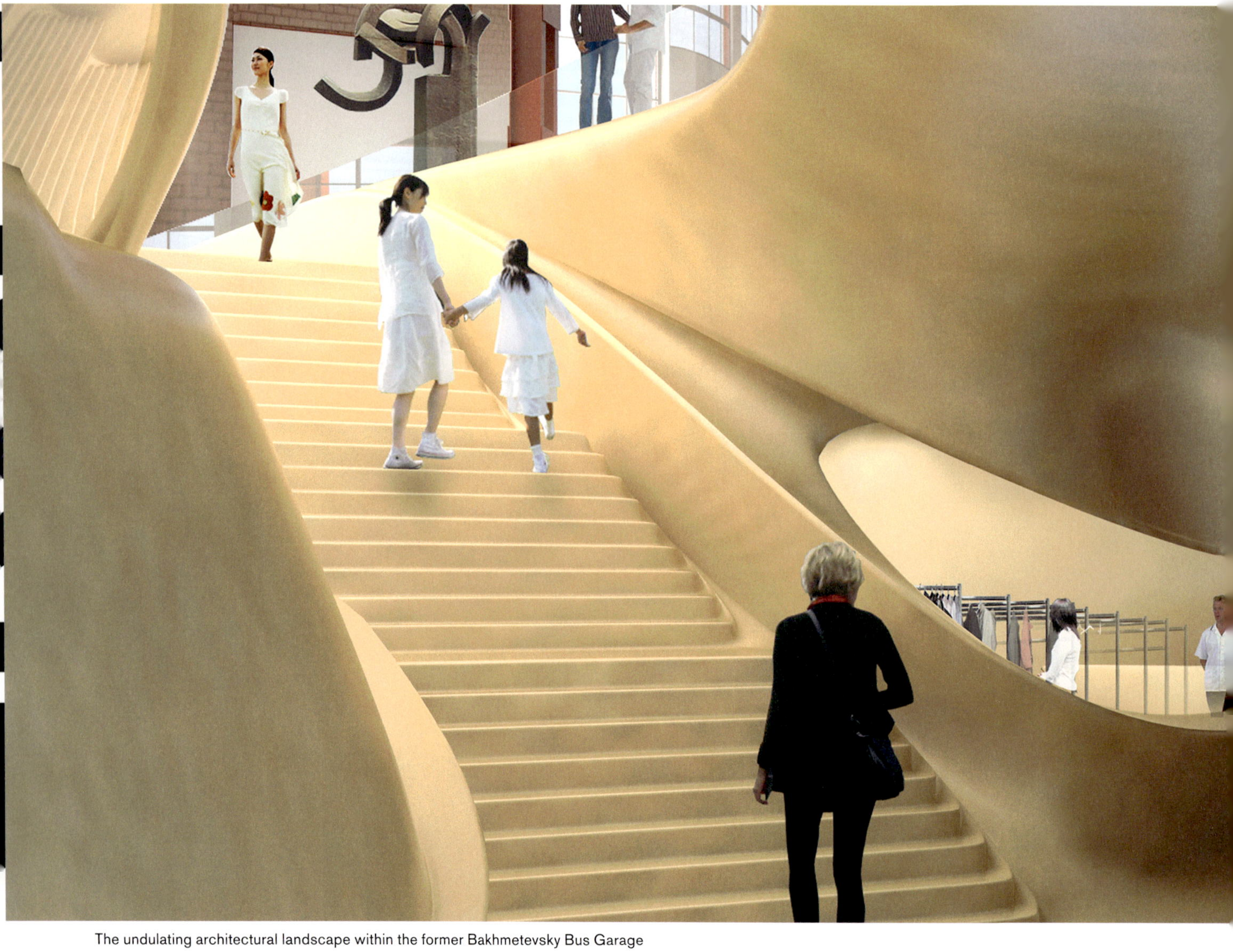

The undulating architectural landscape within the former Bakhmetevsky Bus Garage

The enormous, 154 x 54m structure will become the new home of the Russian Jewish Museum, accommodating a series of museum studios, a museum for children, a learning center, large multipurpose areas, temporary exhibition spaces, an 800-seat auditorium and smaller lecture halls, a restaurant and bar, a museum shop and space for office administration and museum staff. GRAFT's concept focuses on aspects that exemplify the diverse cultural roots of Russian Jewish society, the relationship between the historic and present-day affairs of the Russian Jewish community, and how to respect the heritage of a building like the Melnikov Garage—an icon of Russian constructivism—while repurposing it as the symbol of a new institution that communicates the history of Russian Judaism.

Entrance area

GRAFT's proposal leaves the existing structure untouched, intact and clearly recognizable as a monument to Russian heritage. Within this shell, the architectural concept creates an undulating landscape that animates the garage's interior and serves as a highly versatile event space able to host an array of functions, from temporary exhibitions and art fairs to concerts and conferences.

Formal contrast between the new museum spaces and the existing architecture of the original building

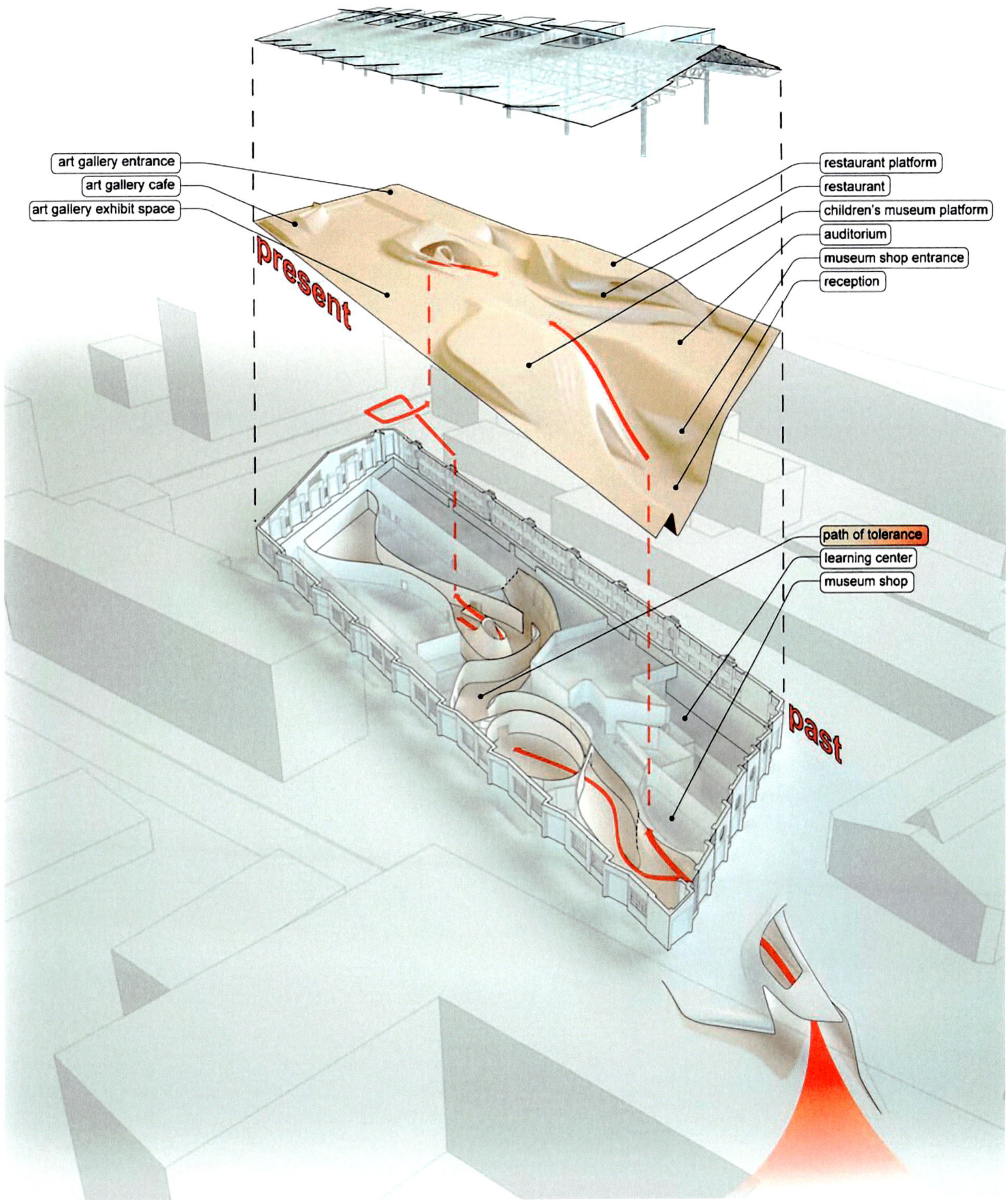

Concept and pathways for Russian Jewish Museum

The intervention expresses a direct and literal relationship between the past and present: Historical material is exhibited in a series of underground rooms, while the floor above serves as a flexible platform for presenting the activities of today's Russian Jewish community. The formal contrast of the interior spaces is enhanced by the architecture of the original building, metaphorically evoking the tumultuous history of the Jewish population in Russia. In bringing together two architectural identities and striking a complementary balance between them, the design creates a new, harmonious synthesis.

PLATOON Kunsthalle, Seoul, South Korea

PLATOON KUNSTHALLE

Project: Exhibition space, bar and restaurant, office and workshop space, container architecture
Location: Seoul, South Korea, and Berlin, Germany
Client: PLATOON.ORG
Year: 2009 (Seoul) & 2012 (Berlin)
Status: Completed

The PLATOON Kunsthalle buildings are designed as experimental spaces for artists, creatives and members of the PLATOON Network; they host art projects, workshops and events.

View into PLATOON, Seoul, South Korea

Section and floor plan of PLATOON, Seoul, South Korea

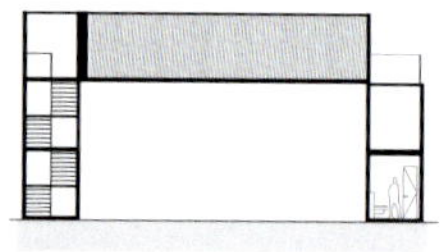

Section B

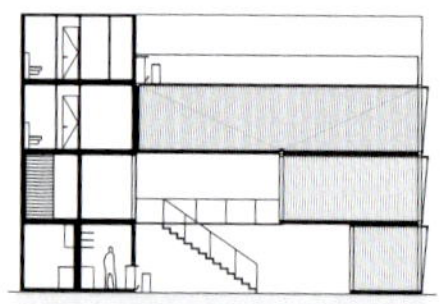

Section A

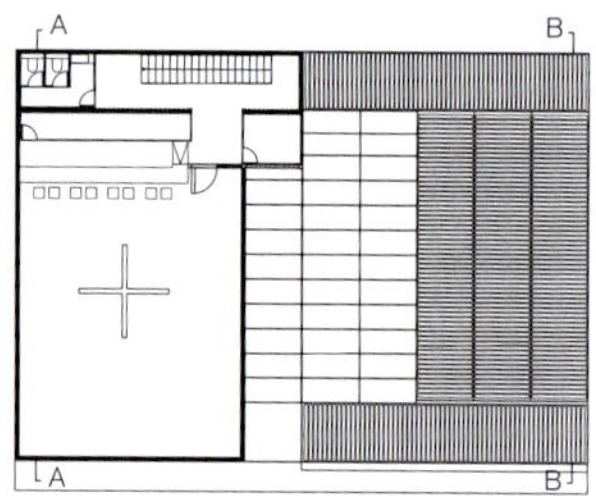

Fourth floor plan

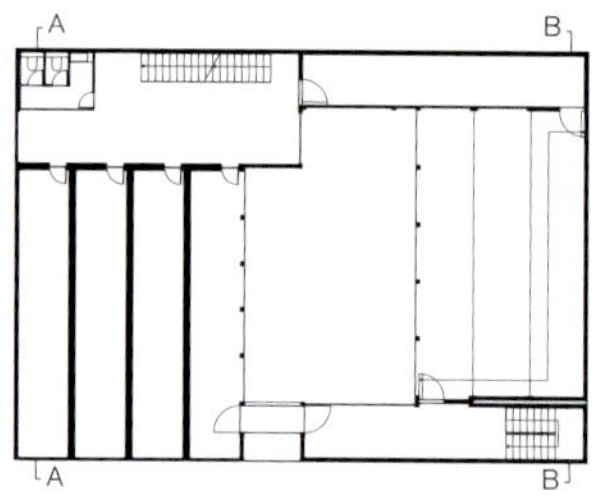

Third floor plan

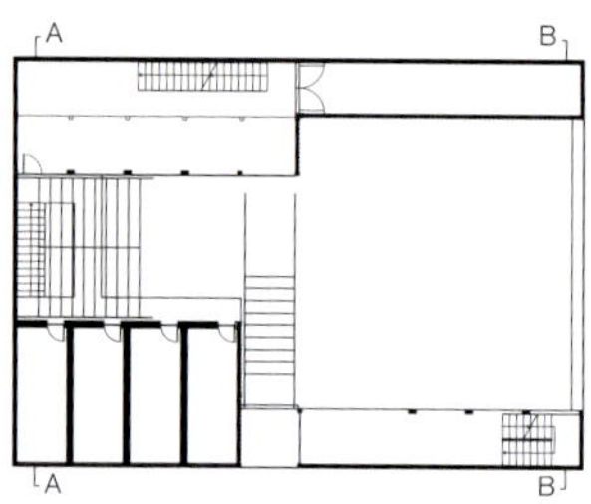

Second floor plan

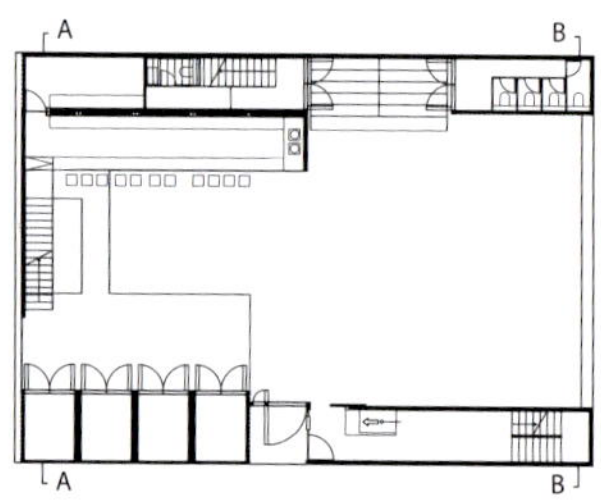

First floor plan

The PLATOON Kunsthalle Seoul opened in 2009 as a space to harness and develop the creative potential of subcultures in South Korea and other Asian countries. Its programmatic orientation towards cultural movements under the radar creates a dynamic space where new ideas are born and presented.

The project is built of 28 intermodal shipping containers. As icons of a flexible architecture in a globalized culture, the stacked containers form a unique construction that can be rebuilt anywhere else at any time.

Exhibition space made of 28 stacked shipping containers

Flexible interior space

Interior of PLATOON, Berlin, Germany

Entrance area of PLATOON in Berlin, Germany

Sections and floor plans of PLATOON, Berlin, Germany

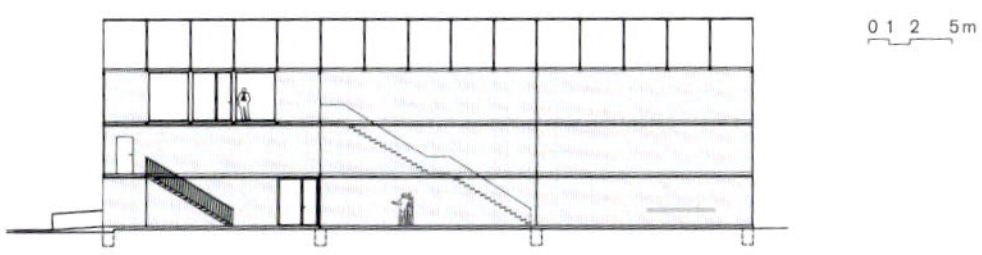

Section B

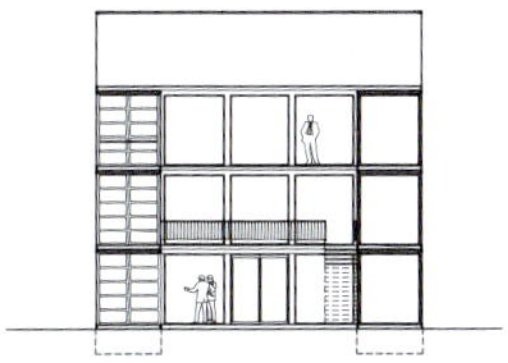

Section A

In 2012, GRAFT also assisted PLATOON in the architectural development of the PLATOON Kunsthalle Berlin. It is likewise a modular structure comprised of 34 shipping containers and serves as a platform for contemporary creativity.

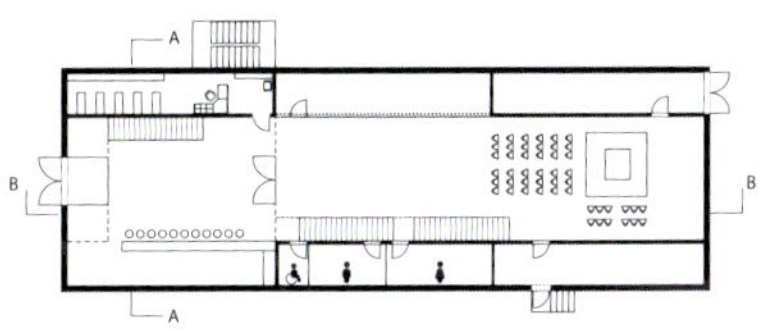

First floor plan

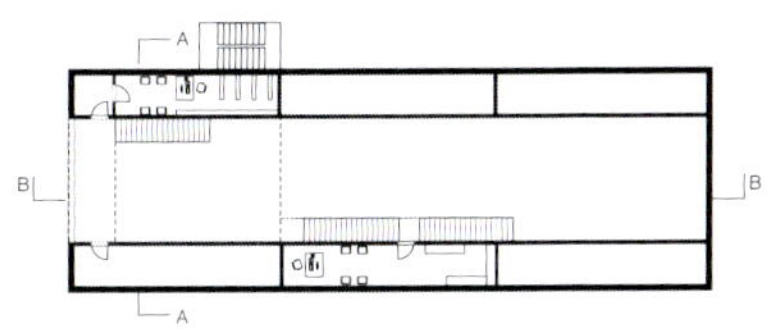

Second floor plan

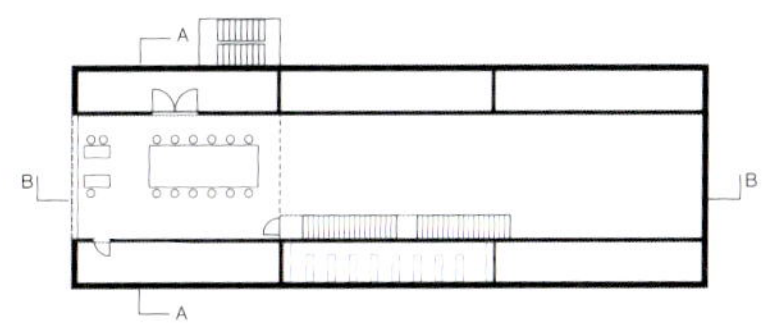

Third floor plan

PLATOON in Berlin, Germany

Unlike typical "white cube" art institutions, it provides a home for subculture initiatives: Events, exhibitions, workshops, lectures and discussions on urban street art, graphic design, performance, fashion, digital art, music, film, club culture and political interventions.

Opening of PLATOON Kunsthalle Berlin in summer 2012

AUFGEKAUFT !!!
P
50 CENT / 60 MIN

SHOWPALAST MUNICH

Project: Commercial, event space
Location: Munich, Germany
Client: APASSIONATA Park München GmbH & Co. KG
Year: 2017
Status: Competition 1st prize; completed
Size: 5,000m^2 (GFA)

After winning 1st prize in the competition for the Showpalast theme park in 2013, GRAFT completed the first major building of the complex in 2017, following a construction period of around twelve months.

The Showpalast is located in the Fröttmaning district of Munich near the Allianz Arena soccer stadium and is the first of 13 pavilions that will constitute an extensive adventure playground and amusement park dedicated to the theme of horses.

Façade detail

The 40-meter-wide Showpalast stage

A wooden structure in the adjacent amusement park

A wooden pavilion in the adjacent amusement park

The Showpalast arena seats 1,700 spectators in front of a specially designed, 40-meter-wide stage. With its limited number of rows, its layout ensures that all visitors are given clear, close-up views of the unique show.

While the stage and backstage areas are designed to allow horses access to the show space from all directions, modern projection technology augments the real with the virtual, creating a flexible and immersive theatrical experience.

Clad with undulating timber slat screens, the façade of the Showpalast appears to take flight—like a galloping horse in motion—especially when illuminated by a light show.

Dynamic light installation
by Kardorff Ingenieure
Lichtplanung

Lobby light installation by Kardorff Ingenieure Lichtplanung

With its strong visual language, the Showpalast forms the centerpiece of the amusement park and enters a symbiotic relationship with its surroundings, establishing a positive connection between the natural and the artificial.

Despite their different functions and characters, the other pavilions will share a similar material palette and design DNA, creating a harmonious ensemble and lending the brand a sense of spatial identity. The use of wood as a natural, familiar material makes the avant-garde forms of the pavilions more approachable.

Lobby

Showpalast Munich at dawn

GRAFT's design gives the remarkable horse show a distinctive and instantly recognizable public face. The successive addition of pavilions housing a horse care center, a horse museum, a blacksmith, a veterinary center, a science center, a riding hall and lunging circle, a 360° cinema, a foal station and numerous stables was completed in 2019.

UNBUILDING WALLS. FROM DEATH STRIP TO FREESPACE

Project: German Pavilion,
16th Biennale Architettura di Venezia
Location: Venice, Italy
Client: Bundesministerium des Innern, für Bau und Heimat (BMI)
(Federal Ministry of the Interior, Building and Community)
Year: 2018
Status: Competition 1st prize; completed
Collaborator: Marianne Birthler

Anamorphic wall installation in the German Pavilion at the 16th Biennale Architettura di Venezia

To mark the year that Germany had been united for as long as the Berlin Wall existed (1961–1989), GRAFT and Marianne Birthler curated the exhibition UNBUILDING WALLS at the German Pavilion at the 16th Biennale Architettura di Venezia.

The exhibition responded to contemporary debates on the meaning and sociopolitical relevance of national borders, on protectionist temptations and the pitting of visions of cultural homogeneity against multiculturalism and globalization.

In the German Pavilion, GRAFT and Marianne Birthler took the parallel as an opportunity to explore the effects of division and the process of healing as dynamic spatial phenomena. With reference to "FREESPACE," the central theme of the Biennale Architettura proposed by Grafton Architects, special focus was given to outstanding examples of urban and architectural design that address aspects of division and integration.

By analyzing architectural projects on the former border strip, the curators examined developments in this unprecedented void in the middle of a reunified country and a new capital. The heterogeneity of the many approaches, typologies, protagonists and results showed the breadth of architectural debates and solutions.

Wall fragments displaying architectural projects on the former border strip

German Pavilion (16th Biennale Architettura di Venezia)

Wall fragments of the anamorphic installation

Taking the experience of the Inner German border as a starting point, the exhibition also examined historical and contemporary barriers, fences and walls beyond Germany's specific national perspective.

As part of the preparations for UNBUILDING WALLS, a team of journalists traveled to border walls around the world.

People have been building walls since humans became sedentary—to protect themselves, to keep their property safe and to give spatial definition to a sense of belonging. Every wall therefore postulates an "us" and a "them." Walls divide. Whether they are good or bad, and for whom, depends on the reason they were built and the function and meaning they assume. Do they serve to protect people or do they limit their freedom and render it worthless? In the latter case, walls become prisons, instruments of exclusion and division that separate what was previously connected. This applies to the wall the GDR government built in 1961 around West Berlin and along the Inner German border to prevent its citizens from leaving. Its protective function primarily served those in power; for the people of the GDR it was incarcerating.

The Berlin Wall in particular quickly took on a symbolic meaning over and above that of the actual construction. It not only represented the division of a city and an entire country, but also came to symbolize state repression, forced separation, autocratic despotism and the inhuman potential of political ideology. Walls seal off authoritarian regimes from the rest of the world with a frequently deadly border or are the product of decades of conflict, failed diplomacy and a lack of will or ability to seek peaceful and humane solutions.

Since February 5, 2018, the Wall that divided Germany for 28 years has been gone for longer than it existed. This symmetrical moment in history presented an opportunity to reflect on developments on the former border strip since the fall of the Wall.

Exhibition panel

Wall fragments

The former border strip in Berlin

The "Wall of Opinions" video installation in the German Pavilion (16th Biennale Architettura di Venezia)

The Wall and its border installations eradicated all traces of the past in order to turn it into a deadly zone aiming to hinder any attempt to flee the GDR. A year after a peaceful revolution brought about the fall of the Wall on November 9, 1989, this military zone between the two parts of the newly reunified country lay empty like a vast open wound. At the same time, it also represented a unique opportunity to shape the process of the growing together of Berlin and the rest of the country—both spatially and programmatically.
Looking back, we can see a complex variety of different approaches. The revolution and the fall of the Wall happened suddenly, catching both German states unprepared. There was no master plan for the path towards unity. As in many other areas of society during the process of reunification, the work of the planning disciplines was not entirely even-handed, which left many GDR citizens unhappy and remains a cause of resentment and social tension to this day.

The initial intention was to create free spaces where the Wall and former death strip used to be. Alongside state-initiated gestures of connection, such as Axel Schultes' design for the Federal Ribbon, a complex process of democratic wrangling ensued regarding the future of this new urban space. Should people be allowed to live on a former death strip? Should this brutal, built testimony to a difficult and contentious period of German history be eradicated or should it be kept for future generations?

The approaches to dealing with the space left by the Wall are rife with ambivalent concepts: East and West, separation and connection, prominence or integration,

Exhibition catalog UNBUILDING WALLS. From Death Strip to Freespace

Gunther Adler (left), State Secretary at the Federal Ministry of the Interior, during the inauguration speech of the UNBUILDING WALLS exhibition, with Michael Müller (right), governing mayor of Berlin, and the exhibition curators (center) at the German Pavilion (16th Biennale Architettura, Venice, Italy, 2018)

Exhibition catalog UNBUILDING WALLS. From Death Strip to Freespace

forgetting or commemoration, leaving empty or habitation, reconstruction or transformation.

Solutions between these poles have since been found: Sometimes a conscious coexistence of old and new, sometimes a connection of the two, and sometimes something entirely unexpected.

The pluralism of architectural approaches along the former death strip over the last 28 years is the built manifestation of this debate. It documents a struggle for self-conception and identity—of the respective protagonists and of a reunified Germany and its people. For us, its variety is an expression of richness, a testament to a vibrant, pluralistic society.

At the same time, this process is still ongoing: Walls that have been overcome still cast a long shadow. The urban and architectural concepts are inseparably bound up with the social upheavals and transformations in the former GDR, the success of reunification and the disruptions and changes in people's personal lives. The "wound" that resulted from the Wall and the death strip must heal, and not just along the former border. It is a continuous, highly complex social, economic and cultural process that is by no means finished. Statistical surveys show that the country is still alarmingly imbalanced in many respects, whether in the distribution of power, regarding earnings or voting patterns.

The question is thus: How can we unbuild walls—physically, spatially and mentally?

Wall fragments of the anamorphic installation

The "Wall of Opinions" video installation in the German Pavilion (16th Biennale Architettura di Venezia)

TRANSCENDING THE LOCAL / GLOBAL DIVIDE

A CONVERSATION WITH REM KOOLHAAS

OMA is soon to complete the outstanding Springer Campus in Berlin-Mitte under the direction of Rem Koolhaas. Situated along the course of the former Wall, the building has an enormously significant role, not only in terms of its location, but also in terms of Berlin's history and identity. The client, media group Axel Springer SE, shaped the area during the years of German division, as well as during the period of growing together both spatially and semantically. GRAFT examined the divided and reunited Germany as a social and spatial phenomenon as part of their curatorship of the German Pavilion at the 16th Biennale Architettura in Venice. The exhibition's central sculpture will now be on permanent display in the foyer of OMA's new Springer Campus. GRAFT took this cooperation as a starting point to talk to OMA founder Rem Koolhaas about Berlin's identity and its development in both a local and a global context. What is the role of an internationally active architect in the ever-changing market economy, which identities are on the rise, and how do digitization, surveillance and commercialization feed into different modes of identity?

GRAFT For our Biennale contribution, we looked at what happened architecturally after the Berlin Wall fell. We researched the process of rebuilding, which was dominated by a strong nostalgia and the attempt to recreate a heterogeneous cityscape. You were very vocal about the fact that the Wall should not have been demolished entirely, because having this very contextual, unique space and erasing it also meant erasing a critical part of the history of Berlin.

During our research however, we discovered that this void, this blank canvas, had become an essential part of Berlin's identity. Even though there haven't been many architectural highlights erected on this empty space since the Wall came down, it still grew to be a major point of identification and the basis of many subcultures in Berlin. Looking back now, would you still consider the demolition of the Wall as a lost opportunity, or are the new fragments that have been created where it once stood interesting to you?

REM KOOLHAAS My interest in Berlin is not only an interest in the Wall. My interest goes back way before this and is related to Berlin as the birthplace of radical ideas and their partial implementation. What I objected to was more in the context of preservation, or at least that's how I would read it today. If preservation is a process that enables you and later generations to understand what happened in history, then the erasure of the Wall was a massive mistake. I simply thought that getting rid of the entire Wall was part of a premature attempt to impose the winners' aesthetic and the mentality of a given regime.

GRAFT Berlin was unable to bear the *horror vacui* of this scar after 28 years of emptiness along the death strip. That's why the decision to close this unique gap in the urban fabric was taken, even if it would eventually be seen as one of the biggest wasted opportunities in Berlin's recent history. At the same time, the way this area has been filled in the last 30 years shows how much the attempt to edit out and suppress the memory of its existence was a grave mistake. Today, the discovery of an original part of the Wall or an unknown escape tunnel is considered a sensation. But right after reunification, almost every single bit of the Wall was demolished and any remains were ignored. You were among those who supported a different approach, for instance during your participation in the jury for the Potsdamer Platz master plan. What was so controversial about those discussions?

KOOLHAAS I recall it very clearly. On the one hand, Hans Stimmann positioned himself in an incredibly strong, almost authoritarian way. He was adamant that certain proposals were terrible and that others ought to win. It was the brutality with which he succeeded in hounding the jury to a single conclusion that became so controversial. On the other hand, I have a slightly revised understanding and almost respect for Stimmann, in terms of him being able to protect Berlin from the most vulgar aspects of neoliberalism. Berlin today is remarkably free of grotesque architecture, and I think that is in part due to Stimmann's influence.

OMA's Axel Springer Campus in Berlin, Germany

GRAFT On the other hand we are surrounded by a lot of banality. Stimmann kept a lot of good architects out of the city and prevented projects that could have been fantastic.

KOOLHAAS Of course, there is a lot of banality, but there's a lot of banality in the world. In China, there is currently a contentious debate about "weird architecture." I think that Stimmann was really able to prevent a lot of weird architecture in Berlin. I'm not saying he did the right thing. If you compare Milan with Berlin, you see that in around 1990, Milan had a very intact result of a city with a lot of interesting modern interventions. If you look at how the market economy affected Milan—with buildings by Zaha Hadid, Daniel Libeskind and so on—compared to what happened in Berlin, you have to admit that somehow the maintenance of the local mentality and Berlin in itself was very smart, even if it was completely misguided and the arguments didn't make any sense. In retrospect, it was a shrewd choice. It killed a lot of creativity, a lot of thinking, but at the same time one effect of that dogmatism was positive.

GRAFT As a Berlin office, we see a lot of missed opportunities. After several years as an advisory consultant for a developer at Checkpoint Charlie, we have a good impression of how much a successful project depends on a synergetic discourse between the client, the authorities and the public. Public projects of such an important nature need to be driven by a common interest, a positive attitude and an optimistic curiosity for a place, its history and its future. In a confrontational environment, it is virtually impossible to successfully negotiate how to interpret a collective historical heritage and propose its future. However, your recent project in Berlin, the extension of the Springer publishing house with a digital campus, is one of the most exciting buildings along the former death strip. Axel Springer and his media house played a significant role in the history of the Wall. Springer's high-rise next to the Wall was a very political intervention, and an important contribution to Berlin's history—it connected architecture to the ideological struggles that were happening at the time. This was in stark contrast to Aldo Rossi's nearby project on Schützenstrasse, which tried to ignore the reality of the Wall to interpret what he thought was the true lost Berlin, the Berlin of the 19th century. You also proposed a building on the former death strip, just a few blocks away. It used the course of the Wall as a motivational factor and geometrical starting point for the inner logic of the building. The framework of a horizontal city that was laid down as a basic rule in Berlin should not be used, in our eyes, as a justification for limiting the pluralism of styles and, by extension, identities. It was more Stimmann's idea that we all had to entertain the same architectural and formal expression. We see it as a Potemkin village of an intact Berlin that ironically never existed. The interesting question, though, is how much pluralism can a city absorb? Should a city be a vessel for a democratic expression in architecture?

ONE OF THE TERRIBLE EFFECTS OF THE MARKET ECONOMY HAS BEEN TO ERODE THINKING AND TO REPLACE PLURALISM WITH VARIETY OR DIFFERENCE.

KOOLHAAS Pluralism is an interesting word because, in the latter part of the 20th century—let's say from the 1970s—it became an extremely vital concept. It suggested that there were many ways of thinking and that there could also be a society that would stimulate and enable many different ways of thinking. One of the terrible effects of the market economy has been to erode thinking and to replace pluralism with variety or difference. It's also naive to think about pluralism as if it still were a rigorous doctrine in the current discourse.

GRAFT In your book *Delirious New York*, you described the "culture of congestion" as an urban phenomenon caused by dense social energy. In light of the current pandemic, the culture of congestion doesn't seem to apply anymore. Do you think there is also a culture of isolation, perhaps with regard to rural versus urban identities?

KOOLHAAS Obviously, the corona crisis throws light on our project "Countryside: The Future" in a certain way, but I don't want to be too opportunistic and say, "I told you so." Of course, there is an implication, which I wouldn't directly or indirectly call an argument for a culture of isolation. The culture of congestion is rather being replaced by a culture of surveillance. This has become the culture of our cities, and to some extent also that of the countryside as an escape from the urban. The countryside is not necessarily a form of isolation, but a form of slightly less oppressive environments and regimes of control.

GRAFT In 2000, we did an exhibition in New York about surveillance, called "Enemy of the State," where we showed the cones of vision of surveillance cameras. Using graphics and painted interventions in public areas in New York City, we illustrated which spaces were under surveillance and which ones weren't. The project uncovered small, unmonitored spaces where people could behave as anonymous citizens. The protection of privacy is still seen as one of the cornerstones of Western democracies. Architects, however, have no influence on the politics of surveillance, yet digital developments have made the issue a subject of strong debate. Surveillance measures have to be discussed and legally agreed on, constitutions provide strict rules against misuse, etc. On the other hand, we see how effectively countries like South Korea, for example, where the acceptance of digital technology is much higher, were able to react to the current Covid-19 crisis. This might alter the course of the discussion in Europe and the United States. The unprecedented circumstances of this health crisis are forcing us to judge globalization and urbanization differently, and we will see the ways in which this will affect public life in the future.

KOOLHAAS My prediction is that when this is over, it will have contributed enormously to the ascendency of Asia and have given us all a reason to be humble, as the approach in South Korea, for instance, was obviously more intelligent and effective than anything we did in Europe.

I feel that globalization was perhaps a Western formula, the term having been invented by the West. It was initiated with great enthusiasm and success after the Wall fell, viewed as a complex phenomenon with good and bad impacts. Now, at a time when everyone else has embraced it, whether they wanted to or not, we are the first ones questioning it. I fear that we in the West will decide that globalization was a mistake in the first place. The phenomenon itself will remain very vigorous, and I even think that much of our future depends on it. My critique of globalization is that while we encourage globalization, we retain and increase our distance from any kind of regime we don't like. There are currently sanctions against Iran, Russia and China, and these ambiguities and contradictions in globalization are the problem, not globalization itself.

GRAFT We often encounter the misconception that globalization leads to a totally standardized world, but it incorporates an underlying promotion of diverse global lifestyles and beliefs—thus globalization is a descriptor of alternative localities. As some people see this freedom as a threat, to them it represents a very unpopular idea. The fear of a uniform global society is widespread and extensively discussed, especially if we look at the economic outcome and the diminishing impact of local measures when responding to global phenomena.

Even before the pandemic, we all knew that we were living in a deeply globalized world, as you said, whether we wanted to or not. Yet the need for local identities has constantly been on the increase in the globalized world. Both our offices benefited from globalization. Being able to establish offices on different continents, working in many cultures, acting at a local level, as architecture always does, is a commitment and a challenge. It's an interesting enigma for us. We are constantly asked to create local identities, yet we act globally. How do you make sense of this conundrum as an architect?

KOOLHAAS We are both very privileged to have been able to do that. It's something I never took lightly. I was always extremely careful to first get to know the conditions of each individual case before I intervened in a different culture. In most cases, we had a ten-year period of getting to understand and really feel these cultures.

IT'S THE ULTIMATE PRIVILEGE TO CONTRIBUTE TO THE UNKNOWN AND THE UNEXPECTED.

GRAFT We always try to be present in the cultures we work in. At the same time, it is also an advantageous position to be an outsider in a given local context. We left Germany to start our office in Los Angeles and, just three years later, when we opened our second office back in Berlin, we felt like—and were also seen as—outsiders to ordinary local conflicts. It was a good way to deal with bias. It's a beautiful thing that, as architects, we can bring something new to a project. It's the ultimate privilege to contribute to the unknown and the unexpected. We believe that in each of the cultures GRAFT has operated in, we did something that, firstly, could only have happened in that place and, secondly, was a positive contribution to that culture. Maybe this is what "grafting" really means for us: Respecting and juggling what you know with what you don't know and need to learn. Sometimes there are unexpected intersections between the two. Or they are contradictory in a way that making decisions or proposing solutions becomes more of a statement than an autonomous architectural decision. That's where identity can be "identified." Either way, a successful solution is only possible with personal dedication: Being informed and developing the affinity necessary for such intimate interactions.

KOOLHAAS I agree, it works in both directions. If you're lucky, you might contribute something to a different culture and this might also have a deep effect on your own perception of things. In that sense, an extended form of knowledge of different political systems and cultures, of scrupulous intervention or collaboration with each other are completely plausible aspects of globalization.

GRAFT How do you perceive the increasing desire for local identities versus international connectedness? A growing number of people seem to make a clear "either–or" distinction rather than showing interest in the ambiguities and overlaps, the combination and coexistence of diverse approaches and findings.

KOOLHAAS Our profession is a pretty complex one. There is never an easy answer to any particular project. There is always an aspect of local or global politics involved. I posed this question at the Biennale in 2014. The collective effect was that even if architects, cultural institutions and political systems work in seemingly international ways, they are inevitably local. If you take a closer look at the apparent similarities of modernism across the world, you see that, actually, there are very, very deep differences that are stipulated and created by local conditions. The effect of the local is not determined by switching to a local style or a local approach, but simply by approaching the local with the same subtlety as the domestic.

GRAFT Our profession should be at the forefront of resolving problems, as architects constantly deal with societal complexity on many different scales. Whether it's the dichotomy of urban versus rural or local versus global, architects are always forced to think in complex ways, a result of their position at the intersection of ecology, economy and culture.

KOOLHAAS I totally agree. If you know my work, you'll have probably noticed that in the beginning I was skeptical about architecture as a profession, and there has been a major change since. As many other professions are flattening, the profession of architecture has a reach that is quite rare. But I don't think we are very confident in deploying that range. And that's due to the virginity of the whole structure, the dependence on and the difficulty to find either clients or support for genuinely ambitious efforts.

GRAFT One approach is to try and be virtuous at the blurred border between culture and commerce. They are both intertwined, and your work shows brilliantly that you don't necessarily need to make that distinction. There is a commercial aspect to culture and vice versa. You can introduce culture into the commercial, and each aspect will benefit the other. It synthesizes the superficial polarity of both categories, which are mostly used to indicate good and bad—or the other way around—depending on your viewpoint. It seems we have to leave such banal frameworks behind.

KOOLHAAS That is true, but I would also like to emphasize that the success or failure of this is entirely a matter of the sophistication and ambition of the client. It's the ambition of the client that is decisive if the combinations that are so often kept separate could also overlap. At OMA, we have theorized these combinations, but in our practical work, the building, these combinations have proved extremely difficult to realize. As a result, many of our strongest works are quite classical in terms of their categorization.

The UNBUILDING WALLS sculpture in the lobby of OMA's Axel Springer Campus

Rem Koolhaas (Rotterdam, 1944) founded OMA in 1975 together with Elia and Zoe Zenghelis and Madelon Vriesendorp. He graduated from the Architectural Association in London and in 1978 published Delirious New York: A Retroactive Manifesto for Manhattan. In 1995, his book S,M,L,XL summarized the work of OMA in "a novel about architecture". He co-heads the work of both OMA and AMO, the research branch of OMA, operating in areas beyond the realm of architecture. His built work includes the Qatar National Library and the Qatar Foundation Headquarters (2018), Fondation Galeries Lafayette in Paris (2018), Fondazione Prada in Milan (2015/2018), Garage Museum of Contemporary Art in Moscow (2015), the headquarters for China Central Television (CCTV) in Beijing (2012), Casa da Musica in Porto (2005), Seattle Central Library (2004), and the Netherlands Embassy in Berlin (2003). Current projects include the Taipei Performing Arts Centre, a new building for Axel Springer in Berlin, and the Factory in Manchester. Koolhaas directed the 2014 Venice Architecture Biennale, is a professor at Harvard University, and, in 2019, opened a major exhibition for the Guggenheim museum entitled Countryside: Future of the World.

APPENDIX

GRAFT founding partners Thomas Willemeit, Wolfram Putz and Lars Krückeberg (left to right)

GRAFT partners Thomas Willemeit, Lars Krückeberg, Dennis Hawner, Georg Schmidthals, Sven Fuchs and Wolfram Putz (left to right)

ABOUT GRAFT

GRAFT was established in 1998 in Los Angeles, California, by Lars Krückeberg, Wolfram Putz and Thomas Willemeit. Further offices followed in Berlin, Germany, in 2001 and Beijing, China, in 2004. In 2018, GRAFT expanded its management team, welcoming Sven Fuchs, Dennis Hawner and Georg Schmidthals as new partners.

GRAFT is conceived as a studio for architecture, urban planning, design, music and the pursuit of happiness. Since its establishment, it has been commissioned to design and manage a wide range of projects across multiple disciplines and in numerous locations. Although the company's core enterprises gravitate around the field of architecture and the built environment, GRAFT has always maintained an interest in crossing the boundaries between disciplines and "grafting" the creative potential and methodologies of different realities. This is reflected in its expansion into the fields of exhibition and product design, art installations and academic projects,

UNBUILDING WALLS curators Wolfram Putz, Marianne Birthler, Lars Krückeberg and Thomas Willemeit (left to right) at the German Pavilion during the 16th Biennale Architettura, Venice, Italy, 2018

UNBUILDING WALLS team and curators, with Gunther Adler, State Secretary at the Federal Ministry of the Interior, Michael Müller, Governing Mayor of Berlin, and representatives from the Federal Ministry of the Interior at the German Pavilion during the 16th Biennale Architettura, Venice, Italy, 2018

Opening of UNBUILDING WALLS at the German Pavilion during the 16th Biennale Architettura, Venice, Italy, 2018

GRAFT team excursion to UNBUILDING WALLS in fall 2018, Venice, Italy

as well as in their variety of project locations around the world. GRAFT's collective professional experience encompasses a wide range of building types, including residential, cultural, educational, institutional, commercial, master plan and healthcare projects. GRAFT has won numerous international awards, and now numbers some 150 members of staff from over 20 nations.
Lars Krückeberg, Wolfram Putz and Thomas Willemeit have held several guest professorships in the USA and Germany and are members of the expert team of the Zukunftsinstitut think tank.

In 2007, together with Brad Pitt, Bill McDonough and the Cherokee Foundation, GRAFT established the Make It Right Foundation, whose objective was the rebuilding of New Orleans' Lower 9th Ward after Hurricane Katrina.
GRAFT's self-initiated projects also include SOLARKIOSK, a company founded with the German lawyer Andreas Spiess in 2009 to bring clean energy, connectivity and solar products to rural areas in sub-Saharan Africa. And in 2015, GRAFT co-founded Heimat2 with H. W. Pausch, Sven Rawe and Dr. Gerd Ellinghaus, which aims to bring dignified housing solutions to refugees in Europe.

In 2014, in collaboration with branding expert Linda Stannieder, GRAFT's founding partners set up the GRAFT Brandlab agency, enabling an additional focus on communication design, brand strategy and consultancy while staying true to GRAFT's multidisciplinary approach and working methods. Through progressive brand innovation concepts and a multidimensional approach, the agency places greater focus on enriching the interface between digital and physical brand experiences within constantly evolving markets and cultures. Today, the agency is led by Nikolaus Hafermaas and Rico Zocher.

Lars Krückeberg, Wolfram Putz and Thomas Willemeit wrote IDENTITY together with Nora Zerelli, who manages communication at GRAFT, and PR team member Nadine Cordial Settele, who was in charge of illustration editing.

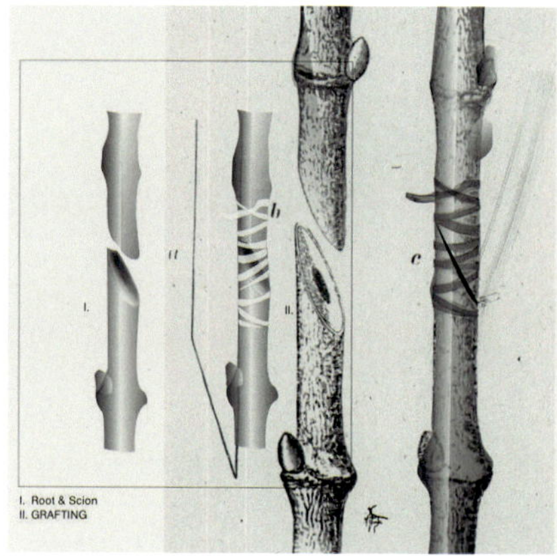

Grafting techniques: The English word "graft" has a variety of meanings. It stands for transplants in the field of medicine, but also for hard work. In botany, grafting is described as the addition of one shoot onto a genetically different host, in order to combine the positive properties of two genetically different cultures in a new biological hybrid. Applying this to architecture results in a refusal to accept contingent boundaries between disciplines and opens up new creative possibilities.

Wolfram Putz (left) and Thomas Willemeit (right) with former GRAFT partner Christoph Körner (center) at the "21 years GRAFT" anniversary celebration at Holzmarkt, Berlin, in 2019.

Thomas Willemeit (left) and former GRAFT partner Gregor Hoheisel (right) at the "21 years GRAFT" anniversary celebration at Holzmarkt, Berlin, in 2019.

Michael Müller, governing mayor of Berlin, at the "21 years GRAFT" anniversary celebration at Holzmarkt, Berlin, in 2019.

"21 years GRAFT": 2019 marked the 18th anniversary of GRAFT's Berlin office, exactly 21 years after the company was founded in LA.

The GRAFT office in Berlin

The GRAFT football team during the ABC Cup 2018, Berlin

Staff list April 2020

GRAFT

Achim Krayl
Agata Filipowicz
Agata Glubiak
Agnieszka Szymanska
Aleksandra Kiszkielis
Alexander Moritz
Alexandra Baack
Alexandra Bunescu
Amit Rivlin
Ana Galvez
Ana Lopez de Rego Curros
Andreas Blödow
Andrei Dan Musetescu
Angelika Rehe
Anja Frenkel
Ann-Sophie Heuer
Anna Wittwer
Anna Yeboah
Anna-Maria Grabi
Annabell Pfeifer
Anne Kleinlein
Annette Finke
Antonio Luque
Arne Wegner
Bas Kahlert
Benedikt Boschert
Berke Inöntepe
Bertrand Malpel
Besher Alyoussef
Bojan Zdravkovic
Caroline Lefèvre
Caroline Lossack
Casey McSweeney
Chrisanthi Karta
Christoph Korner
Claire Sattler
Costanza Governale
Daniel Finck
David Wehrmeister
David Wurth
Dennis Hawner
Dorian Mandzukic
Ema Neimarlija
Emma Rytoft
Filipa Leal de Carvalho
Friederich Atanasoaie
Georg Schmidthals
Gregor Hoheisel
Haotian Yang
Harpreet Kaur
Heike Heister
Inga von Türckheim
Irene Aguilera Blanco
Izabela Kordyka
Jacek Jara
Jan Kadziela
Jannis Jaschke
Javier Nieto Cano
Jerzy Gabriel
Jesus Navarro
Julia Kraffert
Julie Hoffmann
Karsten Littau
Kathrin Starcke
Katja Mydlach
Katrin Stahn
Kris Ki Yoon Kil
Kristian Taaksalu
Kudzai Magoche
Lars Krückeberg
Leon Seibert
Leonardo Nahuel Musso
Lorenzo Cristoforetti
Luis Tomas
Mahasa Niki Möller
Maike Wienmeier
Marc Paulin
Marco Falzoni
Marco Migliavacca
Marie Poth
Marta Piaseczynska-Karaivanov
Marta Wegner
Martin Bernard
Mathilde Catros
Mathilde Dewavrin
Matthias Eckardt
Matthias Rümmele
Melissa Swick
Nadine Cordial Settele
Natalie Dillon
Nikolaos Xenos
Nikolas Krause
Nils von Minckwitz
Nora Zerelli
Ödül Akyol
Paula Rosch
Peter Buche
Philip Weibhauser
Philippos Michael
Raluca Ana Maria Constantin
René Lotz
Ricardo Valencia Paez
Riccardo Russo
Roman Puzicha
Sara Gomez
Sarah John
Sascha Krückeberg
Sebastian Gernhardt
Sebastian Massmann
Sharareh Ghanavizchian
Simon Hendel
Sorin Gabriel Gosa
Stefanie Götz
Sven Bauer
Sven Fuchs
Théophile de la Presle
Thomas Willemeit
Tobias Hein
Tolegen Batentayev
Ulrike Seifert
Vera Pabst
Veronika Partelova
Viktoria Delovska
Vincent Krause
Wolfram Putz
Zsolt Gondos

GRAFT BRANDLAB

Alexandra Parger
Alexandra Uzunoglu
David Steingrüber
Felipe Wagner
Helene Haas
Jana Lux-Mahnke
Jörg Dengler
Kara ten Hoevel
Linda Stannieder
Lucas Confurius
Marvin Bratke
Maximilian Grieb
Miruna Turbatu
Moritz Behrens
Nikolaus Hafermaas
Rico Zocher
Sean Ketchem
Sabrina Ziep
Simon Bollongino
Tanja Schaub
Victor Pang

We would like to thank all current and former GRAFT designers, architects and artists that GRAFT has had the privilege of calling co-workers and friends over the years.

The GRAFT team on Brocken Mountain, the highest peak of the Harz mountain range, Germany, winter 2016

The GRAFT Christmas party 2017 at BRLO BRWHOUSE, Berlin

Illustration credits

All images, drawings and diagrams © GRAFT, except for:

06 Nora Zerelli
07 Snøhetta
08 Chess Boxing Global Marketing CBGM
12 Jeff Granbery, M2G Media
13 BigRep GmbH (left)
13 Helena Willemeit (right)
15 Tobias Hein
16 Tobias Hein (left)
16 Noam Rosenthal (right)
17 Nikolay Kazakov for Volocopter / Skyports
18 Ronald Grant Archive / Alamy Stock Photo (left)
18 Syd Mead, Inc. (right)
19 Magdalena von Saleski
32–34 Tobias Hein
35 WES LandschaftsArchitektur
48–51 Nikolay Kazakov for Volocopter / Skyports
52 Nikolay Kazakov for Volocopter / Skyports (top)
52 Raphael Olivier (bottom)
53 Raphael Olivier
54–55 Nikolay Kazakov for Volocopter / Skyports
60–61 Jeff Granbery, M2G Media
69 terra0 (www.terra0.org)
70 WoeLab
71 SES / SOLARKIOSK
72 Design Research Lab, Berlin (top)
72 Jörn Alraun (bottom)
75 Gesche Joost
76–81 HERE Global B.V.
84–86 SOLARKIOSK
87 Media Stock Masters / Shutterstock (top)
87 SOLARKIOSK (bottom)
88–91 SOLARKIOSK
92–93 Simon Mulumba / CMONCY IMAGES
94 Gais S et al., Nat Neurosci. 2000,3(9): 1335–39
Figueroa-Ramos MI et al., Intensive Care Med. 2009, 35: 781–95.
94–95 Tobias Hein
96 Tobias Hein
97 Quote from Saladin A J Acoust Soc Am 2011; 6:3754 3760 213 (left, top)
Shilo L et al., Am J Med Sci 1999, 317(5): 278–281 (left, center)
Sleep Medicine Center of Charité CCM
Tobias Hein (bottom)
98–99 Tobias Hein
99 Shilo L et al., Am J Med Sci 1999
Sleep Medicine Center of Charité CCM
102 WeWork
103 TRILUX
104 Ricky Ridecos
106 Public Domain
107 Katja Zimmermann for Berlin Food Week
109 WeWork
110–119 TRILUX
120–125 Ricky Ridecos
126 GRAFT Brandlab
127 GRAFT Brandlab
128 Arup
168 Bauwelt 1953 Heft 1, Artikel 'Das Bayer-Haus in Berlin' (top, left)
168 Marco Migliavacca (bottom, left)
180 Waldemar Titzenthaler / ullstein bild
181 Waldemar Titzenthaler / ullstein bild (top)
181 Max Wagenführ: Der Admiralspalast und seine Bäder. In: Moderne Bauformen, 11. Jg. 1912, Heft 3, S.136–152, hier S.140 (bottom)
190 Pablo Mason
192 hiepler, brunier,
193 Live Love
194 Landesarchiv Berlin, F Rep. 260-03, Nr. A 1710 (top, left)
194 EMBASSY, Berlin (www.embassyexperts.com) (top, right)
194 Stiftung Stadtmuseum Berlin (bottom, left)
194 Marco Leitermann (bottom, right)
195 Madeleine Brunnmeier
196–197 hiepler, brunier,
200–201 hiepler, brunier,
202–205 Napat Pattrayanond and Soopakorn Srisakul
206–207 hiepler, brunier,
208–209 Dartford: Copyright of Mercedes Benz Cars UK Limited – kindly reproduced with permission; Budapest, Heilbronn, Hong Kong: hiepler, brunier,; Den Haag: Ronald Tilleman; Bangkok: Napat Pattrayanond and Soopakorn Srisakul
212 Marcus Schwier Architekturfotografie
214–215 hiepler, brunier,
216–217 Tobias Hein
218–219 hiepler, brunier,
220–221 Tobias Hein
222–223 Tobias Hein
224–226 Andi Albert
227–228 Tobias Hein
229 Andi Albert
230–231 Tobias Hein
233 DONE STUDIO – Ulf Saupe
234 Tobias Hein
235–237 DONE STUDIO – Ulf Saupe
238–243 Heinemann
244–245 Christian Barz
246–249 Yang Di
254–257 Ricky Ridecos
258–259 GRAFT Brandlab
260–261 Archimedes
262–265 GRAFT Brandlab
269 Jan Bitter (3 x top, right)
269 Kirsten Bucher (bottom, left; bottom, right)
272 SHF / Stephan Falk (top, left), ANSA (bottom, left)
274 Philip Lange / Shutterstock
275 Massimo Parisi / Shutterstock (left)
275 Kirsten Bucher (right)
276–283 Michael Moser
289 Tobias Hein
288–289 Urban Nation
290–291 Tobias Hein
292–293 Aurelio Schrey
294 Tobias Hein
295 Urban Nation
308–315 Tobias Hein
320–327 PLATOON
328–329 Stefan Müller-Naumann
330 EQUILA (top)
330–333 Stefan Müller-Naumann
334–335 EQUILA
336–343 Jan Bitter
344 Max Schmieding, PROXI.ME
345 Jan Bitter (top)
345 Max Schmieding, PROXI.ME (3x bottom)
346–347 Jan Bitter
349 Courtesy of OMA / Photography by Laurian Ghinitoiu
351 Courtesy of OMA / Photography by Fred Ernst (bottom)
354 Pablo Castagnola (top, left)
354 Marie Weikopf (top, right)
355 Jan Bitter (3x top)
356 Marie Weikopf (4x bottom, left)
356 Tobias Hein (top, right)
356 Sebastian Wells, Ostkreuz (bottom, right)
357 Tobias Hein